D1558325

On My Honor:
Lesbians Reflect on Their
Scouting Experience

edited by

Nancy Manahan

Illustrations by Lynne Tuft

WITH A FOREWORD BY

VICTORIA A. BROWNWORTH

Madwoman Press, Inc.
Northboro, Massachusetts

Cover by Phoenix Graphics, Winter Haven, Florida

Printed in the United States on acid-free paper.

Library of Congress Cataloging-in-Publication Data
On my honor: lesbians reflect on their scouting experience / edited by Nancy
    Manahan; illustrations by Lynne Tuft; with a foreword by Victoria A.
    Brownworth.
            p.   cm.
        Includes index.
        ISBN 1-886231-02-8 (alk. paper)
        1. Lesbian Girl Scouts—United States.   I. Manahan, Nancy, 1946.

HS3357.L4705 1997
369.463'086'643—dc21   97-36697
                                                                            CIP

CONTENTS

DEDICATION

✳ ✳ ✳

To my friend and mother, Ruth Hinchon Manahan, in appreciation for her love, acceptance, and encouragement in all my endeavors. Her integrity, hard work, generosity, and enthusiasm for life have been my most profound influences. I am particularly grateful to my mother for helping begin Girl Scouting in our hometown, Madelia, Minnesota, the year after I was born.

And to my sister Pat Manahan Anderson, who taught me Girl Scout songs, helped me earn badges, and (as "Patches") kept me safe one summer when she was the camp nurse, the waterfront director, and the swimming, canoeing, and boating instructor at Girl Scout Camp Tukawah.

And to the Girl Scout Troop 56 mothers and leaders, as well as the other volunteers and staff of the Peacepipe Girl Scout Council, for making Girl Scouting available to girls growing up in southern Minnesota then and now.

In Memory

Josephine Alexander (1909–1993)

Beloved friend, activist, and writer of *America Through the Eye of My Needle* (Dial Press, 1981) and essays in *Fierce with Reality: An Anthology of Literature on Aging*, ed. Margaret Cruikshank (North Star Press, 1995).

For every tree used in the printing of this book, two trees will be plan' ed.

ACKNOWLEDGMENTS

✳ ✳ ✳

Thanks to Seal Press for permission to reprint Judith McDaniel's "Scouts on the Saranac" under the original title "Down the Saranac with Sixteen Paddles" and Carol (Heenan) Seajay's "Becoming a Canada Tripper, 1965" from *Rivers Running Free*, eds. Judith Niemi and Barbara Wieser, 1992; to Jorjet Harper for permission to reprint "Lesbian Girl Scouts: 'You Don't Bring Your Lover to a Troop Meeting'"; to Cindy Dasch for permission to reprint the chorus of "On My Honor"; and to the Tierra del Oro Girl Scout Council for permission to reprint terms from their Glossary of Girl Scout Terms.

I appreciate all the help I received with this book. My deepest thanks to

- My partner Becky Bohan, author of *Sinister Paradise* and *Fertile Betrayal*, for having the idea of a book about lesbian Girl Scouts; for encouraging me at every stage of the three-year process of gathering, editing, and writing material for the book; for contributing invaluable advice whenever I asked; and for giving me loving support on the home front.
- my friends Ruth Baetz, author of *Wild Communion: Experiencing Peace in Nature* (1997), for editing nearly every piece in the book; Myra Williams for putting me in touch with African American Girl Scouts; Lauren Coodley for giving me perceptive feedback on the introduction; and several professional Girl Scouts, who asked to remain anonymous, for reading and commenting on the manuscript.
- my brother, Jim Manahan; my sister, Margaret Manahan-Gert; and Cynthia Graham and LaVerle McAdams, for copyediting the manuscript.
- my brother, Bill Manahan, and my sister-in-law, Diane Manahan for financing part of the book promotion tour.

Thanks to all the women who contributed to this book. I appreciate your courage and generosity in sharing your stories and photographs as well as your patience with my editing suggestions and the rounds of revisions.

Thanks finally to Diane Benison for taking on the project, for making excellent suggestions at strategic points, and for editing and publishing the book with such care.

FOREWORD

by Victoria A. Brownworth

I always wanted to be a Girl Scout.

It wasn't the uniform. I went to Catholic school; I'd had my fill of uniforms. It wasn't the cookies. You could always get the cookies at school from someone who *was* a scout. It wasn't even the badges, though these were intriguing and slightly mysterious—very different from anything one got at school or church.

No, my desire to be a Girl Scout stemmed from something far deeper than these somewhat frivolous accoutrements of the scouting mystique. I grew up in the 1960s when being a girl was still very much about perfecting traits like politeness and even servility; striving as the nuns at my school explained so succinctly, to be "unremarkable." In the 1960s girls were raised to be as homogenous as society could make them (without even the diversity inherent in Girl Scout cookies). Girls did not speak unless they were spoken to, girls did not excel because it might make boys appear stupid, girls did not think about careers except as a hedge against that time when they would achieve the premiere goal for any girl: marriage and family. A girl was groomed from birth to be the perfect wife and mother. The journey to that acme of domestic bliss did not include individuating one's self or broadening one's horizons except as it might increase one's desirability as a possible mate.

In this Ozzie-and-Harriet atmosphere where my destiny as a future Harriet seemed preordained, I yearned to be a Girl Scout because Girl Scouts seemed to have the best of both worlds. Scouting was an acceptable, even laudatory pastime for girls while also offering a variety of experiences not available to girls in other social or even educational contexts. I wanted to be a Girl Scout because in books I read as a young girl (and I was always a voracious reader), scouts did things other girls did not. Girl Scouts were *participants*, not passive observers; they did not sit idle on the sidelines ceding action to boys alone. Girl Scouts went hiking and camping. Girl Scouts could survive if they were lost in the woods by blazing a trail, making a campfire by rubbing sticks together, cooking on a stove made from an old juice or soup can, fashioning a lean-to out of branches and leaves. (This aspect of scouting had particular resonance for me because I spent a great deal of time in the woods surrounding the neighborhood where I grew up.) Girl Scouts were *doers* at a time and in a climate where girls were not allowed to *do* much of anything. And yet scouting was unique in that Girl Scouts received approbation for their forays outside the straitened realm of 1960s girlhood. Scouting gave an imprimatur to adventures and experiences that would otherwise be deemed "unladylike."

Yet beyond my interest in this quest for adventure, where even the scary prospect of being lost in the woods and subject to bear attacks seemed preferable to the stultifying choices proffered to me as a young girl, was the lure of the camaraderie that seemed unique and even vital to scouting. In my youth, a key element of the socialization of girls included being instilled with a wariness of other girls/women. Girls/women would not be competing for jobs or any of the things boys/men competed for in society; rather, we would be competing for boys/men themselves, because our ultimate goal remained securing the right man and raising a family with him. Thus other girls/women had to be kept somewhat at arm's length. For example, in the Archie comic books that were so popular when I was in grade school and junior high, the male characters—regardless of class or intellectual differences—were friends, they hung out together, their camaraderie in being male superseded everything else, including their relationships with and competition for girls. But the girls in these comics were forever baiting each other, in competition for the ultimate life prize—a man—unable to truly share friendship because that wariness of other females had been instilled in them. They were socialized to be distrustful of each other, and thus isolated from true friendship and camaraderie.

While these comic-book girls were reflective of the real socialization of the girls and women around me, scouting seemed decidedly different. Girl Scouts exhibited that same camaraderie boys had; scouting seemed like a secret society in which girls had access to experiences they were barred from otherwise. Without being elitist (because I lived in a working-class neighborhood), the Girl Scouts were a special and unique group, with specific privileges conferred upon those girls lucky enough to be accepted into that select society. Girls Scouts appeared to lay claim to an experiential entitlement the rest of us had no access to.

So I yearned to be a scout, to belong to that singular club where girls were something more than, well, *just* girls. The Girl Scouts held such promise: A world in which girls were real people—strong and independent, able to forge close friendships and share in a broader experience of girlhood than any I had been privy to in my young female life. But family obligations kept me from joining the Girl Scouts.

Some yearnings never go away. I didn't think about my lost chance at scouting for years until my partner and I were going through some old photographs of hers. One photo showed her as a thirteen-year-old, lanky and lean with long blonde hair and a very bored expression as she stood in her green uniform, the sash covered in patches and insignias, a tiny little pin with wings on it at the top. Her mother stood next to her, smiling a motherly smile, looking warm and matronly in her own green uniform. Thus I discovered that my lover had been a scout (first a Brownie, then a full-fledged Girl Scout, hence the little wings for moving up the scouting ladder). Her mother had been a troop leader.

For years I was fascinated by this photo. Periodically I would ask to see it. Part of my fascination clearly related to the juxtaposition of images: the bored teenager with the overly engaged mother; the hippie-style hair and macramé friendship bracelet with the uniform from an earlier, more traditional time. I was simultaneously attracted to and envious of the younger version of the lesbian woman who was my lover in the uniform of that secret girl society to which I had wanted, so wanted, to belong. But the vicarious attachment to scouting through my partner was tempered by the still palpable sense of loss that I had never been a scout and thus could not share that past, and as I still imagined it, magical experience of scouting with her. Why couldn't I have been a scout, too?

Not only was my partner a scout, but as I began to talk to women friends about this book I found my closest friends had all been Girl Scouts, as well. Now I realized just how deprived my girlhood had been. My two closest friends, both lesbians, had been scouts—one in a small, rural town, another on the outskirts of a big, urban center. Both were working class.

These two women are extremely successful professionals today. Their experiences of scouting were positive and affirming. One friend, now in her early fifties and executive director of a social services agency for abused women, notes that scouting gave her "a very strong sense of self. I think it

taught me that girls could do things, be strong. It was definitely empowering."
She would have continued to be a scout for many more years, she added, but
the poverty of her small town made it difficult to get troop leaders. "I loved
scouting," she said. "I think most girls, no matter where they live, no matter
what their sexual orientation, would really benefit from the experience."

The other friend, a law professor and writer, notes that scouting offered
one of the only avenues for girls to be together without boys. "Before Title
IX," she noted, "there were so few choices for girls, so few ways in which girls
could get together to work and play without the influence of boys on the
group and on the dynamic, because boys always changed the tenor of things
for girls, they always repressed the natural way in which girls behave on their
own without that heterosexual pressure. There were few places for girls to go
that were just for girls. Girl Scouts was one of those places."

When Nancy Manahan asked if I would write a promotional blurb for this
book, the complicated nature of my emotional relationship to scouting was
revisited. A jumble of scouting-related memories came flooding back. Like
scouting itself and its iconic presence in my girlhood, there were the
accoutrements as well as the deeper questions. There was that photograph of
my lover, of course; and then memories of all the girls I had known in school
who were scouts and how envious I had been of them; the many books I had
read in which the interesting girls, the adventurous girls, were always scouts,
or the grown-up girl sleuths had learned their wit and wiles from their earlier
roles as scouts.

And there were other memories. I remembered sitting around my first
campfire at a lesbian festival; I had wondered then if this was indeed what
being a Girl Scout was like—that camaraderie with strangers in the woods,
singing songs in the moonlight, feeling that intrinsic sense of belonging. I
remembered being a reporter more than a decade ago and talking to a woman
who had been fired from her job with the Girl Scouts because she was a
lesbian.

This myriad of disparate thoughts came to me as I considered what I might
say about a book on lesbians and scouting. What could I say?—after all, I'd
never actually been a scout.

Nancy's earlier book, *Lesbian Nuns: Breaking Silence*, had been revelatory
for me. I was the first reporter in the U.S. to write about lesbian nuns; *Lesbian*

Nuns: Breaking Silence came out a few years after the series I wrote for the *Philadelphia Gay News*. I had long considered becoming a nun and struggled to figure out a way in which I could do so; had spent years in Catholic school and been irrevocably imprinted by that experience. Reading about those lesbian nuns had a tremendous impact on me; it was acutely personal. I felt an intimate kinship with them and an intrinsic spiritual and emotional validation in knowing that they existed—they were there.

I have always been drawn to communities of women, lured by the dual promise of camaraderie and independence. Had Nancy asked me many years ago to write a foreword for *Lesbian Nuns: Breaking Silence*, I would have known exactly what to say—I was that close to the subject, engaged in the personal, spiritual and political ramifications of that book.

But scouting was something else; how could I write appropriately and provocatively about something I had not experienced? I had only ever stood outside the window of the scouting world with my face pressed longingly against the glass. Yet as Nancy and I talked about the book, we both came to the same realization—I had a great deal I wanted to say about the Girl Scouts; that even though I had never, in fact been a scout, the lure and promise scouting held for me as a young girl had created its own mystique and momentum in my life.

Just as *Lesbian Nuns: Breaking Silence* caused a furor when it was published in 1985, so too, I'm certain, will this volume, and for very similar reasons, because it breaks its own kind of silence by acknowledging what many of us have long known: There are lesbians in the Girls Scouts.

Of course there are—there are lesbians everywhere. But acknowledging lesbians as cashiers in supermarkets or as linewomen for the telephone company or as instructors at health clubs or brokers on Wall Street doesn't have the same impact as acknowledging that lesbians are a fundamental part of that all-female society, the Girl Scouts. There is, in the minds of many, a causal link between *homosocial* (that is, same sex) groups and *homosexual* behavior. The lesbian and gay community calls this "queer fear"—the heterosexual concern that if no members of the opposite sex are present in a particular group (whether all-male or all-female) then homosexual urges will rise to the fore and somehow subsume (or at the very least taint) the entire, previously heterosexual group.

There are no clear data on how this fear developed, although it fairly conclusively evolved out of post-Freudian concerns about the dangers of homosexual behavior; "queer fear" is decidedly a product of twentieth-century psychology impacting on mass culture. In more recent times, notably since the late 1980s and the rise of the Christian Coalition and other extremist groups within the Religious Right, "queer fear" has been transmogrified and given real credence by being referenced by these groups as "the homosexual agenda" (a term coined by Pat Buchanan when he spoke at the 1992 Republican National Convention).

A charter element of that so-called "homosexual agenda," according to those who promulgate the theory, is "infiltration" by lesbians and gay men into the most sacred arenas of heterosexual culture and society—marriage, the family, the schools, the churches (the Religious Right in the United States is definingly Christian) and any other groups in which children can be imprinted with so-called homosexual ideology—like the Boy Scouts or Girl Scouts. The construct of the theory of the "homosexual agenda" posits that because lesbians and gay men can't have children of their own, they must find ways to "convert" the children of heterosexual parents to the "homosexual lifestyle." (Taking this theory as seriously as possible, however, the basic tenet is inherently flawed. Statistics indicate fully one-third of gay men are parents, while over a half of all lesbians have children. These children are the result of previous heterosexual relationships, adoptions and alternative insemination.)

Within the political contextualizing of the "homosexual agenda," lesbians and gay men are perceived as predatory; not child molestors *per se* (though gay men are frequently targeted as molestors even though the overwhelming majority of sexual abuse of children of both genders is perpetrated by men who identify as heterosexual), but women and men who want to co-opt— and, by extension, corrupt—children. The unrelenting message of the Religious Right has been that lesbians and gay men threaten the fabric of American life as we know it, and are most threatening to the children of America who are too naive to comprehend the complexities of the "homosexual agenda."

This dramatic fear of lesbians and gay men has affected all sectors of fundamentalist Christianity in the United States. In June 1997, the Southern Baptist Convention, the largest single Protestant fundamentalist denomination in the country, voted unanimously to boycott The Disney Corporation, the largest family entertainment company in the world, because Disney has made domestic partnership health benefits available to its lesbian and gay employees and owns ABC, which airs the sitcom "Ellen," starring openly lesbian comedian Ellen DeGeneres and in which DeGeneres's character, Ellen Morgan, recently declared her lesbianism.

The Religious Right and fundamentalist Christians were also prominent voices in a well-publicized lawsuit brought by a decorated gay Eagle Scout against the Boy Scouts in 1993. The scout was barred from becoming a troop leader because of his sexual orientation; Christian Right groups argued that a gay troop leader would be likely to molest his charges as well as tarnish the name of the Boy Scouts by associating what they termed "a Christian group" with homosexuality.

It is not surprising in this atmosphere, then, that there are real fears among lesbians in the Girl Scouts that this book will somehow damage both scouting and the role of lesbians within the Girl Scouts. Outing is always an alarming prospect; but so is remaining in the closet. The argument is often made that secrecy allows lesbians to continue to act as role models while outing would make that impossible. But there can be no real nurturing in secret; the very fact that lesbian troop leaders or administrators must lie and hide their sexual orientation in order to nurture lesbian scouts disabuses any young scout of the notion that lesbianism is something to nurture. Being in the closet only reinforces the concept that something is inherently "bad" about being lesbian. Thus this book ultimately can only do good, by exposing the truth and allowing girls and women to make real choices, not choices informed by bias and distorted stereotypes. The idea of choices for girls, of course, is what the Girl Scouts has always promoted.

This book defines and explores the need for such openness within the Girl Scouts. The range of experience lesbians have had in the Girl Scouts is vast. By and large, those experiences have been good, as this volume explicates. But there is no avoiding the bad experiences and their roots in homophobia, which is, undeniably, a form of prejudice.

So how do we answer the questions posed by both lesbians and the Religious Right regarding the role of lesbians in the Girl Scouts?

The answer to lesbians is simple: Hiding is never good, the closet is an increasingly dangerous place; it only takes one person to rip open the door of the closet and expose the lesbian hidden within. Far better to step out willingly, honestly and proudly into the light than have someone with their own homophobic agenda damage one's good name through innuendo.

As for the Religious Right, history answers all their questions and addresses all their fears. Lesbianism poses no threat to the integrity of scouting as so many girls—myself included—have envisioned it over the years. In the eighty-five-year life of the Girl Scouts of America there have been many lesbian scouts and many lesbian troop leaders and administrators who have helped sustain and advance the organization. They, however, have not always received the same kind of support. As a few of these tales explain in raw, often poignant language, there are young lesbians who have been treated very badly and traumatized by the homophobia inherent in some (not all, as many of the other pieces declare) troops.

Ultimately, however, the Girl Scouts isn't *about* sexual orientation, but something else entirely, and that fact forms the foundation for this book. Scouting remains an engagement in something beyond simple sexual expression—lesbian or heterosexual. Scouting is about helping to establish the *self-esteem* and *self-worth* of girls by making them feel significant and whole as individuals while also encouraging them to feel integral and essential to the group as scouts—regardless of their race, age, intellect, religion, economic or class status, or physical ability (there are groups of disabled scouts). Part of establishing that self-esteem would be to allow discussion of homosexuality so that lesbian girls could feel as comfortable as their heterosexual counterparts—*and*, as has been proven over the years in the arenas of race and class, obliterating some of the prejudices girls are acculturated with by society. The Girl Scouts is a great place to explore and celebrate difference.

And that is what the Girl Scouts is about, celebrating difference (girls are different from boys; girls are individuals, different from each other) as well as exploding myths (girls are less important than boys; racial, ethnic and other differences make one girl less than another).

It's been thirty years since I first wanted to be a scout and a great deal has changed for girls since I was a child. The pressures on girls are significantly different than they were when I was growing up; girls are still expected to marry and have children, but they now bear the added responsibility of having a career as well. Studies over the past few decades indicate that girls are still very much discriminated against in every aspect of social life. Girls get inferior education in co-gendered classes where both male and female teachers are predisposed to be more attentive to male students than female students. Girls suffer from verbal and sexual harassment as early as first grade. Title IX has given girls entree into the arena of subsidized sports which studies show makes them far more able to compete in other aspects of life, but in recent years high schools and colleges have begun filing lawsuits to have that equal opportunity measure invalidated so that the money spent on girls/women can be diverted to men's sports. The position for women once they enter the work force isn't much better: Women make only a few cents more on the dollar today than they did when I was in elementary school; the glass ceiling is real and visible to women of every class and race.

The emotional and sexual pressures on girls are equally powerful. According to many experts in the field of abuse, one in four girls is a victim of incest or sexual abuse. Girls are increasingly victims of violence at home and on the street. Teen pregnancy remains higher in the United States than in any other industrialized nation. There are more new cases of AIDS among young women and teenage girls than among any other group. More girls are smoking and taking drugs than ever before in history.

In this new and dangerous territory girls need the solidity of groups like the Girl Scouts far more than they did when I was a girl and roles for women and men were more clearly defined and segregated. But groups like the Girl Scouts need to be accessible to *all* girls, not just white, heterosexual, middle-class girls. Some studies have indicated that the suicide rate among lesbian teens may be as high as ten times that of young heterosexual women. Access to role models and open integration into groups of teens where the threat of homophobia is mitigated by discussion and exploration of different sexual orientations is essential for these young girls' survival. Traditionally the Girl Scouts has presented a haven for girls with no other access to the warmth and camaraderie provided by scouting; shouldn't that access be extended to young lesbians?

There are those who will be outraged at the prospect of open lesbians in the Girl Scouts hierarchy, those who view lesbianism as a perverse "lifestyle" choice, rather than an inherent sexual orientation. But there were probably many Southerners outraged, when I was a young girl, at the prospect of black girls integrating previously all-white scout troops; the Girl Scouts survived that period, they will survive this one as well. Just as racial integration was furthered by that acknowledgment of racism (although no doubt a book could be done on the variant perspectives of black women on their experience with racism in the Girl Scouts), *acknowledged* integration of lesbians into the Girl Scouts (they've been there for eighty-five years) will help to mitigate the biases of homophobia.

I began this foreword by saying I had always wanted to be a scout. Reading this book hasn't changed my opinion; the sad pieces are painful to read, but they speak to the larger issue of homophobia in our society and how the Girl Scouts is a part of that society. Overall the book is tremendously affirming of the role scouting has played in the lives of young lesbians, and most young women, as my partner and friends assert. *That* reality underscores the need for acceptance of lesbian troop leaders and administrators as well as scouts. If scouting was an overwhelmingly bad experience for girls, there wouldn't be such a need to anchor a place for lesbians within the group.

Scouting still offers girls choices unavailable to them elsewhere. The last three decades have engaged women in infiltrating one male bastion after another. But in the last decade it has also become clear that there is great value in gender-specific groups for girls and women. We now know, for example, that girls do better academically in classes and schools without boys. Scouting carries the same weight as other sex-segregated experiences—teaching girls to be themselves without looking over their shoulders for the approval of men; teaching camaraderie; teaching sharing, trust and integration. In the inner city, scouting offers girls a refuge from the pressures of the street; in rural areas, scouting offers respite from the isolation imposed by geography.

What will happen when people discover there are lesbian troop leaders and lesbian girl scouts? Initial outrage from some quarters, perhaps. But the boycott of Disney has already been unsuccessful; the desire for the commodity overwhelmed the politics of the boycott; most people can't explain to their children that they can't go to see *Beauty and the Beast* or *Hercules* because the company that made these movies treats all its employees equally. It would be a difficult task for most parents to deny their girl children scouting privileges for similar reasons. Fear of homosexuality will always obtain wherever a group is comprised of one gender only; but conversely, the fear also exists that wherever there are two genders present heterosexuality will predominate—and statistically there are more chances of girls being molested by men than by women (according to the 1995 Department of Justice statistics, 97 percent of all sexual abuse of girls is perpetrated by men; of the percentage perpetrated by women, nearly one hundred percent of those incidents occurs at the hands of mothers or other female relatives). No group is inherently incorruptible, but as groups go, the Girl Scouts is as pristine as they come in terms of protecting girls of any sexual orientation from sexual abuse.

One also cannot say that just because some Girl Scouts and troop leaders and administrators are lesbian that scouting is a queer thing. It's a *girl* thing. It fosters important female identity for *all* girls, lesbian or heterosexual. It empowers *girls* to be *girls*—not pseudo men, not cookie-cutter girls but independent, thinking young women who will be able to take the personal and survival skills they learn in scouting and—like my very successful partner and friends—apply them later in their lives, regardless of their sexual orientation.

Scouting is, as many of these pieces explore, first and foremost about gender equity. It's about strengthening a girl's sense of herself and her place in the world, allowing her the space to be herself with other girls, away from the pressures of the sexual world.

This was what I so yearned to be a part of when I was a young girl. I didn't know I was a lesbian yet. I didn't understand my own sexuality on any level in those years. But what I did understand with unrelenting clarity was how narrow the world seemed for women as compared to men, for girls as compared to boys. Scouting represented an alternative choice to me, an opportunity to do more in the world. I believed Girl Scouts had entrée into a world that was far more expansive than the one to which I was privy. Girl Scouts could canoe down a river and survive in the woods; those were skills that could lead somewhere beyond the horizons that were set for girls when I was growing up.

Not every experience in this book replicates my rosy image of scouting, but that isn't surprising; no single experience is perfect for everyone. But it is clear from the majority of these pieces that scouting does open a new world for young women—regardless of their sexual orientation. But this book is about breaking silence, something Nancy Manahan understands in a way few other editors do. Once again she has taken on the exploration and examination of lesbian experience within a community of women that is as American as apple pie (or Girl Scout cookies). As she touched on our spiritual center in *Lesbian Nuns: Breaking Silence*, she touches on our cultural center in this book. This is a book all lesbians should read, because it is about our experience and history as lesbians, it forms part of our cultural identity. But it is also a book *all* women should read, whether they (or their mothers, daughters, aunts, cousins, friends) have been scouts or not. Because it is, more than anything, about what it means to be a girl and woman in our society, what the struggle for personal, gender and sexual identity means for women and how we empower ourselves through speaking out, through breaking silence, through understanding what honor among girls and women really should mean.

Victoria A. Brownworth
Philadelphia, Pa.
September 1997

Victoria A. Brownworth is a Pulitzer Prize-nominated journalist and one of the most widely published lesbian writers in the United States. A contributing editor and columnist for several newspapers, magazines and journals, her writing appears regularly in both the queer and mainstream press, including Ms., the *Village Voice*, OUT, POZ , *The Baltimore Sun, The Philadelphia Daily News*, and *LBR*. She is the author of seven books and editor of five. Her book *Too Queer: Essays from a Radical Life* was nominated for a Pulitzer Prize, an American Library Association award, the Robert F. Kennedy Book Award, and was a double finalist for the 1997 Lambda Literary Awards. She lives in Philadelphia with her partner of ten years, filmmaker Judith M. Redding.

On My Honor:
Lesbians Reflect on Their
Scouting Experience

INTRODUCTION

✳ ✳ ✳

A Simple Question
of Justice

Nancy Manahan

 In an Indian restaurant one evening, the curry prepared with coconut milk reminded me of Girl Scout "cake." I regaled my partner with a description of the big squares of unsliced white bread dipped in sweetened condensed milk, rolled in coconut, speared with a freshly-sharpened stick, and toasted over the camp fire. This, my favorite camp dessert, tasted like fluffy angel food cake with coconut frosting.

Becky said, "You look so happy when you talk about the Girl Scouts. Why?"

I tried to explain the joy of Girl Scouting. I told Becky about troop meetings, day camp, trips to Camden State Park, and the magical week at Camp Tukawah each August. I loved everything about the Girl Scouts: the uniform and badge sash; the sturdy green handbook full of practical knot-tying and lashing techniques; the sense of community as we constructed a kaper chart or sang around a campfire; the ideals of international peace and friendship; and the happiness of sitting on a dock beside Mary, my camp friend, our legs dangling in the cool, clear water.

I was flooded by memories of two Girl Scout Roundups, with thousands of tents sheltering scouts from all over the world. And once again, I felt the draw of traveling to Our Chalet (the first international Girl Guide/Girl Scout[1] center) near Adelboden, Switzerland, and to Our Cabaña (the first Girl Guide/ Girl Scout center in the western hemisphere) in Cuernavaca, Mexico. Although I never visited either center, my imagination was stirred by the dream of meeting girls and women who said the promise in other languages and, in their differently colored uniforms, tried to live by the same scouting laws I did.

An hour later, over Indian tea, I softly sang, "Make new friends, but keep the old / One is silver and the other gold," a round espousing one of the many Girl Scout principles that have guided my life. I remembered the bittersweet end-of-camp ritual when we held hands around the fire and sang with passionate, choked voices:

Each campfire lights anew
The flame of friendship true
The joy I've had in knowing you
Will last a whole life through.

Becky watched me wipe tears from my eyes. "You know," she said, "I've noticed that lesbians tend to get very emotional about their scouting experiences. What is it about the Girl Scouts that affects so many lesbians?"

I thought for a moment. Even though I hadn't realized I was a lesbian during my Girl Scout years, my joy in scouting stemmed partly from being in an all-women environment for at least a week every summer, the only time I didn't have to cope with men, boys, or the pressure to date. At camp, I met a few counselors who, in retrospect, I think were lesbians although they gave no indication of that by word or action. Those counselors acted as a powerful antidote to the poison of homophobic self-hatred already dripping into my veins. I could see with my own eyes that they were wonderful, good-hearted, principled women. Although I didn't know the word "lesbian," I knew I was interested in girls *that* way. From those few camp counselors I absorbed the unspoken but reassuring message that being a sexual minority wasn't so shameful after all.

"This sounds like your next book," Becky said, as we paid the bill.

"Oh, no," I replied, "I'm sure someone has already done it."

During the next few weeks, I looked for books on the connection between lesbians and scouting. I found nothing. I looked for articles. I found nothing. I checked out data bases. Still nothing. After meeting Madwoman Press' Diane Benison, who expressed interest in publishing a book about lesbian Girl Scouts, I began announcing the project in magazines, newsletters, and at women's bookstores. Over the next two years, almost one hundred women responded.

On My Honor: Lesbians Reflect on Their Scouting Experience contains stories from thirty-three of those women, documenting the contributions lesbians have made to the Girl Scouts, the impact scouting has had on lesbians, and some of the problems undermining the relationship between lesbians and scouting. Most of these stories are written by women who, like me, haven't been involved in scouting for years. Other contributors currently hold professional or volunteer positions with the organization. They range in age from thirty-one to sixty, represent a variety of ethnic backgrounds, and live in all parts of the United States.

The stories they tell are in most ways no different from those of heterosexuals involved in Girl Scouting. Girls from dysfunctional families found a haven of sanity in their scout troops and at camp. Girls from healthier families received additional support to take risks, develop leadership skills, and serve others. Both types of girls found role models, good values, camaraderie, a service ethic, and the joy of the out-of-doors. As adults, many of the women in this book became camp counselors and troop leaders, taught girls camping and leadership skills, and helped raise money for wider Girl Scout opportunities. Some became professional Girl Scouts, choosing a career with the organization they loved. All of them knew that as Girl Scouts, they were contributing something worthwhile to their communities and to the next generation of girls.

Breaking the Silence

With all these commonalities, what makes the stories in this book different from the stories heterosexual women might write? The contributors to *On My Honor: Lesbians Reflect on Their Scouting Experience* are breaking a taboo. For many years, lesbians in Girl Scouting–as in the larger society–have been warned, explicitly or implicitly, not to reveal their sexual orientation. Bad things would happen if they came out of the closet. Parents would withdraw their girls from the organization. Program directors and camp counselors could lose their jobs. Volunteer leaders could have their troops taken away. Professional Girl Scouts could lose not only their livelihood, but the entire career upon which their lives, their friendship network, and their identity were built.

The taboo against being openly lesbian originates in society's ignorance,

Margaret Manahan (l),
Nancy Manahan (r)
1962

fear, and hatred of homosexuality. Just the phrase "lesbian Girl Scout" can raise in the homophobic mind the specter of a deviant predator seducing an innocent girl. Abuse can happen anywhere, of course, but statistics show that a girl runs a far greater risk of being molested by a male relative or neighbor than she does during any number of years with a lesbian troop leader or camp counselor.[2] In fact, as some of the women in this book can attest, Girl Scout camps across America provide havens of safety where, for a week or two each summer, girls are free of the sexual abuse taking place in their own homes.

Perhaps an even deeper reason for encouraging lesbian Girl Scouts to remain in the closet is misogyny–fear and hatred of women, especially of powerful women (no matter what their sexual orientation) who embody independence from men. An all-female group like Girl Scouting, which teaches girls to chop their own wood, build their own fires, carry their own canoes, and run their own organizations, threatens sexist social arrangements by empowering females. Not revealing that this group includes lesbians–women independent of men in a most basic way–may seem to be a prudent choice in a misogynist world. Today, however, I believe that encouraging lesbian members to stay in the closet damages Girl Scouting more than it protects the organization.

Girl Scout Lesbian Policy

Many people mistakenly assume that the Girl Scouts and Boy Scouts are twin organizations with the same anti-gay policy. Former United States Surgeon General Joycelyn Elders, for example, when asked in a 1994 cover story interview with *USA Weekend* if the Boy Scouts should admit homosexuals, replied that they should and that she also thought "lesbians should be allowed to join the Girl Scouts."[3]

USA Weekend received eighty letters in response to that story, including one from then-Girl Scout national executive director Mary Rose Main and then-national president B. Larae Orullian, who contended that Elders' statement "creates confusion about the Girl Scouts' stance on sexual orientation." Main and Orullian stated that "Girl Scouts of the U.S.A. is totally separate from the Boy Scouts of America," and that, "while the Girl Scouts do not recruit lesbians, we do not discriminate. We respect the beliefs of our members and do not intrude into personal matters. We do not have policies on sexual orientation."

"However," Main and Orullian cautioned, "we do not condone or permit sexual displays of any sort. Neither do we permit the advocacy of a personal life style or sexual orientation. Girl Scout leadership," they concluded, "must at all times serve as appropriate role models for girls."[4]

The fundamental stance of the organization is that sexual orientation is not an issue; appropriate behavior *is*. The position is further explained in the Girl Scouts of the U.S.A. book *What We Stand For*, designed to "answer some commonly asked questions about Girl Scouting, its principles, and practices."[5] In addition to the principles Main and Orullian voiced, this document says that "personal lifestyle or sexual orientation . . . are private matters for girls and their families to address."[6] The Girl Scout position, in a nutshell, is "don't ask, don't tell."

Girl Scout Lesbian Reality

Girl Scouts of the U.S.A., should be commended for publicly stating that it does not discriminate against lesbians and for adopting its then-progressive "don't ask, don't tell" position in 1980. It requires courage and integrity for

Nancy Manahan,
Boundary Waters Canoe Area,
1993

a mainstream organization dealing with children and dependent on public goodwill and public funding to take such a position. Nevertheless, articulating a position is not the same as establishing a policy or encouraging the 320 local Girl Scout councils (all independent from the national office and from each other) to adhere to that policy. Sexual orientation is not included in the official Girl Scout of the U.S.A. nondiscrimination policy, along with other protected classes like age, race, color, ethnic background, sex, religion, national origin, and socioeconomic status.

True, in some councils, lesbian staff and volunteers find acceptance and freedom from discrimination; they do not need to be completely in the closet to retain their positions. In most councils, however, lesbians fear that if they were ever open about their sexual orientation, there would be trouble.

This discrepancy between position and practice is analogous to an organization addressing anti-Semitism by stating that it is open to all individuals regardless of their religious beliefs. Such an organization might say that while it does not recruit Jews, it does not discriminate or intrude into personal matters such as religion. It does not, however, condone religious displays of any sort, nor does it tolerate the endorsement or any particular religion. It says that religion is a private matter for members and their families to discuss. Meanwhile, this hypothetical organization honors Christian holidays with office decorations, parties, and days off. It discourages members from mentioning Judaism or openly discussing the organization's history of dismissing members who admit to being or are rumored to be Jewish. No doubt many Jews could pass as Gentiles in this imaginary organization, just as many lesbians can pass as heterosexuals in Girl Scouting. But an organization that encourages passing and whose members risk repercussions for not passing is practicing discrimination.

Perpetuating this sort of discrimination violates basic democratic principles such as freedom of speech (a person should not risk losing her position for what she says or writes); freedom of assembly (a person should not risk losing her position for participating in a meeting, a rally, or a parade); and separation of church and state (a person should not risk losing her position because of some people's religious objections to her life choices).

Although Girl Scouts may not endorse a particular lifestyle, the organization *does* "permit the advocacy of a personal life style or sexual orientation," *as long as it is heterosexual.* Recent handbooks discuss heterosexual dating, dealing with boyfriends, and (hetero)sexual questions. Husbands are not only talked about; they may be an integral part of the troop life, participating in camping trips, cookie sales, and other activities.

This sort of double standard was also practiced in the early days of the National Organization for Women, which told lesbians who were involved in NOW that they could participate in the fight for women's equality as long as they stayed in the closet. NOW feared that if lesbian women were open about their orientation, they would drive away other members and discredit the organization. Lesbian activists, with the support of heterosexual feminists like Gloria Steinem, finally prevailed on the question of lesbian visibility. The National Organization for Women now has a solid lesbian rights plank. Those who were opposed to lesbian visibility have expressed regret at their former stance and have acknowledged both the contributions of lesbian members and the importance of opposing all forms of injustice.

Although very different in membership, mission and funding, the Girl Scouts, like NOW, must deal with societal anti-lesbian prejudice that appears to jeopardize the good work the group does for women and girls. Both organizations include members who reflect majority positions, those whose primary concern is to protect the organization, and those who would push the bounds. Perhaps the Girl Scouts can take courage from the National Organization for Women's success in pushing the bounds on the issue of homophobia.

Girl Scouts and the Military

Another significant difference between the Girl Scouts and NOW is that Girl Scouting is based on a paramilitary model.[7] Its inspiration was the British Girl Guides, modeled after the Boy Scouts, established by a retired British army general, Lord Robert Baden-Powell. Girl Scouts of the U.S.A. inherited and retained some of the military trappings. Begun in 1912, Girl Scouting expanded rapidly during World War I as members provided essential wartime services such as producing food, rolling bandages, and selling war bonds. Girl Scout founder Juliette Gordon Low wore a military-style uniform. A film she helped make in 1918 shows uniformed scouts crisply saluting each other and marching in formation.[8] Even in the 1950s and 1960s, I remember standing at military attention around the flag pole each evening during Camp Tukawah's solemn lowering of the United States flag. I learned to fold it into a perfect compact triangle, holding my breath lest a corner of the sacred flag slip from our fingers and touch the ground.

The United Sates military and Girl Scouts of the U.S.A. have more in common than patrol structure, uniforms with insignia, and patriotic flag ceremonies. Both organizations have trained, encouraged, and rewarded many lesbian women for outstanding service–as long as they stayed in the closet. Both institutions have conducted periodic witch-hunts, purging some of these same dedicated women, closeted or not, from the ranks.

Lesbians in the military are finally telling their stories. Randy Shilts' book *Conduct Unbecoming* (1993), details the long and distinguished history of homosexuals in the service and describes the shameful treatment they have received in return. Winni S. Webber's *Lesbians in the Military Speak Out* (1993) contains personal stories from lesbians serving in all branches of the U.S. armed forces, and Nanci Little's novel *Thin Fire* (1993) tells a moving story about an army lesbian that resounds with verisimilitude. *Serving in Silence*

(1994), the autobiography of Colonel Margarethe Cammermeyer, became the basis for Barbra Streisand's made-for-TV movie starring Glenn Close, which was seen by millions of Americans in 1995.

In addition to the media examination of the subject, gay and lesbian military personnel are pressing their case in the courts, in marches, and in a widespread campaign to educate the public and to bring about an end to discrimination in the United States Armed Forces. Perhaps it is time for Girl Scout leaders to expand their efforts to offer education on this issue to adult members and the communities they serve.

Lesbian Girl Scouts in Print

An article about lesbian Girl Scouts *had* been published but didn't show up when I was doing my initial search: a 1989 essay by Jorjet Harper in New York's defunct *Outweek*, reprinted in this book (Chapter 21). A lesbian Girl Scout story by Judith McDaniel, "The Juliette Low Legacy," later appeared in *40 Contemporary Lesbian and Gay Short Stories* (ed. Irene Zahava, Westview, 1994). See Judith McDaniel's non-fiction account of a lesbian Girl Scout in Chapter 1 of this book.

Also in 1994, *The Lesbian Connection* (a twenty-year-old bimonthly news and opinion magazine) printed a spirited exchange of letters about the importance of Girl Scouting to many lesbians. Some of the writers praised the organization for fostering their strengths, encouraging them to be themselves, and in some cases, providing a refuge from unbearable family situations. A few letters depicted an astonishing atmosphere of acceptance. For example, an openly lesbian vice president of an Eastern Girl Scout Council described her council's affirmative action policies, which include the promotion of positive role models, both lesbian and straight, and zero tolerance for sexist, racist, ageist, or homophobic behavior.

Some of the contributors to this book have had similarly positive experiences with the Girl Scouts. They have served at camps where lesbian staff were welcomed and have found an accepting women's community in Girl Scouting. For example, when Roberta Garr, an American Girl Scout, applied for a residence visa in Norway so she could be with her Norwegian partner (Chapter 27), the leaders at Our Chalet, the Girl Guide/Girl Scout international center in Switzerland, where both women had worked, wrote a letter attesting to their long-term relationship. In Wyoming, an out-lesbian couple, both lifetime Girl Scout members (Chapter 29), lead a Senior troop with the support of the girls' parents, the executive director, and the council president. Dawn Ace (Chapter 30) worked for the San Francisco Bay Girl Scout Council, where nobody objected when her partner Phoebe stopped by the office. Even more remarkable, Beth Toolan (Chapter 32) was hired by a Massachusetts Girl Scout council as an open lesbian and has successfully integrated her family and professional life.

Other lesbians have not been so fortunate. A woman in graduate school (Chapter 22) was warned by her boss that if she contributed to this book, she would never again get a job or volunteer position with any Girl Scout council. Prejudice cost Rachel Wetherill (Chapter 20) her Girl Scout troop. Kristen Renn (Chapter 26) lost her job with a Girl Scout council, not because of behavior or inadequate job performance but, she learned from inside sources, because of her sexual orientation. Fortunately, experiences like this are more the exception than the rule, but the threat of exposure and prejudice clouds many members' professional and personal lives.

For Whom Is This Book Intended?

I hope this book makes the cost of institutionalized homophobia clearer to the Girl Scouts. The stories here detail not only personal suffering, but also the enormous talent and financial drain caused by the loss of dedicated, competent, experienced lesbian volunteer and professional members. The *de facto* "don't ask, don't tell" policy on sexual orientation also does a tremendous disservice to girls who need more, not less, sophisticated help in living in an increasingly complex and diverse world. By silencing what may be the largest minority in the organization, the Girl Scouts are missing a valuable opportunity to model respect for diversity and justice.

The book is especially for adult lesbians and their supporters currently in Girl Scouting. Thank you for your courage and leadership. Please help the organization–which does so much to empower girls and women–take the next steps in treating its lesbian youth and adults with integrity.

This book is for girl members. I hope you are learning to appreciate diversity and to oppose injustice of any kind. I hope you find support and encouragement to be completely yourselves. If it's important to you, I hope you can find an adult lesbian role model who is serving the organization she loves, and who is helping you and your friends become strong, self-accepting, independent women, no matter whom you choose to love.

The book is also for lesbians who no longer are or never were Girl Scouts. I hope you enjoy these stories of self-discovery, love, and courage. They supply a missing chapter of our history, depict another facet of our culture, clarify another aspect of our oppression, and offer inspiring examples of integrity.

On My Honor: Lesbians Reflect on Their Scouting Experience is also intended for readers at large, women and men in large and small towns, who may be moved by the courage in these stories. I hope you will offer support to lesbian and gay youth and adults. I hope you will stand up against injustice the next time a teacher, minister, or scout leader in your community is persecuted. I hope you urge your elected representatives to vote in favor of bills prohibiting discrimination on the basis of sexual orientation.

Finally, the book is for the thirty-three contributors: a chance to tell their stories, to reflect on the meaning of Girl Scouting in their lives, to thank an organization that helped them become the women they are, and to publicly urge that organization to live up to the values they learned there: fairness, honesty, and respect.

Conclusion

On My Honor: Lesbians Reflect on Their Scouting Experience is not saying that all or most Girl Scouts are lesbians. The vast majority of the millions of girls in scouting grow up to be heterosexual, and the vast majority of the hundreds of thousands of adult volunteers and paid staff who keep the organization running are heterosexual. There may be more, fewer, or about the same percentage of lesbians in Girl Scouting as in comparable groups. Since the Girl Scouts' founding in 1912, almost sixty million girls have been members. If, as researchers estimate, between two and ten percent of the general population is primarily homosexual in orientation, then anywhere from one to six million Girl Scouts may have been or have become lesbians. This is the first book to tell their stories.

The women here give voice to Girl Scouts empowered through contact with nature, all-female environments, and strong role models (Part I). They carry these experiences with them into adulthood, taking their place in the long green line of American leaders and activists in whose lives the ideals and values of this extraordinary organization are fulfilled (Part II). They represent scouts who have suffered when those ideals were not fulfilled– women disillusioned by racism, those who lost positions when their sexual orientation became known, and those closeted in an organization that is not safe for them (Part III). And finally, they speak for lesbians who have found acceptance, a supportive Girl Scout community, and an opportunity to successfully integrate their personal with their volunteer and professional life (Part IV).

It is time for Girl Scouts everywhere to try, on their honor, to do their duty to end overt–and covert–discrimination against what is probably the organization's largest minority. It is time for Girl Scouts of the U.S.A. to affirm its lesbian members, openly and proudly. A good beginning would be to listen carefully to the women in this book.

Nancy Manahan, 1997

[1] *Juliette Gordon Low, founder of Girl Scouts of the U.S.A., learned about Girl Guiding from the founder of the Boy Scouts, Lord Robert Baden-Powell, and his sister, Agnes Baden-Powell, who established Girl Guides in England in 1911. The American organization, begun in 1912, was called Girl Guides in America until its name was changed in 1915 (Scouting for Girls, 4th ed. New York: Girl Scouts, Inc., 1923, p. 1). Girl Scouts of the U.S.A. is one of 136 member countries of the World Association of Girl Guides and Girl Scouts (WAGGGS) with a world wide membership of eight and a half million.*

[2] *According to the U.S. Bureau of Justice, 97 percent of sex offenders are male. "Bureau of Justice Statistics," March 1996, <http://www.ojp.usdoj.gov/pub/bjs/pdf/wopris.pdf> (June 30, 1997). A pioneering study at the University of Colorado Health Sciences Center indicates that a child is more than one hundred times as likely to be sexually abused by the heterosexual partner of a relative than by a gay adult. (Marilyn Eliss, "Child Molesters Rarely Homosexual," USA Today, July 12, 1994, Internet ed., p. 1D)*

[3] *"Listening to Elders," USA Weekend, June 3-5, 1994.*

[4] *B. Larae Orullian and Mary Rose Main, "No Bias in the Girl Scouts," USA Weekend, July 1—3, 1994, p. 12.*

[5] *Girl Scouts of the U.S.A., What We Stand For. New York: GSUSA, 1994, p. 5.*

[6] *Girl Scouts of the U.S.A., What We Stand For. New York: GSUSA, 1994, p. 10.*

[7] *Barbara Smalley, sociologist, personal interview, January 5, 1994. (Smalley herself lost a job with the Philadelphia Girl Scouts over the issue of sexual orientation.)*

[8] The Golden Eaglet: The Story of a Girl Scout. Videotape. Girl Scouts of the U.S.A., 1952.

PART I

* * *

Empowerment

Empowerment

Many women have found Girl Scouts empowering. First, and perhaps most importantly, Girl Scouting is a gateway to the natural world. Spending a week canoeing on a wilderness river, backpacking on a mountain, or just living in cabins at the edge of a forest can open the door to a deep connection with nature. The exhilarating, challenging, and deep spiritual force of nature is alien to girls accustomed to, at best, city parks. Girl Scouting can provide not only the introduction to that force, but instruction in being competent and at home in the wilderness.

In addition, Girl Scouting is the gateway to an all-female world. For many girls, scouting is their first and only experience of women doing all the important, creative jobs, making all the decisions, and modeling all aspects of leadership. Strong, competent female role models are especially important for girls growing up in a world in which men still make most of the decisions and hold most of the power.

Although most scouts are heterosexual, some are lesbians. The word may never be spoken, and no one, perhaps not even the young people themselves, may be aware of their sexual orientation. But for lesbian youth who desperately need a role model, a lesbian camp counselor or troop leader may provide the first clue that heterosexuality is not the only option, that diversity is acceptable, that a woman can love and build a life with another woman.

The ten women in Part I recount their stepping through the door of Girl Scouting into the freeing realms of nature, female strength, and lesbian role models.

CHAPTER 1

Down the Saranac
with Sixteen Paddles

Judith McDaniel

An adult volunteer recounts a typical Girl Scout experience: guiding a group of teenagers on a wilderness trip. Lesbian volunteers do exactly what heterosexual volunteers do: teach girls camping, canoeing, and group skills, passing on to the next generation what they themselves have learned in scouting.

"**Y**ou're going to do what?" my friends asked when I announced my summer recreation. "With how many Girl Scouts?" And, "What do *you* know about canoeing?"

Not a lot, I had to admit. I hadn't been in a canoe for ten years when I went on the spring trial run with others who had also agreed to lead a short canoe trip on the Saranac River. I am more often behind a desk or at my typewriter, but my canoeing muscles hadn't been *too* out of shape, I remind myself as I stand looking at the piles of gear stacked around the first two girls to arrive. Another car pulls up and deposits two more girls. As Mary's mother gets back in the car, Mary pulls out a huge portable radio and starts to turn the dial. I signal her mother to wait and edge toward Mary.

"Gee, Mary, I don't think you'll have much time to listen to that. And we wouldn't want it to fall out of a canoe, would we, hmmm?" I maneuver her toward the car and she very reluctantly deposits the radio with mother. So does her friend Julie, to Mary's distress.

"Oh Julie, why'd you have to tell them you have one?" Mary pouts. "You know I can't sleep without a radio on."

As I wave good-bye to the departing mother, I hear Beth's undertone, "Never mind. I brought mine with me and my mother is already gone." They all look relieved. I file the information for later. At 10 a.m. our sixth canoer arrives and we heft our gear and set off down the path to the tents we will occupy for this one night before our outing. By 10:30 the girls are out in canoes on Hidden Lake, getting checked out by the resident canoe staff on how much they remember about their strokes and canoe safety from last year's lessons. I take half an hour to reconnoitre.

Checking through the gear, I realize that most of it is borrowed from the other volunteers. This is an all-volunteer camp, sponsored by the Adirondack Girl Scout Council. The staff has run the camp for three years now, more elaborately each time. This year the girls who were trained in camp last year are eligible for an out-of-camp canoe trip, which is why I'm here.

At noon the girls troop up to the boat house where I've laid out peanut butter and jelly for sandwiches. Mary tells me she doesn't eat peanut butter. I explain that it is all we will have for lunch for the trip, since it doesn't spoil. I'm irritated with her already because of the radio incident, because she seems so lethargic and whiney.

"What's for dinner, then?" she asks, looking with distaste at the sandwich counter.

"Barbecue chicken," I tell them enthusiastically, "won't that be good?"

But Mary doesn't eat chicken either. "What do you eat?" I inquire with some rancor.

"Oh, steak," she replies languidly, then more animatedly, "and pizza." I grind my teeth. It is time for the food statement.

"Look," I tell the group as we sit on the dock for lunch, "the food for this trip was planned for nutrition and easy preparation over a campfire. There will always be plenty to eat. If you don't like some things, eat what you do like. The main thing is, I don't want to hear complaints. Okay?" They say okay. Mary eats two stale Girl Scout cookies in silence.

After a rest, I put them in the water for swim tests. They are all water rats. They love the water and undergo instant and complete personality changes when they're soaking wet. Mary and Beth want to learn the butterfly so they

Judith McDaniel and
scouts on Saranac
River trip, 1980

can try out for the swim team when they start ninth grade. Julie is a gymnast and takes her lithe young body through a marvelous series of contorted dives, then asks, "Can I do a cartwheel dive off the end of the dock?" I suggest it might be a little narrow and unsteady. She settles for a handstand backflip. I feel stiff just watching her.

Sally arrives in the late afternoon. She is the other adult who is going with us. The girls come up from the lake, tired, but less cranky, it seems to me. Sitting around a table in the kitchen area, I try to set a few rules for the next three days, just a few so we can all relax. Buddies at all times. No swimming without the lifeguard (that's me) present. Camp jobs get traded off—fire, cook, cleanup. When I get out the map, they begin to believe we are really going. I trace our path from the put-in at Second Pond, up the Saranac River to Oseetah Lake, then through the inlet to Kiawasa and the lean-to there.

It's dinner time and they cook. We all eat chicken, even Mary. After dinner I go through the gear each girl wants to take. We leave home Mary's seven extra T-shirts, Elaine's five pair of blue jeans and Beth's radio. She gives it up with good grace. I am looking forward to our trip.

The next morning we are up at six, packed and canoes loaded by eight. The girls sleep most of the drive north, but start to wake up as we drive by the Lake Placid Winter Olympic sites and are ready to go when we pull into the unloading ramp. I let the girls untie the canoes and start carrying them down to the water, while I worry to myself about how to pack and tie down our gear in each canoe, something I'd thought a lot about, but never done before. It seems to me to be common sense—the gear has to stay dry and with the canoe—but the task makes me feel all thumbs and the end result was not the neat packaging I had imagined. Nonetheless, we stow all of our gear and shove off into Second Pond.

The sun is hot, the humidity high as we paddle up Second Pond to the lily pads where we take a right and meander over to Cold Brook. One of the canoes is making a crisscross rather than a straight path, as Mary's stroke is so strong in the bow, Beth can't hold a course. It looks like they are canoeing twice as far as the rest of us! After lunch we canoe through "dead-tree-lake" and down to the state locks, the highlight of Mary's day. The iron gates clang shut behind our four canoes and the floodgates in the front open.

As the water pours out and our canoes begin to descend, Mary asks longingly, "Oh, wow, can we come back this way when we go home?"

"Why?" I ask. "Now you've already seen it?"

"I know, I know," she says, "but I want to go the other way. I want to know what it's like to be elevated." We all agree that may not be possible for Mary and paddle on laughing.

We come out of the locks into the marsh of Oseetah Lake, lily pads and purple-spiked flowers. The sun is even hotter than at noon, and our heavily loaded canoes move slowly around the point to the creek into Kiawasa. In midafternoon we reach the lean-to, find it uninhabited, and even, Sandy tells us all proudly, find a roll of toilet paper in the latrine. General rejoicing. I promise them a swim as soon as camp is set up. Tents spring up miraculously. I check the swim area with mask and snorkel and then we spend the next hour jumping and diving off a large rock.

Out here the girls seem to me very independent and capable. They fix and eat dinner with no complaints and little direction from Sally and me. They are considerate of one another. Although four of the more lively girls bond instantly, the other two are never left out, or teased, but given room to enter in as they wish. They all seem to be slowly sloughing off bits of that "civilized" behavior I found so irritating back in camp.

At dusk I sit writing in my journal, resting under the pines on this beautiful and silent lake. The girls are fixing popcorn around the fire up at the lean-to.

I wake at dawn to hear a single white-throated sparrow greet the first light and wake the other birds. I lie for a half hour listening to each separate chorus enter the cacophony. The last of the night's rainfall drips on the tent fly.

Elaine and Sandy rise with the birds. I suggest that it *is* their one morning to sleep in, if they want. But Elaine is practicing with the hatchet, to her sister's disapproving, "Elaine, not now, go somewhere else, you're such a *twerp!*" from inside the tent. Sandy is washing out the pillowcase that got muddy when she used it in the canoe as a kneeling pad. She is the only girl on the trip I have not yet seen laugh.

After cold cereal and hot cocoa we head to Pine Pond. The morning is grey, but still. I am afraid of a storm, though it is more overcast than threatening.

We beach the canoes in marsh mud and walk into the woods carrying our paddles, lunches, raincoats and watermelon. Paddles are hidden behind a log and we quickly walk the half mile to the pond. As we come over a rise and look down at the water, we are all amazed. This incredibly pure and beautiful pond with a natural sand bottom and beach is breathtaking. The morning is still grey, and we are hungry after the canoeing, but we swim for nearly an hour before I insist on a lunch break. I feel totally relaxed, at ease, and sense the girls feeling a new freedom. After lunch we slice the watermelon and Sally starts a vigorous watermelon pit spit. They are all easily roused, love the attention and the forbidden pleasure of spitting their watermelon seeds at one another.

I wake from a catnap on the beach to see Elaine covered with sand from her shoulders to her feet, the five other girls gravely smoothing the wet sand over her entire body, admonishing her not to breathe too hard or she'll cause an earthquake. They decide she will be Dolly Parton and I watch as they mold her enormous breasts, smoothing each fondly, placing a nipple on top, consulting about whether they are lopsided or not. "Can you see your toes, Elaine?" Beth asks, "Cause if you can, they're not big enough yet." Sandy giggles with embarrassment and glee behind her hand.

I go over and suggest Dolly needs a belly button, craft one carefully in the appropriate zone, but Beth chides me, "Judith, Dolly Parton wouldn't have an inny belly button, hers is an outty," and she corrects my sculpture accordingly. Elaine decides she has to breathe and an earthquake finishes off Dolly.

I have to flog them out of Pine Pond. No one wants to leave, but it is late afternoon and the sun is gone again. I am afraid to take more of a chance with the weather. But it is too late. When we pull away from the cove, out past the protective point, a gusty wind hits our canoes broadside. An enormous thunderhead lowers in front of us, the wind is picking up even more, but I see no lightning, hear no thunder. I decide to head for home and turn to see how the girls are. They are paddling ferociously, putting their shoulders and backs into the effort as I have never seen them before, and I lead us out across the choppy lake toward our inlet. Virginia is in the bow of my canoe and in my anxiety I shout directions at her: "Pull right, Virginia, now left. Virginia, put your shoulders into it," screaming at her in frustration. "Feather your paddle, it will help me." As a gust of rain hits us, I catch a glimpse of her face. She is grinning with exhilaration.

The rain comes harder, but no one thinks of rain gear. We are all soaked and if we stopped we'd be blown clear back to Pine Pond. Still I hear no thunder. When we make the narrow channel a fisherman calls out to offer us shelter in his camp. We are only a half a mile from camp now, so we shout no and head for home. As we beach the canoes at our lean-to, the rain comes down in sheets and I hear the first thunder blowing across the lake.

"They loved it," Sally says in amazement as we flop into our tent to recover after drying off the girls and giving them hot chocolate. "They weren't scared. Just Mary. She kept asking me, what will Judith do if there's lightning?" She pauses, then turns to look at me. "What would you have done?"

"Put in," I answer emphatically. "We'd still be sitting in the rain on a shoreline somewhere waiting for this to pass. Were you scared?"

"Nervous," she allows.

"Me too," I confess, "me too."

The rain quits in the early evening while we make dinner and sit around the campfire toasting marshmallows. When it starts to pour again, we all go to bed. In the grey morning we cook French toast and start to break camp. I contemplate the peanut butter for the day's sandwiches, eye Mary, and ask, "Anyone prefer pizza for lunch today in Lake Placid Village?" Mary's whoop echoes in the trees and her enthusiasm carries us back down the trail, packs the canoes and sets us off again.

We vote to go back through the locks, retracing our steps, hoping to give Mary a real "elevation" like she'd asked for. As we start up the inlet, we all cheer to see the sun come out through the clouds, shining on just us. I know that when we get to the village Mary will start to whine and complain about her wet sleeping bag, she and Julie will point at every teenage boy we drive by, and Beth will spend fifteen minutes in the only ladies' room at the pizza place combing her hair while five of us are waiting to go to the bathroom. But for now I let the girls lead the way out into the marsh, enjoying the sparkle of the water as it comes off their paddles, watching the reflection of their firm and strong stokes in the rippled water.

Judith McDaniel

✳ ✳ ✳

CHAPTER 2

Camp or Bust

Martha McPheeters

A neurobiologist describes falling in love with the wilderness at age eight and trying ever since to return to her nirvana.

I despised the after-school Brownie program, making sit-upons and learning the Brownie Smile song when I could have been playing cowboys or football with my boy friends or writing poetry on my father's Smith Corona. When I was eight, however, my parents sent me to Girl Scout camp, and I changed my mind about the scouts.

Ten Brownies slept in a cabin in the woods. The bigger girls slept in tents, and the biggest girls slept on the ground and cooked over a fire. We ate s'mores and paddled canoes. I learned the buddy system for swimming, the correct glue for woodcraft jewelry, three hundred songs, and at least ten ghost stories. My counselors were named Brook and Shakespeare.

At the end of camp, when my parents pried me out of the woods and into the car, misery overtook me. Why couldn't I stay? Why did camp have to end? Why couldn't we go home today and come back tomorrow with the new batch of campers? My parents consoled me all the way home.

Martha McPheeters
(about 1963)

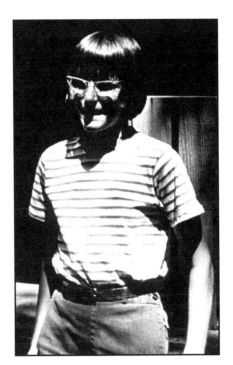

At camp, I had tasted whole wheat bread for the first time. Now there were multigrain breads in our breadbox. I had eaten my first oatmeal at camp. My mother thought oatmeal was vile, but she cooked it for my breakfast whenever I asked. In preparation for sleeping in a tent the next summer, I pestered my parents until I was allowed to sleep under a blanket-covered card table in the backyard.

In those two weeks at Girl Scout camp, I had glimpsed nirvana. Living outdoors, sleeping on the ground, hiking, canoeing and swimming were heaven. My parents continued to introduce me to academic and artistic pursuits like the mathematical puzzles in the back of *Scientific American*, oil paints and canvas, and flute lessons. But the passion burning in my eight-year-old heart was for the outdoors. Today we call it a love of the wilderness. I called it "to camp or bust."

I vowed I would return the next summer for the entire season: six whole weeks. My parents explained the impossibility of my proposition. They just didn't have enough money. The finances were strained with one two-week session, but because I had had such a wonderful time, they would see to it that the money was there again for a two-week session next summer. My work was cut out for me. How could I spend six weeks at camp for the price of two?

I can't claim a great entrepreneurial spirit or a precocious knowledge of the adult world. I was just an eight-year-old, after all. However, I was a kid who asked questions.

What was a scholarship? What was a grant? Did kids ever get to work at camp for their tuition? How old did I have to be to babysit? Exactly what was my allowance for? What could I do to get it raised?

The school year passed, and the questions slowly got answered. The next summer my parents paid for one session. I wrote an essay (I thought it was silly) about why I wanted to go to camp, and so earned a scholarship to the second session. My offer to stay and help the camp director with chores got me that coveted third session. I was exuberant.

Camp Amahami was even better the second year. The preprimitive unit was my home for the season. I learned how to clean latrines and kerosene lamps, important life skills for this new outdoor recruit. I thrilled to the scream of a mountain lion, perfected my canoe strokes, learned to build a one-match fire, and went on my first overnight hike.

Raising money for the next summer was simple because I was finally old enough to sell Girl Scout cookies. The girls who sold the most cookies got an automatic scholarship to camp. After school, I pounded the suburban streets, knocked on doors, acted cute, and made sales. I felt I was prostituting myself, but the end justified the means.

Perhaps to help me learn about means and ends, camp was a letdown this summer. I wasn't allowed in the pre-primitive unit again, and I wasn't old enough for the primitive unit. Despite a summer of discontent, I began to develop two very important life skills: the art of convincing twenty girls to swim before breakfast (or hike after dark, or collect honey from a beehive) and, when things got boring, the subterfuge to slip away from a group and explore the woods on my own.

After a winter of reading books about camping and again selling Girl Scout cookies, I was accepted into the primitive unit at Camp Amahami. My excitement was almost uncontainable. I didn't eat for nearly a week before camp.

After loading luggage and provisions onto a barge for the trip across the lake, we said goodbye to our parents and pushed off to our uncharted wilderness campsite. I was on my way to heaven.

The campsite had a brook nearby. We had to haul water to drink, cook, clean up, and boil all eating utensils in our ditty bags. The health department had decreed that all dishes not going through an industrial dishwasher had to be kept at a rolling boil for twenty minutes. Our counselors enforced this rule with bucket brigades and firewood piles replenished to their shoulders daily. We soon tired of the bucket brigade, and, using the only tools we had available—axes, saws, knives and twine—we built a trough that delivered unlimited supplies of water to our kitchen area. The water entered our system many yards upstream and flowed gently all the way to the campsite, arriving at waist height to directly fill the immense pots. I thought our rickety construction of crisscrossed sticks lashed to trees, supporting a split rail trough made leak-proof with pine sap was beautiful.

Gathering the massive amounts of firewood required was pure pleasure, a chance to get away from the group and explore by myself. As the session continued, my pleasure increased as I had to travel greater distances to find firewood. Back in camp the big logs were sawed and split. Day by day I gained competence with the axe and saw. I dreamed of building a cabin in the woods, stocking it with firewood, and engineering a water system.

At home my mother had attempted to introduce me to the feminine arts of homemaking. I never paid her any mind. But at camp I cooked with gusto. Over the fire, I grilled burgers, boiled vegetables and created my childhood favorite, macaroni and cheese. With the help of a reflector oven, I produced bread, biscuits, cookies, and brownies. We caught and ate fish. Wild greens became salad or tea. We picked and ate every berry as it ripened. There was a long stretch of blueberry items: pancakes, muffins, pie, cobbler, jam. At the end of that week, my enthusiasm for gathering had waned a bit.

So had my enthusiasm for backpacking. We trekked ten miles in two days on hot dusty trails to climb a fire tower and look at the vista. I vowed my next camp would be in a cooler environment where girls traveled by canoe rather than on foot.

The following summer, tuition wasn't the problem; transportation was. In the spring, after I had sent in my money and been accepted at a camp far north in the Adirondack Mountains of New York, my parents informed me that they couldn't drive me there. The camp was on an isolated highway, miles from the nearest town and even farther from a bus stop. Undaunted, I calmly convinced a buddy that we should go to camp together. She thought it was a fine idea, and her parents agreed to drive us.

Lake Clear Girl Scout Camp provided the cool climate I desired. I learned about portaging and swamps and bugs and being windbound. It was a very fine summer. On a rare backpacking trip we climbed Whiteface Mountain. On the way down, we ate at a gorgeous camp on Lake Placid, one used exclusively for training girls to be camp counselors. I had my next goal.

Inquiries about this non-Girl Scout camp confirmed my suspicions: Woodsmoke was expensive. The two women who ran it needed to break even at the end of each summer. They catered to girls from wealthy families and charged a tuition appropriate to their clientele.

The director offered me a full scholarship if I would convince two full-paying girls to enroll. I took on the challenge despite the fact that I didn't know any girls who could afford it.

My parents pointed out, however, that there were girls on my swim team whose families could afford to pay Woodsmoke's fees. I had not noticed this class difference, but with a bit of parental nudging, I attempted to bridge it. Befriending these girls felt even more like prostitution than selling cookies. I wrote to the camp director, said that I was not successful, and asked for other means of getting to camp. She phoned and somehow convinced my mother to host a gathering of appropriately well-heeled girls and their parents at our house! The director would give a slide show and shmooze with the rich folks to get the two required sign-ups upon which my scholarship depended.

The evening presentation came and went with no sign-ups. Crestfallen, I started making alternate summer plans. A week later the camp director called again.

"Do you still want to go to Woodsmoke?" she asked.

" YES!" I shouted.

"Then I'll apply for some New York State funding. If it comes through, you can go to Woodsmoke on a full scholarship," she said.

That summer, I attended Woodsmoke for an enthralling eight weeks. My seven fellow campers were daughters of the rich and famous. They had familiar last names and a sophistication I had seen only on TV. Our counselors and instructors were equally exclusive. We learned water skiing from the reigning national water ski champion. Our swimming teacher had coached the winning team for the national synchronized championships. Our tennis teacher had competed at Wimbleton. When we hiked the Appalachian Trail, we were led by the director of the Appalachian Mountain Club. Our counselors worked us from early morning to late night. We studied, learned our lessons, and practiced being counselors. It was the best summer ever.

After Woodsmoke, I was never a camper again. I became a student at Outward Bound, a counselor, a trip leader, a solo trekker, and a wilderness educator. But the lessons I learned working to get to camp each summer have made everything since then possible.

Perseverance and asking questions smoothed my passage through graduate school in neurobiology. The biggest "silly" essay I ever wrote was a Ph.D. thesis; but like that long-ago essay that got me to camp, it was a ticket to work that paid enough for me to continue my passion for the wilderness during the four months I wasn't being a scientist. The willingness to ask for what I want from authorities has shown its usefulness repeatedly: getting into graduate school without Graduate Record Exam scores, leaving school for a fifteen-month tour of communes, getting paid to paddle Arctic rivers, and finding my current hermitage on Black Sturgeon Lake in northern Ontario.

These traits also helped me follow my feelings when I fell in love with a woman for the first time. I knew I could trust my heart, and I felt confident that I could overcome whatever roadblocks were put in my path. This confidence allowed me to speak about being a lesbian in the early seventies when the "L" word still wasn't uttered in polite society. In addition, my early experience with class difference made it easier for me to recognize and cope with sexism and homophobia.

In my Girl Scout years, I met many positive role models. In retrospect, I find many of them were lesbian. In fact, my very first camp director was fired from her job as a high school art teacher after she admitted to being a homosexual. Perhaps on some subconscious level she and other lesbian Girl Scouts opened me to the possibility of loving women. My hormones, or whatever it is that triggers sexual interest, did not become active until after my Girl Scout days. My guess is that counselors and campers around me were falling in love or having affairs. I just absorbed it as part of the delightful ambience of camp.

For the last fifteen years, I've spent eight months indoors each year as a research scientist and four months in the wilderness. I've instructed and guided for adventure education organizations such as the National Outdoor Leadership School, Woodswomen, and Outward Bound. Some years I've gone on major paddling expeditions in the Arctic. Other years, rock climbing or skiing have been the focus. In these various outdoor activities, I run into an astounding percentage of other lesbian Girl Scouts and Campfire Girls. For example, my friend and lover of twenty-five years, Marcia Munson (chapter 14) started the first wilderness adventure organization exclusively for lesbians. It was based in Oregon in the early 1970s and was called Keep Listening. My friend and lover of ten years, Anne Dal Vera, was a member of the first team of women to ski to the South Pole. Marcia was a Girl Scout, and Anne was a Campfire Girl.

Today I find myself in transition. I feel that I've sold enough cookies to be able to live the life I want. I've recently cut my official ties with academia and am beginning the familiar struggle of making a dream come true. This time I want to live in beautiful wilderness areas for twelve months each year. Wish me luck as, once again, I try to get to camp or bust.

Martha McPheeters

CHAPTER 3

Camp Fires

Jeanne Córdova

A love-lorn Catholic teenager found God, joy, and love with the Campfire Girls (a sister organization to the Girl Scouts) on California's Mount San Gorgonio.

I was fifteen and I was depressed.

I wasn't dejected because I was the second oldest of twelve children or because my explosive father chased us through the house with his belt. I wasn't depressed because I was led to believe that everyone in the world was Catholic, that West Covina was the center of the known universe, or that I didn't have a boyfriend. I thought these arrangements, especially not having a boyfriend, were normal.

My mother said I had a skewed views of things from the first day she brought me home from the hospital. I longed for freedom, intimacy, and the company of women.

Mother understood none of this, so she was particularly perplexed when I fell into a non-responsive state in the spring of my sophomore year. I crawled out of bed in the morning with none of my usual *joie de vivre*. I ceased interrupting teachers and sulked home from school, skipping softball practice.

I sat at the dinner table mute even when my brothers stole meatballs off my plate. I, too, was baffled by my sudden lack of interest in anything. Teenagers in West Covina in 1964 didn't kill their parents, do drugs, or know about depression.

If Mother had asked, I was naive enough to have told her, "I'm sad because Miss Cukras went away." My high school English teacher who doubled as my softball coach had been the light of my life for a year and a half. But Mother didn't ask because Mother always knew best. She decided all on her own "what to do about Jeanne."

She conscripted me into the Camp Fire Girls.

When I got off the bus at Camp Nawakwa outside of Big Bear, California, one month later, I was not impressed. Sure the pine trees danced against a china-blue sky, the air was aromatic with earth spices. Who cared. I was supposed to be cured by spending two weeks in the company of silly uniformed girls in starched white shirts and ridiculous red scarves. At least pining over Miss Cukras had its own obsessive endorphin high.

I was too old to begin at the usual buttons-and-badges level, so my mother had entered me in the only program available to girls in their mid-teens. The other new recruits for the Counselor-In-Training (CIT) program and I were herded into the big wooded lodge which looked like a larger version of my family's dining room. I was sure my life was about to repeat itself.

But something magical happened in those mountains over the next three summers. I discovered there was life outside of the values my parents espoused. I discovered I was more than one of twelve, "the trouble maker." I found freedom and intimacy. I found *Jeanne.*

Why did Jeanne stop rebelling and become the model counselor leading her fifth graders singing "Kumbaya" around the campfire? Who was she, I wondered, as I strained my well-developed softball calves up the countless switchbacks of San Gorgonio with a twenty-pound pack on my back. Where did the fire in my soul come from as *Jeanne* the poet lay exhausted above the timberline?

I had become someone else. Or was I always this way, I wondered, as I lay on my cot each night breathing in the pine, exhaling to the stars.

Perhaps I was different now because I had been given a troop of young girls for whom I was solely responsible. I, their unit counselor, was the first

Jeanne Córdova, 1968

one up at dawn, gently rousing them from their sometimes scared sleep. I, no one else, was supposed to pick them up when they tripped over rocks and fell. *Jeanne* was the one who sang them to sleep at night, and made up stories that would "not be boring,"—but plot-less enough to go to sleep by.

Maybe it was Strawberry, a seven-year-old with a button nose and freckles too large for her face, who adopted me as Mom-away-from-Mom. I went to sleep at night scheming of ways to make her happy. I awoke each morning to her bouncing not so quietly on my toes at the bottom of my cot. Strawberry became my first "daughter."

Or maybe I was transformed by "Greyback" herself. That was the name we gave our new god, San Gorgonio, the mountain. She had a bare charcoal spine, high above the timberline. And it was there, beyond where living things grew, that I came alive. It was there that I was close to God. There were no stop signs, no roads, no fences on Greyback. My fellow CITs and I skipped along her boundless ridge riding the vertebrae of the mountain like elves on the wind. Through summer rain and gale-driven nights we sang ourselves to sleep tucked in bags rolled tight against each other for heat. Elbows would poke into our bellies if someone decided to turn in the night, teasing would echo until dawn. Yet there was always a tenderness in the way we cared for one another, even when competing for who'd get to the top first.

My body felt reincarnated every time I reached the summit, my mind expanding to an animal freedom beyond thought. Greyback, in her eleven-thousand foot majesty, brought the power of nature into my soul and body. Mine was still a Catholic God at the time. There on the mountain, I saw for the first time that God was more than suffering on the cross. Nature was holy.

Snuggled inside my bag, guided by a weak flashlight I wrote a love poem to my earth-god;

> Oh peaks of foreign majesty
> My eyes know not thy bold ascents.
> My spirit soars, like bird of heights
> To cling to cliffs with sights unparalleled.

But woman does not live by majesty alone. No matter how Godly. So perhaps the new *Jeanne* came to be because of the magical women at Camp Nawakwa.

There was "Mama" Carol, a plump, seemingly elderly lady at thirty-five. As Camp Director, she wanted us to be excited about life at Nawakwa. Mama Carol rarely leaned on her counselors. She stayed in the background and made us grow up. But we always knew Mama Carol was back there, somewhere. The safety net.

And there was my best friend, Jane Bjerum, who didn't like me on first sight. She was a veteran, a second year CIT when I arrived. And no one but she was going to lead songs around *her* camp fire. But what really threatened Janie was that the captain of our CIT unit also *liked* me. Charlesita Mann measured six feet tall in her worn hiking boots, and her height was augmented by a serenely commanding presence. "Charlie" never had to ask you to do something twice.

At first I was both attracted to and afraid of my twenty-two-year-old captain. Our unit's grapevine told me, long before she spoke to me personally, that she was going to be a nun in the Immaculate Heart of Mary order. I, too, was planning to join the I.H.M.s, the convent of the famed peacenik pop artist, Sister Corita. This was magical! Charlie and I were destined.

But destiny threw me a curve. I was never to see Charlie again after we left Nawakwa, even though I looked for her when I joined the I.H.M.s three years later. No, our destiny took place at Nawakwa.

It was my second year at camp, and I had finagled Mom into letting me spend the entire summer instead of just two weeks. It was colder that summer as we second year CITs lay nightly outside of Charlie's tent. Charlie, and her assistant Clair, had rank. They made their bunks inside a spacious, but rough canvas tent. I grew gradually sicker with a cold and finally Charlie heard me one night whimpering in pain. She made me bring my cot and sleep inside with them until I got better.

Charlie offered to rub my aching shoulders and back. I'd always thought backrubs were the priviledge of grown-ups. My young sister often rubbed my father's always aching shoulders, but no one else in my family touched much. Perhaps my mother's attention was forever diverted by my ten younger siblings, or perhaps it was because Latin fathers don't touch their daughters, and Irish mothers don't touch at all.

In any case, Charlie's touch was the first real intimacy I had ever known.

Once inside the tent, my cot a few feet from hers, Charlie would talk me to sleep at night. We'd whisper about the CIT unit programs, who was assigned to what, which kid was having a crisis and how to assuage it. Gradually our midnight conversations would segue to God and his mysteries, and we soared into dreams about our future at Montecito—the Santa Barbara novitiate of the Immaculate Heart nuns.

Some nights found me sitting on Charlie's cot-edge rubbing her flannel covered shoulders and neck. During these earth-bound séances of the spirit we'd philosophize about city life "down-the-hill" and how we loved it on our mountain. Los Angeles seemed another world.

There came one special night in a summer of unforgettable intimacy. Charlie was sitting on my bedside that evening as we watched the Little Dipper, our favorite constellation, slip into view through the open tent flaps. She was rubbing my shoulders after a particularly grueling hike up and down Greyback. My back ached from carrying one of the youngsters down the last mile. But my restless heart felt safe as always to be back home with my unit and Charlie. The sweet tingling of my massaged muscles danced like the dawn winds. We drifted, I dozed, my spirit on its way into subconsciousness.

"I love you, Jeanne," came the whisper.

I awoke with a start. Had I really heard those words? Had Charlie said them?

"Goodnight now, kiddo." My cot creaked as a weight lifted and I heard footsteps shuffle softly toward her bed.

I had heard sacred words!

No one had said those words to me since I was a babe on my mother's lap. Presumably my infant ears had heard them then, but at sixteen, that night at Nawakwa, the campfires of my heart were lit. Someone I loved also loved me!

Charlie transformed me because she gave me the freedom to be who I was and the intimacy to make it safe.

Later that summer, Charlie would say the sacred words again, and I would say them to her. By my third summer at Nawakwa, Charlie had left to seek her future. But Janie, Charlie's other special camper, and I had become best friends. She and I would say the sacred words to each other and keep vigil with the stars. Years later, when Janie and I were both old and wise at twenty-two, we would complete those words with our bodies in a dorm at Harvard.

My idyllic summers at Nawakwa with my young charges, with Charlie, Janie, Greyback, and God never included the complications of adult love. Those were the summers of intimate innocence, the campfire of freedom that led me to myself.

Young men are drafted into the army, but I believe young women should be drafted into Girl Scouts or Camp Fire Girls. Boy Scouting is seen by parents as a way for young men to learn a sense of honor, responsibility and male bonding. But the Girl Scout or Camp Fire experience is too often dismissed by parents as irrelevant, by girls themselves as

Jeanne Córdova

"silly." But what do kids know? What did I know at fifteen? I certainly didn't know that campfires were caldrons of good witches who brewed joy and empowerment. No one told me Mother Nature could offer me the globe in all her glory in a way my mother never could. There ought to be an 11th Commandment for women: Thou shalt place thy female offspring in the company of women. For here shall they find safety and intimacy suitable for life.

CHAPTER 4

One Entry Point
to Lesbian Nation

Margaret Cruikshank

Writer, scholar, and teacher Margaret Cruikshank reflects on the connections between Girl Scouts and loving women, from her fascination with her butch Brownie leader to the scout-camp-familiarity of her first lesbian bar.

My Brownie leader Betty Arnold wore men's clothes and had slicked back short hair. No other female on Park Point[1] looked like that in the 1940s. "Are you a man or a woman?" puzzled kids would ask Betty. I reacted strongly to the question, with embarrassment, confusion, fascination, curiosity. Today I know why their question sticks in my memory: Betty Arnold was a dyke; I was a dyke-to-be; and scouting was our common ground.

Perhaps because my mother was grateful that someone else had taken on the Brownies, she did not fault Betty for her butch look. But she must have wanted me to know that Betty was not quite acceptable, because she told me that our Brownie leader did not pay her library fines and even worse, had piles of unreturned books at home. That these were hideous character faults was made plain to me.

I was intrigued by Betty's sturdy shoes, man's belt with big buckle, glistening hair, deep voice, and swagger. Such veiled lesbian images were present for me from the very beginning of my days in scouting. Nothing dramatic ever happened to reveal unmistakably the link between scouts and loving women, but I was aware of passionate feelings in myself for other girls and women and just as aware that those around me were also feeling deep attachments.

As a Senior Scout at Camp Fannie Bailey Olcott (named for the daughter of one of the 19th century timber and mining barons of northern Minnesota), I had a counselor named Mic, who was big and broad shouldered. She talked tough. This made an impression on me because ladylike speech was one of many requirements at the convent school my mother insisted I attend. The speech teacher said several times a week, "Her voice was ever soft, gentle, and low, an excellent thing in a woman," quoting a line from *King Lear*. The voice of Mic was anything but soft, gentle, and low. Once as twelve campers sat at our lashed table eating supper, she glanced at me and roared, "Eat your carrots, Cruikshank; they'll give you hair on your chest." I was mortified. How *could* she? Mic was a 1950s gender bender. Hair on my chest was her metaphorical way of predicting that in a few years, I'd be as queer as she was—if I were lucky. Significant, too, was her use of last name only; no female I knew talked like that. Mic was signalling her difference.

She dragged us out of bed to dreadful calisthenics, enjoying our discomfort. She had us sing hearty wake-up songs. "God has created a new day/Silver and green and gold...." At the time I thought her zeal excessive. Now I suspect she was indulging in campy humor. Our unit lived on an island where Mic had absolute power. We paddled back and forth to the mainland camp in a war canoe, ten paddlers. Mic barked commands. Bending the elbow of the arm that held the shaft of the paddle was simply not allowed. Hard as it was to keep my elbow straight, I forced myself to conform so as to escape notice.

By the time I was a junior counselor at Camp Olcott, Mic was assistant camp director, and her gruff, deep-voiced directives no longer scared me. I didn't know that most of the counselors were lesbians. The word was not in my vocabulary; the concept was not in my consciousness. James Joyce said that the novelist should be nowhere visible but everywhere apparent. Lesbianism was like that at Camp Olcott in 1960. For example, even though I thought I was unlike the scout leaders I vaguely knew were "different," the way I spent my breaks from camp showed how like them I was. During one break, I visited a woman I'd had a passionate, though nonsexual, affair with in high school. On another break, I drove into Duluth for an event that had been heartbreaking in the anticipation: the woman I loved in college was entering the convent. Watching the ceremony I felt sad and alone. Getting back to Camp Olcott was a relief.

That summer our little band of invisible lesbians had great esprit de corps. Hilarious laughter seemed always to ring out in the clean pine air. Counselors had names like Sam, Bongo, and Sarge. I was Yogi Bear. We counselors formed a community that felt whole. Did my twenty-year-old self ask why, in a world without men, everyone was so happy? Dimly I knew I belonged in such a circle of women free of preoccupations with boyfriends, but I had no way of explaining that to myself.

That was the summer when glamorous, witty, and sexy John Kennedy was running for president. In Protestant Minnesota there were many jokes (and perhaps a few genuine fears) about the Pope taking over America if JFK were elected. My friend Judy Niemi[2] (who was further along in figuring out her lesbian identity in that she had a "particular friend" among the counselors) played an elaborate joke on me, with the help of her PF. Niemi and Jay had a male friend in Denver pose as a priest and send me letters about my role in the coming takeover by Rome. The counselors' plot grew more elaborate. I received phone calls from the "priest" in Denver (in 1960 a long distance phone call was still a dramatic occurrence). Through the mail came a large cartoon of Charlie Brown in a Roman collar, hand raised as if to give a blessing. Suspecting that my funny, anti-clerical, and anti-Kennedy aunt in Seattle was behind the plot, I enthusiastically told Niemi and Jay all about it, never suspecting that they were the schemers. I don't know how I finally learned the truth, but I felt exhilarated to have had such attention lavished on me. An unspoken message of the plot was that women have hilarious fun together.

That summer I too had a particular friend. Mary Jane was beautiful, brainy, and Irish. She was drawn to my blue eyes. I loved her passionately. I didn't have a name for the feelings, but their intensity was unmistakable. She gave me her sweatshirt—or did I give her mine?

During the Christmas holiday in 1960, Olcott counselors had a reunion at the home of Muggs, our camp director. Judy and Jay slept on the floor side by side. I was uncomfortable with that. I sensed that the few straight counselors disapproved. I wanted no one to think me odd or perverted. But what *were* perverts? I respected Judy as much as anyone I'd ever known. I felt queasy, though, at the thought of women together. That was icky, dangerous,

Margaret Cruikshank

mysterious, maybe even pathetic.

Seven years later, I had outgrown these fears and settled in happily with a lover, although we were secretive and knew no other lesbians. "Not icky," I sang exuberantly to Marcia as we rolled in the sheets, "just sticky." We visited Camp Olcott at the end of the summer, after the campers had gone home. The lesbian camp director, my friend Corky,[3] was still there with another woman. No one said a word about being gay; it was still a taboo topic, and scouts was the perfect cover. My lover and I stayed in the main lodge. An urban soul, Marcia had never seen darkness as total as the darkness of a northern Minnesota night. She was actually scared. I was her brave protector. How satisfying to show her the scene of one of my happiest summers. At that point, I could not really *claim* my lesbianism as an identity, but taking Marcia to camp showed that I got the connection between loving women and staying in scouting.

Another seven years pass. I make my first cautious trip to the lesbian bar in Minneapolis. "No one will know me here," I assure myself as I step inside. The atmosphere? Unbelievably wholesome. *This is just like scout camp*, I think with surprise and relief. A few minutes later a woman comes up to me. "Hi, Peg," she says with a grin. "I always wondered about you and Mary Jane[4] at Camp Olcott."

✳ ✳ ✳

Epilogue

By coincidence, Mic and I were neighbors in the same Maine village in the summer of 1995. She was in town with her long-time partner. We all became close friends who explored Maine together. In the presence of a complex, multi-faceted, delightful, and sometimes uproariously funny companion, I realized how limited and one dimensional my camp sketch of her is. I feel grateful that I can update my impressions of Mic. After forty years, "EAT YOUR CARROTS, CRUIKSHANK" is still good for a laugh between us.

[1] *Park Point is the island in Lake Superior connected by bridge to Duluth. Queers, artists, and people from the British Isles lived there when I was growing up. Gentrification has changed the atmosphere.*

[2] *Judith Niemi, women's studies teacher, scholar, writer, wilderness guide, is the editor, with Barb Wieser, of* Rivers Running Free, *canoe stories by women. An extraordinary woman. [Editor's note: See Judith Niemi's "Lesbians, Lightning, and Bears," Chapter 11.]*

[3] *Corky was a teacher in North Dakota in the off season. In those days, mid- to late-1960s, car dealers loved teachers because of our steady jobs. Corky walked into a car dealership in North Dakota, pointed to a Thunderbird, said "I'll take it," and drove off in triumph. Lesbian bravado. Surely Girl Scout camp fostered that spirit.*

[4] *Mary Jane, though certainly drawn to me at camp, went on to marriage and motherhood. We are friends.*

CHAPTER 5

Becoming a Canada Tripper, 1965

Carol (Heenan) Seajay

A non-scout fell so in love with camp and canoeing that she became a Girl Scout and helped organize an eight-day canoe trip into Canada.

Maybe the rest of the campers were at Crafts. Maybe I was headed back to my tent for something I'd forgotten. I don't know where I was supposed to be, but I wasn't intended to be walking up the path alone. I heard the sharp crack first, then looked up to see the counselor pick up another length of wood, set it on the stump, swing the ax high and bring it down. The wood split neatly in two, flying away from the ax as the clean crack filled my ears. She reached for one of the pieces, balanced it on the stump again as she freed the ax from the home it had found in the stump. She held the ax in front of her, looking at the wood for a moment, then once again lifted her arms in a fluid movement, bringing the ax high over her head and down again with a sharp crack.

I had never seen anything like it. I'd never seen anyone split wood; I'd certainly never seen a woman split wood—or do anything as bold as pick up an ax and use it. Washing machines and vacuum cleaners, yes. And the endless round of canning all summer. But nothing like this tall, lean woman stretching her body, lifting her arms, swinging the ax high and splitting the wood cleanly.

I stood there in the path watching while she split the rest of the wood and stacked it away. Then I still stood there, staring into the clearing as if I could see in the pattern of trees or the pattern of the light in the air, how the future had just changed for me.

I didn't mean to become a canoeist; I hadn't wanted to go to Girl Scout camp at all. The other kids in the neighborhood were going to Van Buren County youth camp, a subsidized program for city kids. My brother had gone the year before, and he came home with exciting, terrifying tales of stealing girls' panties, and running bathing suits up the flagpole. All the kids were going, it was the thing to do. Maybe my mother wanted something different for me. As the years passed, I came to see that she wanted something better for all of us than just getting by, than fear, than the early pregnancy and early marriages that grade school sexuality promised. Whatever her reasons, she pounced on the Girl Scout camp flier she found in my coat pocket and campaigned for my willingness to try "this other camp." I wanted to go where my friends were going. I didn't want to go away for two whole weeks—one was enough! But I must have nodded my head at a wrong moment one sleepy night, because by the time I got up in the morning, she had already mailed the deposit to the Girl Scout camp. I never did remember agreeing to go.

But I did go. And at nine I fell in love with trees, with the out-of-doors, with something I later called community—living and working together, sharing projects and goals, succeeding at firebuilding, outdoor cooking, scavenger hunts. When the other girls complained of being homesick, I'd say that I wasn't homesick but that when I got home I would be "campsick." I'd carry on about how I'd be "Mac-sick" ("Mac" being the graceful ax-wielding counselor) until my tent-mates would tell me to shut up.

Back home, I raved about camp until my mother made me a deal: if I could save half of the fee for next summer, she and my dad would come up with the rest. How they expected a nine year old on a ten cent a week allowance to come up with twenty-two dollars, I never knew. Perhaps the point was that I wouldn't be able to. But that fall we moved to a rural school district with new adventures like school buses and hot lunch programs. I found that if I bought a carton of milk with the sack-lunch kids, and mooched

Carol (Heenan) Seajay, 1959

a piece of bread or peanut butter sandwich from a kid who did buy the hot lunches, I could save up as much as twenty-five cents a day. I made my twenty-two dollars easily. There was no stopping me.

As a non-scout I had to wait until after a certain date to apply, but I went every summer. Being tiny, I called myself "Shrimp" and after the first couple of years, all the returning staff knew me by name, would greet me when I arrived. I fell in love, again and again, with camp, with the counselors, with the particular quality of energy, with sharing, with acceptance, with having a place and knowing what to do in it.

Home again after the third summer, I sat on the back porch and thought about boarding school kids (I'd just seen *The Parent Trap*) and how they lived in one place all winter, and then went away to summer camps, but still called "home" the place they went at Christmas and for a week here and there. I decided that if they could call "home" someplace they only spent a few weeks a year, then I could call Girl Scout camp my real home, and know that I was just "staying" at this other place the rest of the time.

I had a regular summer gang of girls who went to the same session year after year, and ended up in the same units. At fourteen we were finally old enough to sign up for the canoeing units. Somehow I missed the word that we were all going to sign up for the intermediate trip. I carefully followed the rules and signed up for the beginner trip, and ended up without any of my usual pals. There was one girl from my school, however, and she and I became tent and canoeing partners. Dot didn't *get* canoeing. Didn't get why, if you paddled on this side, the canoe went the other way. So even though I was far smaller, I ended up in the stern, learning to guide the canoe, to compensate for her odd and erratic strokes, and to load the canoe to make up for having the heavier paddler in the front.

We had the worst trip possible. We were an odd group of girls who never did click together. It stormed the entire time we were actually out on the river, and we had to get off the river any time the lightning was at all close. Our clothing and gear were soaked and we camped in farmers' barns both nights. We probably canoed a total of eight miles in three days. Describing the trip afterwards to my friends, I talked about my excitement at being on a real river, the intensity of the lightning and how we'd had to drag the canoes over downed trees in the river. They were skeptical and asked about being cold and wet, about soggy peanut butter and jelly sandwiches, about whether we'd seen any whitewater *at all*?

They came home from their trip later in the summer radiant and sparkling, full of tales of Pooh, the canoeing counselor, doing headstands on the bow as they floated lazily downriver on hot sunny days. They heard tales from the counselors of our ill-fated trip and laughed at and with me. "Shrimp is so into canoeing that she has a good time even when it's awful!" was the word. "Next year," they said. Next year they wanted to go on a canoe trip to Canada. They'd heard that the camp had run a trip to Canada a few years earlier and decided that it could happen again, for us. By hook or by crook. And I was going. Forget the progression of trips. If I could canoe with Dot through the rain, I must be ready for Canada.

Most of the gang went to the Catholic girls' school, located conveniently across the street from the Girl Scout office and very handy for lobbying for a special trip. "You aren't even Girl Scouts," they said in the office. We all promptly found troops and joined up. "It costs too much," they said. We agreed to pay a higher camp fee. "We have no way to know the trip will fill." We called everyone we knew who had ever gone on a canoe trip and guaranteed eight of the twelve places. I think we wore them down with our sheer persistence. They didn't know where in Canada to take us. They couldn't find staff with enough whitewater skills. Finally they came up with the

Boundary Waters Canoe Area (BWCA) on the border of Canada and Minnesota, where we could do an eight-day lake trip in real wilderness. We wanted a river trip. BWCA was their final offer. We agreed jubilantly. We were going to Canada!

As the Canada Trippers we were the elite of the camp. Each session, all the campers gathered to wave the current group of "Trippers" off. When the canoers returned to camp, the dinner bell was rung, and everyone gathered from all over the camp to greet them. Only the Counselors-in-Training ranked higher. But that summer we Canada Trippers outranked even the CITs. Canada was exotic. Going on the trip was brave. Very few in the entire camp had been in a real wilderness before. It was a two-day drive, including a four-hour ferry trip across Lake Michigan, just to get there. The few days in camp before the trip were heady. We did canoe drills, paddled hour after hour to build strength; we practiced portaging. This was not going to be an easy downriver ride. At last we set out.

We drove across Michigan and Wisconsin, into Minnesota, farther away from home than I'd ever been before. On the drive we spent hours planning chore-charts and a rotation of tasks so that everything would go smoothly. We camped in the woods near the outfitter's parking lot, and it wasn't until the next morning as we were loading gear into the canoes that I believed we were going to canoe into Canada.

This was like no place I'd ever been before. We were a gang of young women, mostly fifteen, our counselors barely twenty-one. No one had offered us this trip—we'd thought of it, lobbied for it, planned it, and practiced for it. Finally, there we were: pushing off into the wilderness, the lake and the vast sky stretching out before us in welcome invitation. We were on our own, with stars and sun, compass and map to guide us.

On this trip, we couldn't simply follow the current downstream—every direction was a real possibility in the maze of lakes. Someone turned out to be good at reading the maps and compass. I think it was actually a committee of three or four who watched the contour lines and the compass, comparing the islands and shorelines to the map to determine where we were, and where we should head next. I was content to follow their lead, paddling back and forth cheerfully looking for a portage, only to have it turn out be around the next bend. I didn't care if we went on a side trip to see the Indian Rock paintings or which route we chose to get to the next chain of lakes. We were here. Everywhere was here. Sky and water, trees and waves. Loons laughing and calling, diving and surfacing. Our silver canoes glinting in the sun. I had, in those moments, everything I had ever wanted in my entire life.

We saw a bear on the shore that first day. A small, unconcerned black bear, but very exciting to us. None of us had ever seen a wild bear before. We decided to camp on an island. It seemed safer. Others had done that before us, and after we had unloaded all our gear we realized there was no firewood on the entire island. Four of us took a look at the driftwood on the opposite shore and set out in empty canoes to bring it back.

Only later did we realize that we had blown the careful pretrip plan of patrols and chore-charts that organized all of us into "fair" and rotating divisions of camp chores. By the time we got back with the firewood, the tents were set up and dinner was ready for the quickly-built fire. Someone had initiated an inventory of the food and gear packs from the outfitter and repacked them to distribute the weight evenly. (It had taken two of us to even lift the one filled with canned goods and four of us to get it over the first portage.) Someone else had started rethinking menus.

After that first night we wordlessly dropped our carefully made chore-charts and began another system of pitching in to do the work at hand, each one following her own inclinations but mindful of all that needed to be done. I loved (and still do) building fires more than almost anything. So did a lot of us, so I did a lot of tent staking to share it around. Skills were shared informally. Someone always had a new and better idea for pitching the tents, for stringing up the food at night. "That works, but try it this way," was the approach. Any three of us could get a fire going no matter how much it had rained. I knew almost nothing about cooking, but others did and the rest of us were there to chop and stir and keep the fire below the pots burning steadily. If you saw something that needed to be done, you did it. If you were too busy, you mentioned it to someone else and she did it. Even after all these years I'm still amazed if I find myself in a group of women that *doesn't* function on this model.

I'm sure it wasn't always golden—it rained a lot, and we suffered some anxiety before we realized it was a weather pattern, that it would sprinkle every afternoon and clear off about four. The nights were the coldest I'd ever known and few of us had sleeping bags made to accommodate the low temperatures. We tried every combination of doubling up and tripling up under sleeping bags. The only night I recall being warm was when I snuggled up to Minnie's broad and warm back. She didn't want to do it again, though, and I didn't understand why.

The days were filled with paddling and scanning the forest and shoreline for wildlife. We saw a mother bear with two cubs. I watched loons diving and flying, landing on water and taking off. We paddled on and on, in the solitude, in the beauty, day after day, as if we were the first people there.

We rarely saw other people, but the night we decided to go skinny dipping in the pool beneath a waterfall we were invaded by a troop of Boy Scouts who camped noisily on the other side of the small lake. We hated them. But the next day, when Ruth slipped on a portage and twisted her ankle, we were glad enough to have the Boy Scout leaders nearby. Even collectively, our first-aid skills were theoretical. They knew how to set the broken (we thought) leg, how to make splints from tree branches and pad them for comfort. I was strangely embarrassed by our ignorance and never wanted to be vulnerable and dependent like that again.

Ruth's fall came two days from the end of the trip. Despite the splint—or because of it—she was in considerable pain. When it became clear that a couple of aspirin weren't going to help enough, we decided to do two days of paddling in one, and try to get her back to the outpost that night for real medical attention. We were now much stronger than when we set out. We made our strokes deep and powerful, singing all the canoeing songs we knew to keep our rhythm steady and our spirits high. We finished the last portage by late afternoon. Motorboats were allowed on the U.S. side of the border, and we flagged one down, asking them to tell our outfitter that we'd had an injury, that we were trying to get in that night, and to please send the pontoon boat out for us. Then we paddled on, eating another lunch for dinner, paddling through the sunset, into the long northern twilight and into the darkness.

I think we would have paddled all night if we'd had to, but finally a beam of light and the roar of an outboard motor invaded the stillness. We flagged them down with the flashlights we'd steered by. There was an hour of unloading, tying the canoes all over the edges and the top, and fitting fourteen tired scouts on board. Then the pontoon boat turned around and roared us slowly, but much faster than our tired arms could take us, back to civilization.

We did other trips after this one, including a Senior Scout trip with no adult supervision and a canoe trip on the fastest river in lower Michigan. But eventually we began going our separate ways into adulthood. I felt myself pulled toward college, and for me that meant paying jobs every summer and on weekends during the school year—a necessity that interfered mightily with my camping.

I always meant to return to the Boundary Waters, the place that more than anywhere else gave me the ability to envision and bring my dreams into reality. I'm amazed that the decades have gone by and I've been too busy with all my other dreams to go back.

Carol (Heenan) Seajay

CHAPTER 6

✳ ✳ ✳

Right-Wing Poster Child

Rosemary Keefe Curb

The co-editor of Lesbian Nuns: Breaking Silence *recalls a summer of sensual awakening at Girl Scout camp as forty years later, she drives along Wisconsin back roads looking for the camp again.*

On Saturday, 20 July 1996, the late afternoon hour when the frenzy of crickets screams toward crescendo, I'm kicking up gravel on a back road in rural southern Wisconsin in search of a forty-year-old memory from Girl Scout Camp Juniper Knoll. I had only dreamed I'd return to this spot on the map, but I'd never expected to be here in this fifty-six-year-old body. I've swerved off my Triple-A path from Philadelphia to Minneapolis on a sudden quest. Midafternoon Friday I left the four-week Bryn Mawr summer institute for ambitious women administrators. Late Sunday I'm expected at Nancy Manahan's home. On Monday, I'm speaking at Amazon Books about *Amazon All Stars*, a recently published collection of lesbian plays I've edited.

Having made amazing travel time, I'm indulging in the luxury of this unscheduled nostalgia trip. Since I'm visiting Nancy, who's in the midst of collecting stories from lesbians about their Girl Scout days, the nostalgia isn't unmotivated. I've been musing about the sprouting of my lesbian life in

Girl Scouts. I believe that scouting formed my sense of self-reliance and power from the "twist me and turn me and show me the elf" of Brownie initiation when "I looked in the water and saw ... myself" at age eight to my last summer at Camp Juniper Knoll, when I was a junior counselor at age sixteen.

In those days, I could have been the poster child for the right wing so "faithful to country, loyal to home" was I. From seventh to ninth grades, I did something in the Girl Scout web just about every day. I went from playing big sister at Brownie troops to singing at nursing homes to a whole cat's cradle of meetings. I'd gone for most of the badges in the *Girl Scout Handbook* and was urging those sprouting up behind me along the same path of overachievement. At twelve or thirteen I was a champion Girl Scout cookie-pusher, standing outside the Jarvis Street L stop at rush hour with cartons of sandwich cookies, aiming to win a free trip to Camp Juniper Knoll as one of the top four in Chicago. (I came in sixth.) At the end of eighth grade, I was picked to represent the Girl Scouts of Chicago on Junior Officials Day. Since Girl Scouts got one of the top positions in 1954, I was the Fire Commissioner of Chicago for a day in my green uniform with colorful sash of badges. The 1950s right wing no doubt smiled on the little achiever accustomed to the regimentation of uniforms. In my preteen years, I changed frequently from the navy jumper of Catholic school to the pin and badge-studded green dress of Girls Scouts with no civilian casuals intervening. A few years after I was Fire Commissioner, with a similar ripple of patriotism, I won the "I Speak for Democracy" essay contest with a variation on the "Lord, make me an instrument of thy peace" prayer of St. Francis of Assisi.

What has lured me to the gravel roads of Walworth County, Wisconsin, is neither an obscure badge requirement nor the peace of St. Francis but a raw memory of adolescent libido leaping like late summer fireflies in the humid dusk. Even now, the seductive intoxication of clover and crickets conjure that hot time when I was sticky sweet sixteen. In fact, "Clover" and "Cricket" were probably names of camp counselors back then. I remember a counselor called "Stretch" three or four years—infinitely—older. I remember her tall muscular body gloriously tanned from standing all day on the sunny waterfront deck, power whistle flashing on her tank suit, zinc oxide on her nose.

I don't remember Stretch being particularly friendly or outgoing with the junior counselors. She had that dry butch reserve and self-containment that

Rosemary Keefe Curb, 1954

suggested arcane and exclusive eroticism to me, and I had no words for what I desired. I only knew I wanted to be one of the outlaw bad girls who smoked cigarettes behind the mess hall after dinner, despite the fact that I'd never even held a cigarette. Of course, I knew smoking was unhealthy and, even worse, unladylike. All the more reason to yearn for the badness of smoking.

I can't remember Stretch's first acknowledgement of my existence. I doubt that I could have done more than flash my desire in her direction. Maybe she invited me to her tent. Did she, with a gesture of gallantry, extend the pack of badness in my direction? However our affinity flowered, I did learn to smoke cigarettes and blow smoke rings that summer. Was it nicotine, zinc oxide, or tall tan butchness that prompted me to accept Stretch's invitation to a drive-in movie? There she continued lessons in the culture of cigarettes—how to hold one to look cool, to look tough, to lean in for a light. I remember the heat and glow of my sixteen-year-old body.

Crickets, clover, cigarettes, and even fireflies still conjure that summer of sensual awakening. I wonder if the Republicans of 1996 would be so blasé about smoking if they could remember that it leads to more than lung cancer. If they had a whiff that cigarettes can ignite lesbian desire, they'd be scrambling to ban tobacco.

I left Camp Juniper Knoll in July 1956 never to return. During my four weeks at camp, my family moved from Chicago to Madison, Wisconsin. I arrived at the new house, yearning to return to camp and smoking lessons. Unlike camp counselors of years past, Stretch returned my letters with a phone call. She was coming to Madison to visit me. My mother was less than cordial. What I remember most about Stretch's visit is my mother's reaction: "Get that dyke out of the house," she stage whispered to my dad behind their bedroom door.

A quarter of a century later, while reading the first submissions to *Lesbian Nuns: Breaking Silence*, I asked my mother, "When did you know I was a lesbian?" She said "I always knew." I wondered how sizing up Stretch affected my mother's recognition of her lesbian daughter, but I never asked.

Forty years later, I'm excavating my dyke roots amid the unchanging clover and crickets—no fireflies or cigarettes. On the map from the Wisconsin state line welcome station, I've found Elkhorn, the mailing address for Camp Juniper Knoll. In the convenience store of the gas station at the four-way stop light in Elkhorn, I ask, "How can I find Camp Juniper Knoll?" The woman behind the counter looks blank, so I continue, "Years ago there was a Girl Scout camp here." She mentions a church camp some thirty miles east. "No," I insist, "it was right here. It was a Girl Scout camp." A woman in line behind me speaks up with certainty: "I have lived here all my life, and I've never heard of that camp." I am silenced by the authority of the native. But I know it was all here forty years ago. For this right-wing poster child, Camp Juniper Knoll was my Isle of Lesbos.

✳ ✳ ✳

Editor's note:
Camp Juniper Knoll still exists, right where Rosemary Curb remembered it. Her encounter with local people unaware of its existence probably reflects a common Girl Scout camp practice of maintaining a low profile in the communities near which camps are located.

Rosemary Keefe Curb

CHAPTER 7

* * *

An International Sisterhood

Amanda Kovattana

After being introduced to the ideals of Girl Guiding (the original British scouting organization for girls), in her father's native Thailand, Amanda Kovattana was disappointed by sedate American-style scouting until she discovered an adventuresome troop and intrepid Girl Scout leaders.

My mother was a Girl Guide growing up in England. Mummy loved the camping adventures with the two young leaders, girls not much older than the guides themselves. With her troop, she built rope bridges and pitched heavy canvas tents, learned to use a compass and pocket knife, lashed together camp furniture, and acquired a sense of self-sufficiency that carried her through a lifetime of adventures. As I listened to her stories, I imagined her in her smart blue uniform skirt, long-sleeve blue shirt, yellow tie, brown knee socks, and sensible brown shoes.

As Lord Baden-Powell, the founder of the Boy Scouts, pointed out, the great war had allowed women to show how capable they were. My mother joined the Girl Guides not long after the Second World War ended. For her the war had meant an exciting period of civilian participation in matters of life and death. The Girl Guides was a continuation of such civilian self-sufficiency. Her stories made me eager to join this international body of

58

Amanda Kovattana, 1969

have to wear finky green uniforms and sit in dimly lit basements gluing macaroni to cigar boxes. Our leaders, overweight mothers, sat heavily in chairs and had no intention of taking us for a hike, let alone teaching us how to build a rope bridge. I was aghast that one of the badges required a Girl Scout to clean out the refrigerator. The *Girl Scout Handbook* itself had very little useful information as far as I could see and included, to my horror, pictures of how to get out of a car in a ladylike manner. I began to long for the Boy Scouts. I had my neighbor, whose brother was a Boy Scout, test me for the tenderfoot requirements. Thus began my love of knots and insignia.

The final blow of my Girl Scout experience was our fifth-grade troop camping trip. There were numerous parks in the hills surrounding our suburban San Francisco Bay area town, but the troop leaders had us all bused to San Francisco to a plot of land next door to the city zoo. We waited at the gate of the chain link fence to be let in for our camping adventure. When we walked up the asphalt driveway to our site, we found that the troop leaders had brought their husbands to put up our tents! This was too much. I remember little else about the trip after that except for the introduction of that famous American Girl Scout concoction—s'mores. What a sticky, gooey, impractical invention, especially for camping. I had only encountered marshmallows once before and, like chewing gum, they represented to me a peculiarly American habit that should not be swallowed. Graham crackers were soft, sweet crackers that I did not find as satisfying as a hard English biscuit, and Hershey bars, aside from having no texture, reminded me of the PX and the army brats I put up with in Thailand. The three items melted together were alarming.

I reported all this to my mother, who was horrified, particularly by the fact that the fathers had put up our tents. So much for self-sufficiency. Girl Scouts, I decided, were wimps. I quit. I was having a much better time with my Danish friend, Annette, who had never been a Girl Scout and preferred to climb trees over anything other girls were doing. She was two years younger than I was, which gave me two more years of tree climbing while my peers were getting interested in makeup and being grown up. Bonded by our European heritage and by our parents' strict immigrant values, we started clubs with names like the Fox Patrol. We modeled the skill requirements on the Boy Scout handbook. I taught her all my knots. We went on hikes and acquired pocket knives and bandanas. When I was fourteen, we became members of the Sierra Club and spent a week backpacking. I asked our Sierra Club leader, who showed all the signs of self-sufficiency, if he was ever a Boy Scout. "No," he said, his long hair tucked under a bandana, "I would never join such a paramilitary organization."

The American Girl Scouts were not the only thing that horrified my mother. She was astonished when a teacher at the public school told her I was weird because I did not play with the other kids and just wanted to sit in a corner and read. She also found out that writing exercises were optional; only the smart kids wrote at all and then only for extra credit. When I finished the fifth grade, she decided to remove me from the public school system and enroll me at a private school. There, she reasoned, I would at least learn to write and study a second language before high school. (In Thailand I had been learning French since second grade and writing essays every week).

My eighth grade teacher at the Harker School for Boys and Girls asked why I had not continued in the Girl Scouts. She had been a troop leader, and her daughters had had a great time. I told her of my experience, and she convinced me that not all troops were like that. In fact, she would see to it that I could go to the troop her daughters belonged to, even though I wasn't in the right district. I lived in the unincorporated area of Menlo Park in a working-class district. Harker School was next door in the upscale college town, Palo Alto. The Girl Scouts there had their own building! Palo Alto had had some generous benefactors in the 1940s, and a whole community center was built with children in mind. There was the Children's Theatre, the Children's Library, a fire circle for the Boy Scouts and a rustic lodge for the Girl Scouts. No more dim basements: This redwood shingled lodge had windows, a full kitchen, and a huge stone fireplace.

The leaders were different too, young and fit Stanford graduate students. I joined the Cadette troop. I was modeling myself after men at the time, no longer trusting women to fit my original images of Lord Baden-Powell's frontier women. I tested my leader for wimpiness. Was she afraid of bugs? I asked her, when we were eating our lunch on a hike. She was indignant that I would suggest she was squeamish. She later told us the story of how she had met her husband while canoeing with a girlfriend. They had capsized, and when the men onshore came to their assistance, the two women roughly told them they could manage for themselves, thank you very much. Once they made shore, however, they accepted the men's offer to dry out by their campfire. One of the men, who had admired my leader's spunkiness, asked her out. He turned out to be an explorer she had read about in the paper. She had decided when she read this article that this was the man she would marry. Here he was! I was only partly taken by the romance of the story but was duly convinced that my leader was of frontier stock.

This troop did not fail me. Not only did we go camping, we went to the Sierras in a blizzard! I got to wear my genuine thirteen-button wool sailor pants. We packed our gear in on cross-country skis and snowshoes. We dug trenches for the fire and the tent. We had a ball. I stayed on for another year as I entered a private high school for girls. Our leaders helped us get our canoeing badge and took us to watch sky divers for our aviation badge. I became a patrol leader, told my friend Annette all about our events, and persuaded her to join in time for the trip to Point Reyes National Seashore.

We hiked in even though it was raining. Having set up our tube tent, we came back after dinner to find Annette's sleeping bag soaked from the rain. My bag was dry, protected under the collapsed flap of the tent wall. "We'll have to share my sleeping bag," I announced matter-of-factly. I knew Annette did not share the affection for women that I had been cultivating with Judy, one of my classmates at school, but this was a question of making do, of being self-sufficient. "Okay," said Annette, "but don't tell anybody." I promised. "And don't worry about turning over and waking me," she added, moving into a more sisterly mode. So we slept crammed together in that mummy bag, uncomfortable but warm, and I did not tell anybody of our queer little deed.

There was something uncomplicated and practical about the Girl Scouts, like sharing a sleeping bag out of necessity. At my expensive girls' school such an incident would have been loaded with homoerotic tension. Every act was suspect, simply because we were at a girls' school, and the public school kids assumed we were "lezzies." (I don't know why this assumption was not made of the Girl Scouts.) No gesture was innocent, especially for me, fully aware as I was at fifteen of my desire to embrace girls who were not the least bit self-sufficient or brave in the face of bugs. They were completely different animals, strangely beautiful, feminine, and extremely bright. I admired their academic prowess, while they were attracted to my physical abilities.

I spent hours plotting how to touch them, for it was always left to me to make the first move. There was that night with Judy, who studied Virginia Woolf and knew that Oscar Wilde was the last person in England to be jailed for his being homosexual. "If someone read my journal, they would think I was a lesbian," she had told me when we first discussed our lives as writers. I wrote in my journal that bisexuality was normal at our age. It was considered so in Thailand where machismo gives way to a woman-centered family structure.

I often spent the night at Judy's house ostensibly because we lived so far away from each other, but we both knew we wanted something to "happen" that only the night would allow. We lay on the floor in sleeping bags in her room awake most of the night, edging closer together, every breath tense with awareness of each other. Finally at four in the morning on one such visit, I grabbed her hand. She immediately squeezed mine as hard as she could. That was all we could manage the first time. It took us until we were seniors before we actually worked up to kissing.

I remember prep school as a tortured search for identity and love seething beneath the burden of academic demands. Girl Scouting was a safe haven, a place to shed those burdens and do fun things. Scouting activities were not focused on enhancing college entrance exams or hedging bets for the sobering future. In Girl Scouts we learned what we could do as girls while we still had the energy of youth. For my mother, Girl Guiding had helped ease the traumas of World War II. Similarly the skills I learned in the Girl Scouts gave me some control over the physical world, and encouraged an emotional self-sufficiency that carried me through the surreal trials of being a gay teenager as well as a foreigner. Just going on a hike with my Girl Scout leaders on a rainy day when all the other girls had stayed home affirmed for me my choices. While other girls sought the shelter of convention, I was an individual with fortitude, well on my way to becoming an able frontier woman.

Amanda Kovattana

CHAPTER 8

The Land of Heart's Desire

Jane Eastwood

This Minnesota poet pays tribute to her three most important—and most dramatic—Girl Scout role models, and to the values of friendship "beautifully and blissfully transmitted" by her counselors.

She strode into the room like a general taking command of her troops, which happened to be the hearts and minds of the thirty girls and women who were its occupants. She was a bulldog of a woman: compact, fierce, one-hundred percent muscle. Her jet black hair was short and slicked straight back off her forehead. She wore sensible shoes and a sturdy wool skirt. Her power bored through all protocols of politeness and femininity like a jackhammer. Her voice, loud and deep, resounded. She embarrassed and thrilled me. This strange mixture of fear and adoration later would become familiar to me.

She lived the Girl Scout motto in an exemplary manner. She had to because her looks and power branded her an outlaw from the start. Even if she weren't a lesbian, she might as well have been one. She had to toe the line, live by the rules, not say anything that might suggest impropriety. This was the strange and awful double standard that Girl Scouting demanded. If a lesbian wanted to be with women, use her power, and live a life she loved, she had to be sure she never said or did anything publicly to betray who she really was.

Her name was Barbara (pseudonym), and I remember her vividly because she was the first person I ever suspected of being a dyke. In some part of my young lesbian consciousness, I fell madly in love with her. She was everything I feared and admired. I didn't want to be her *per se* (I was already a declared femme). But I wanted to be powerful and independent, and I longed to be with other women who were the same way. I was seven years old.

Barbara was a lifelong volunteer for the Girl Scout Council in Stillwater, Minnesota, my home town. She was a magnificent role model for me and all who met her. She had a good job as a chemist at 3M and, to my knowledge, never married. That meant she had money and independence, two essential ingredients for self-sufficiency. Her very existence helped me make that early and important connection between job, money, and independence.

Barbara was the first in a long line of heroines and role models that the Girl Scouts gave me.

By junior high school, I was still in scouting, but just barely. Life was troubling, and weekly scout meetings were drudgery. However, in the summer after seventh grade, I went to our council's Camp Northwoods and my life changed forever.

At Camp Northwoods, I took my first whitewater canoe trip and learned about the rigors of deadfalls, the constancy of mosquitoes, and the pleasure of river currents that have their way with you. My best friend Paula and I were canoe partners, and we spent a good deal of our time in the bushes and reeds, unable to navigate the gentle farm river that was our first serious expedition. We returned from our three-day canoe trip as women to be reckoned with: big, powerful, sure-of-ourselves paddlers and scouts. No one could unnerve us, control us, or bring us down. I carried that self-confidence with me through the next grueling year of junior high school.

In the summer after eighth grade, I met a counselor who would become the focus of my attention for the next five years. Simm (pseudonym) was everything a Girl Scout was supposed to be: capable, independent, funny (a quality neglected in the guidebook, but essential), smart, and talented. She'd

Jane Eastwood, 1967

gone to an international leadership program and returned to our council a star. She was beautiful, with deep brown eyes, short black hair, olive skin and a magnificent smile. When she laughed, she shook gently like a willow bough in a spring wind.

I made my first attempts at flirting in the way that junior high kids do—mostly trying to impress, but with a little bit of self-conscious come-on, usually characterized by saying whatever outrageous thought popped into my mind. When Simm chuckled at my jokes, or when she played the folk song that I requested, I felt proud. She noticed me. She liked me. I was special.

When it came time to leave camp that year, Paula and I cried. Simm cried, too, as she hugged us and told us we were important to her. She meant it. She promised to write, and we did too. We all kept our promises.

Ninth grade passed, and I spent my third year at camp. Two other friends came with Paula and me, and we all adopted Simm. She divided her energy equally. After that year at camp, the four of us took up regular correspondence with her, each one taking a turn receiving and sharing her letters.

I still have those missives, written in tiny cramped script on fine vellum paper. When I got her first letter on that paper, I ran out and bought my own supply: lavender with tiny purple flowers. I still have the box with her precious letters. Mostly newsy, they were important because she had made the effort to address each of us individually, acknowledging our importance.

The next year, Simm was less happy, and her correspondence was irregular. She dropped out of college, which surprised us.

Finally we persuaded her to visit. We took a long drive in the country in her dad's big blue station wagon. When we stopped for a picnic, Simm was visibly agitated. Gone was her loose, gentle laugh. Her skin was dull, her body taut with anxiety.

She told us that she had thought about suicide. I remember my throat choking closed. She couldn't explain what was going on with her and why her life had changed so much. Either she didn't know, or she wasn't about to tell four high school kids. But her shame and sense of failure were palpable. She didn't act like the strong, resilient woman who had been our idol. She was crushed and beaten. She said she didn't think she had anything more to give us. She acted like she didn't deserve to be our role model.

Simm eventually disappeared from our lives. Years later I had an insight about what might have happened to her: Maybe she was a lesbian. For someone who had been so "right" by society's—and scouting's— standards, being so "wrong" would have been hard to face.

It would be sad if the demons that haunted her were born of homophobia. It would be a shame if she denied herself the joys of living and loving freely, and more young girls were denied the many riches this woman had to offer. I am grateful that I knew her when those riches were abundant and freely given.

Life at camp continued, and I became a Counselor-in-Training. For me, this was the pinnacle of camp experience. It was like going to an extended camp session and being better than all of the other scouts because you have a special relationship with the counselors. At age fifteen or sixteen, you're within reach of the seductive and mysterious sorority of counselorhood.

The counselors at the camp where I took CIT training were exotic. Take the camp director, for example. Denny's (pseudonym) story reflected some of the bold, sad themes common to lesbian life in the 1950s. At sixteen, she'd run away from home and hitched the rails to New York City where, she'd heard, there were people like her in Greenwich Village. Eventually, she made her way back to the Midwest, and by the time I met her had become something of a camp legend. Denny knew the power of the piercing gaze to melt or thaw an unsuspecting soul and she used this power generously. I trembled when she looked my way and I seemed to be directly in her line of sight often. Her story about how the Girl Scout cookie money built our lodge must have been responsible for selling an extra thousand boxes of cookies each year. She would don an authentic Native American chieftain's bonnet decorated with eagle feathers, given to her by a local Indian chief who, it seemed, was an important friend of hers. (With her black eyes and hair, Denny could have been Native American. If she was, we missed an opportunity to better understand her heritage.)

Denny would tell us how the great Thunderbird spirit up in the sky had used the cookie money to build our lodge. The camp itself had been named in its honor—Camp of the Thunderbird. Each box of cookies we sold gave the great Thunderbird more money to improve the camp and make our lives there happier. It was our responsibility to sell more cookies when we returned home.

Adults and children alike sat in rapt attention when she told the story. Her fierce eyes blazed with eagle power as she strode across the great deck of the lodge. Preacher, healer, and backwoods politician, she stretched the story to epic proportions. I wouldn't have been surprised to see the great Thunderbird swoop down and brand her with its talons. She'd work us up to a tight, fevered pitch with her tale. When she finished, we'd break into Girl Scout ditties with a frenzy akin to speaking in tongues.

When I was twenty-seven, I met Denny again. Three housemates and I, all lesbians, took a drive to a nearby country town that was known for its quaint shops, several of which were lesbian- or gay-owned. We marched into the ice cream parlor, which was jammed to the walls, and there was Denny, scooping cones.

I was dressed to the nines in summer dyke finery: a lavender headband and matching T-shirt, green shorts that looked like Girl Scout "greenies," and Birkenstocks. I looked smashing.

It took an unbearably long time to get to the counter. This gave me substantial opportunity to stare at *her*. She never seemed to look at me, but somehow I knew she was aware of my presence. By the time I reached the counter, more than just my underarms were wet. My knees were making noises like maracas. Like an awkward teenager, I was nearly speechless.

I choked out my order for a chocolate cone, and she took it, but said nothing else. I decided that I had to say something now—there might never be another chance.

"Are you Denny?"

She purred a luxuriant, "Yes, I am."

"I—I know you. I was a CIT at Camp of the Thunderbird. My camp name was Scout."

"I know. I remember you."

I felt a tightness in my chest and shortness of breath. After the obligatory, "Nice to see you, take care," I collapsed at a nearby table. By the time we were ready to leave, she had disappeared into the back room.

I never saw her again. Twelve years later, I met the owner of the shop and asked her about Denny. We talked about her piercing gaze and the way she always made a dramatic entrance into any room, even the camp kitchen. I asked what Denny was up to, and the woman started to cry. Denny, then in her fifties, was dying of cancer. This woman loved Denny the way I had, and she couldn't believe so magnificent a woman soon would be taken away. I'd like to think that if Denny is gone, the Thunderbird finally has branded her and carried her home.

Friendship was the deepest and most important thing to us at camp. It was a value blissfully and beautifully transmitted to us by our counselors, who demonstrated their friendship and abiding love for each other in every way but open romance. It didn't matter that nobody ever admitted they were *in love* with their best friends. The feelings were there in every action, every gesture, every glance, every fond goodnight.

Music was a powerful transmitter of these feelings. We learned hundreds of songs at camp—all the usual ones about life in the wilderness, the obligatory graces and rounds, and the awkward Girl Scout group-it-up songs. The love songs were the ones I clung to, though, and they conveyed the message most clearly. These were the songs we sang to our special friends: "Somewhere" from *West Side Story*; "Softly As I Leave You"; "The First Time Ever I Saw Your Face"; "For Kathy"; "For Bobby, For Baby"; "One Time Only." They were all songs about finding one's true love or having to leave one's soulmate behind.

As CITs, we spent the session break on beautiful Madeline Island, largest in the chain of the Apostle Islands in Lake Superior. We took long walks on the beach, watched the sun bleed red into the water, and drifted off to sleep by the campfire with the songs of love in our breasts, our special friends only inches away. The combination of being in nature and in the company of women, while immersing ourselves in music, created a potent, often erotic, mix. Sublimated feelings and unspoken needs formed a current of desire running through our dreams and powering our daily rituals. We were timeless beings in a timeless land, where the only matters of importance were laughter, wind, water and sun. We were sated by the feast that mother nature offered up and enriched by the wealth of the love we gave to each other.

One song captures my feelings about those years spent outdoors in the company of women I loved. Its last lines ask the question: *Tell me were you ever nearer to the land of heart's desire / then when you stood there dreaming / dreaming there before the fire?*

I know I never was.

Jane Eastwood

CHAPTER 9

✳ ✳ ✳

Mostly Gifts

Nancy Franz

This wilderness guide and volunteer adult trainer from the Wisconsin shore of Lake Superior is grateful for the ways Girl Scouting has shaped her life.

The most important thing I learned as a Girl Scout was that women can be strong and confident without men. This was best illustrated at the camp I attended every summer. The female staff did everything from maintenance to nature programs, and these wonderful role models made sure that we campers learned the skills required for those jobs. I especially enjoyed using an ax and memorizing the night constellations.

Another major benefit of being a Girl Scout was that it built my self-esteem. Early on, troop leaders and camp counselors helped me to take risks and succeed at the things I loved to do. I learned camp craft, no-trace camping, backpacking, canoeing and outdoor cooking. I also learned to interpret signs of the natural world that I found in forests, lakes, stars, and bogs. These experiences expanded as I got older until I felt comfortable tackling just about anything. They were successes that I wasn't able to achieve in school, church, or any other place.

Nancy Franz, 1967

My outdoor experiences in the Girl Scouts eventually led me to earn college degrees in environmental education/ outdoor recreation and natural science education. After college, I worked for the U.S. Forest Service, the National Park Service, and with the Youth Conservation Corps. For the past fifteen years I've been a 4-H and Youth Agent for the University of Wisconsin Cooperative Extension System. What I learned in the Girl Scouts now serves me in my work.

For example, I currently work as an outdoor guide with Women Outdoors (Medford, Massachusetts) and Woodswomen (Minneapolis, Minnesota), organizations that offer wilderness trips for women. Many former Girl Scouts attend these trips, looking for the camaraderie and support they used to find in scouting. These women testify to the value of all-female outdoor activities. They enjoy spending time reliving a common past, whether it's singing old camp songs or remembering how to use a dip bag.

Unfortunately, however, Girl Scouting hasn't entailed only gifts. Lesbian friends have been fired or made to resign without cause. A Black scout professional discovered blatant racism in her coworkers. As a local Girl Scout volunteer, I've noticed a lack of diversity. For the most part, the people in power are white, middle class, and straight, as are most of the volunteers and members. Although badges and handbooks are beginning to illustrate diversity, few adults actually guide young girls in exploring differences.

I often wonder if support would remain for my work with girls and adults if my local Girl Scout council knew about my sexual orientation. I still believe that Girl Scouting is the best place for girls to become strong and self-actualized. I just hope that scouting is ready to become the organization girls today need for a diverse world.

Nancy Franz

* * *

CHAPTER 10

A Trio of Uniforms

Terry King

From Catholic school, through eleven years of Girl Scouting, to a stint in the United States Marine Corps, uniforms marked the stages of this California woman's empowerment and growing awareness of her sexual orientation. (The names of people and Chicago institutions have been changed to protect their identities.)

Scouting began for me in the first grade at St. Moses Catholic Grade School in Chicago. The annotation in my mother's handwriting in my *Girl Scout Handbook* reads May 23, 1951. St. Moses was a Catholic school, one of many in the predominately Black neighborhoods on the South Side of Chicago. All the instructors were white nuns, priests, and lay teachers. All the pupils wore uniforms. Most of the youngsters who attended St. Moses came from families that could more easily afford the tuition than mine.

My family was not well off. My father had been a good provider in my younger years, but as alcohol became his close friend, the family finances became less stable. When I asked to join the Brownies, my mom put me in the troop connected with St. Moses. But we were not able to afford extra niceties available to others in the St. Moses Brownie troop, like buying new shoes and keeping my hair fixed. I complained about that and begged to go to the troop my friend Bensi belonged to on 10th and Wabash, where the

Camarey House Community Center was located. So there I went, and there I remained until I was seventeen years old, wearing first the Brownie, then the Intermediate, and finally the Senior Girl Scout uniform. In my eyes, our troop was the best: we were all Black, and we had a wonderful leader, Mrs. Jancy, a light-skinned woman with freckles. Mrs. Jancy exhibited such warmth toward us that I would have walked on water if she had asked me.

I enjoyed earning badges: literature, folk dancing, play producer, cooking. Our troop excelled in every aspect of scouting. Since Mrs. Jancy's character was beyond reproach, there was never any question of impropriety. I always felt a sort of calm with the troop, my home away from home.

For our Sadie Hawkins dances, we made fliers and posted them around the neighborhood. We sent out handmade invitations to special boys, dressed in Daisy Mae costumes, and wore outrageous makeup. We had a good time teasing the shy boys and even leading them in the dance.

However, it was not dancing, but the out-of-doors that was the real thrill for me. Our troop went to the Kankakee Forest Preserve just outside Chicago at least once a month during the summer for overnight camping and on day trips in early fall. For several summers, Bensi and I went to Girl Scout Camp Chinook in Waukesha, Wisconsin. Being with my troop taught me the essence of companionship and an unselfish approach to life. The feelings inherent in me for other women were nurtured by Mrs. Jancy and other kind, loving women from whom I received instruction, courtesy, and understanding.

In July of 1955, our troop was selected, along with many others worldwide, to participate in the first Girl Scout Roundup in Pontiac, Michigan. The Girl Scout Roundup was the utmost in camping. We brought or made everything we used. There were no men around except for the National Guard, who had been called in to help with the rattlesnakes. One scout who did not heed the warning not to sleep on the ground found a snake in her sleeping bag. I saw a guardsman catch it with a forked stick and give it to a Girl Scout troop from Texas to prepare for a meal to which we were invited.

One of the most uplifting Roundup moments was when all 6,000 of us (5,000 girls and 1,000 leaders) amassed in a bowl-shaped amphitheater and sang "The Bell Song." We later heard from some residents of one of the nearby towns that it really sounded like bells.

My mom had cautioned me not to take showers or be naked around anyone at the Roundup. I did not understand her concern, despite several clues. For

Terry King, 1955

example, when watching movies, I always wanted to be the one kissing or holding the woman, not the other way around. Also, I remember caressing Bensi's breasts on two occasions. These touches elicited a charge through my whole body. Although I didn't know anything about "the gay life," apparently my mom did. When I decided to join the Marine Corps, she did everything she could, including getting ill, to keep me from going.

When my friend Trella decided to join with me, Trella's parents were even more upset than my mother. (Ever since kindergarten, when I was the tallest pupil, Trella had looked to me to protect her from all bullies.) Despite our parents' opposition, Trella and I joined up. I felt right at home in my new Marine Corps uniform. In my spare time, I proceeded to do the things I liked, mainly play softball. My high school had not fielded a girls' team, so I did not excel, but I played, kept score, and learned how to be a trainer. I was also on the Marine Corps volleyball, bowling, and basketball teams.

Quite a few of our sports team members were gay, and although little lights began to pop on for me, I didn't suspect that I, too, was gay until at least a year after I was in the military. One night at a party at a friend's apartment I received my first kiss from a woman. Finally, I understood what my fantasies, longings and electric feelings during all those years had been about.

After that revelation, I read several books, including *The Well of Loneliness*, which I found on the bookshelf at home when I went on leave! I knew I was a lesbian. I started thinking again about a beautiful Girl Scout I'd met at the Roundup. I had kept Denise's phone number and address, and I still had strong feelings for this woman. When I phoned her, I discovered she was, much to my dismay, straight and planning to get married.

I gave up my romantic thoughts about Denise and focused on my life in the Marine Corps. I realized that the Girl Scouts had helped prepare me for the work ethic and the honor parts of military life. But the kindness and conviviality of Girl Scouting were completely absent in the service, and I missed them. I was always in trouble—not in my job, where I received straight 4.0s, but in the area of discipline. I was headstrong and individualistic. One time, when the Major returned from a trip to find me out of town for a baseball game, he fired me. Six months later he had to finagle to get me back because the audit he sent to Washington was a mess.

I still am headstrong, and I still love beautiful women. I am fairly comfortable with my sexuality although I have never directly discussed it with anyone in my family except for one relative who is also a lesbian. We talk occasionally, but others do not pry, and I'm not one to offer unsolicited information.

So there you have it. I've learned a lot from my experiences. Some parts of my life I'd do over if I had the chance. Others I'd keep the same. I believe in following my heart. I believe fear keeps people from experiencing life to the fullest. I believe in God, and I believe in the Girl Scout motto, "Be Prepared."

Terry King

PART II

* * *

Fulfillment

Fulfillment

More than fifty million young Girl Scouts have flowered into adults since the founding of the organization in 1912. Girl Scouting began at a time when the suffrage movement was gaining strength, and the organization has been liberating girls and women from conventional stereotypes and sexist limitations ever since. "Scratch a feminist," says Unitarian Universalist District Executive Anne Heller, "and you'll find a Girl Scout."

Years before becoming a minister, Reverend Heller was at her desk at the Girl Scout council office in Oakland, California when the receptionist announced two women from the Berkeley Women's Health Collective. The women had a remarkable coincidence to report. During a recent staff meeting, they had discovered that amidst all the differences in age, class, ethnicity, regional background, religion, and sexual orientation of collective members, they had one thing in common: everyone at the meeting had been a Girl Scout.[1]

Anne Heller wasn't surprised. She knows that Girl Scouting builds independent women who march to their own drum beat, much like Juliette Gordon Low herself. The women in Part II document how scouting shaped their lives, not only in the past as campers, troop members, and counselors, but in the present as activists, innovators, and leaders. These women still do their best to fulfill the Girl Scout promise and laws, on their honor.

---

[1] Heller, Anne. Pacific Northwest District (Unitarian Universalist Executive Association) District Executive. Personal interview. 24 Aug. 1995.

CHAPTER 11

✳ ✳ ✳

Lesbians, Lightning, and Bears

Judith Niemi

This wilderness guide discovered her life's passion early, and ever since, she has contributed to women's participation and lesbian visibility in the field of wilderness education, leading women's trips from the Amazon to the Arctic.

All of a sudden the woman was getting cold feet about the planned canoe trip. Weeks earlier she and a friend had signed up for a trip in northern Minnesota with a women's wilderness program that I run. It wasn't a rugged trip: it was designed for women of all ages, with easy canoeing and lots of instruction. But now she was on the telephone, canceling. They had reconsidered, she said, because after all there could be lightning storms, and what could you ever do, out on the lake? You'd be helpless! And then she was terrified of bears. And then, she was hesitant to mention it, but, well . . . . What if there were *lesbians* on the trip?

On our end of the line our secretary was being understanding, polite, very professional. But the rest of us in the office had picked up the drift and were rolling our eyes. The second Susan hung up, we started in: "Well, just *guess* which one of those fears is the operative one." "I'll bet she panicked because she was coming with a friend." "Did she actually say someone might make a

85

pass at her?" "Hah! she should be so lucky!"

For a moment I chose to think of it as flattering, and somehow deliciously appropriate, to be linked up with other large exciting forces of nature. Lightning. Bears. Lesbians. I rolled the words around, feeling almost mythic. But in my gut was that familiar cynical, sinking feeling. The depth of fear in some insistently straight people is sometimes silly, usually sad, and generally far off the mark.

Susan had done her patient best; we make a point of being helpful on the phone way beyond the call of duty. Often we're a regular information and referral service: on canoeing, on all the measures to take during electrical storms; on bears. She had told the woman that Minnesota black bears and Yellowstone grizzlies have little in common, and that we often like seeing bears. And yes, she had said clearly, there very probably would be some lesbians on the trip. There usually are. We think that's just fine. *All* women are welcome.

We're always frank about this, and we often add more, a few little pre-packaged lines, to try in a few seconds to cut through a lot of popular nuttiness about lesbians.

"Are you asking will there be lesbians? Oh, sure. And old college friends, and married women escaping the kids, and grandmothers." (Any of whom might, of course, also be lesbians, as were some ministers and the Republican politician, but in a short phone call there's no time to get into that.)

"You can be as out—or as private—as you want to be, about anything. Sometimes we have to remind nonlesbian women that they don't have to keep their husband or boyfriend in the closet either."

"The moose don't care what you call yourself, or whom you love. And it's *their* home."

We figure it's just part of our job as trip leaders to promote an open, caring and sane group, including making it clear that on our trips lesbianism is not "An Issue," just an ordinary part of life. It works out fine; in almost twenty years of leading outdoor trips, I've met only a handful of women as frightened as that caller. But this much frankness is not exactly the norm in outdoor circles. The fact is that among women taking part in adventure travel, especially all-women's trips, the percentage of lesbians must be something like that of dykes in the military. And the subject is just as taboo.

Not that many years ago, I was at a conference of the Association for Experiential Education; AEE members are interested in ethical and social aspects of outdoor education. They run programs for kids at risk and for disabled people; they advocate noncompetitive New Games and talk about diversity. Nothing in the official program or any syllable uttered in the general sessions suggested gays and lesbians even existed. Back then—the mid 1980s—just being a woman got you listed among the "Special Populations," presumably in need of special programming. I was starting to think the trademark of the conference could be the number of exceedingly wholesome young men in shorts who noncompetitively kicked a Hackysack in the lunch line and in the hotel lobby. Then a women's caucus did get formed; we seemed like feisty but nervous outsiders, planning how to get a voice. Even in our own meetings, a word like "lesbian," if spoken (rarely), was ignored. Then a little sign was posted in several women's bathrooms, Magic Marker on torn out notebook pages, announcing a meeting of lesbians in AEE—that night, at a clearing in the woods! Like the witches of Plymouth colony. So there I was, stumbling down a dark wood-chip path, grumbling, "What *is* this cloak and dagger routine? I don't get it!"

But I did get it, of course; I'd been in the closet too many years myself. Silence gets to be a terrible habit, breeding its own fear and powerlessness. We sat in a dark circle. I recognized the voice of a woman who had recently started her own tour company. She was asking, "but how can you *possibly* talk out loud about it? How will straight women react?"

I was impatient. "You really think it's better for a group to feel that there's some big secret hanging around? To let people fret and wonder who is and who isn't? To let women go on assuming that lesbians are a problem?"

Year by year things are improving a little, according to friends who work for establishments like Outward Bound and National Outdoor Leadership School. They can now run staff training sessions on being sensitive toward gay and lesbian students. Instructors who think they've never had any gay clients discover that in fact a few do identify themselves, once the leaders have a little coaching in manners and awareness.

But outdoor leaders are themselves often closeted, fearing for their jobs. One talented, world-experienced outdoorswoman I've worked with, a sweet and sensitive leader of women's trips for years, was once asked by a client, point blank, "Don't you find it hard to be away from home so much? Is there

Judith Niemi,
(about 1948)

a Significant Other in your life?" So she answered honestly, "Yes, I'm in a long-time relationship. It's with a woman who understands how I love my work. It's hard, but here's how we manage...." The shocked client canceled out of a future trip; the guide was promptly fired by her boss (a woman, a lesbian, in fact), for not lying. Dykes are good customers, but being too out could be bad for business. Don't ask, don't tell.

Telling, of course, is exactly what's going to happen when women get together in the outdoors. Oh sure, we climb 10.9 pitches and paddle Class III rivers. (Notice how when you attach numbers to these experiences, they sound just like what the boys do.) But then we're going to sit down for lunch, or around the fire, and there'll be talk. Women's talk, humorous, serious, intimate. Once we get revved up, women's talk is free, revolutionary, and could go anywhere. Politics, great restaurants, lousy bosses, mixed-blessing relationships, menopause. Does anyone actually think that while encouraging women to be free-spirited and fun-loving, you can still selectively squelch them so that the one thing no one will ever mention is *The L word?* Infantile, that's what it is. It reminds me way too much of junior high school, or, much as I hate to say it, Girl Scout camp.

Scout camp. Giggling girls in the bunkhouse exchanging sexual misinformation and dirty jokes. (I rarely understood them; there was one about daddy's flashlight and mommy's cave and looking for a little red dress.) Back rubs while seated around the campfire, which we all knew were amazingly delicious but should go on only so long (just why wasn't clear). Counselors to be looked up to (but Crushes, on the other hand, were shameful). Camp taught us to be strong, to admire women, to expand our horizons. But not too much. At home and school we were encouraged to be nice, to become secretaries and teachers and librarians; without anyone saying so explicitly, camp also told us, "Don't Go Too Far." (Whatever exactly that meant.)

But what are women's wilderness trips about—or Girl Scout camp, for that matter—if not trying out our strength and feeling the freedom of the wilds and learning to trust ourselves and each other? For those of us who feel like born lesbians, there's no strength or freedom or trust if we can't be ourselves, be out and honest. It's deeper, however, than questions of orientation. Courage and freedom is what all women need.

These days I'm a grown-up, enthusiastic wilderness guide. I try to be an honest woman, in all aspects of my life, so, guiding or anyplace else, that generally includes being matter-of-factly out as a lesbian. Usually that's natural and not a big deal. But at times when silence seems easier, I'm adamant with myself; I remember why it is important. I remember because of what I learned at scout camp, mostly by bad example.

Don't get me wrong, I absolutely adored scout camp. My discriminating or cranky adult self mutters darkly about how things should have been, or at least ought to be by now, but the kid in me is full of happy nostalgia. I could still sing you the song my tent pals and I made up forty years ago, to the tune of "Hernando's Hideaway"—"They wreck. Cha cha. The place. With Luster-Lace. It's called our Tumble-Inn. Ole!" Camp was the best thing that happened to many of us.

After all, how did we ever get through the 50s intact? Through that decade of Ike, always smiling, and cheery H-bomb drills at school. ("Heads down, kids, pop under the desk!") Moms were at home making cookies, and in a small town like ours the only organized sport for girls was baton twirling. Those of us who would later dive so exuberantly into the heady Second Wave of feminism and Lesbian Power must have had something keeping our secret baby-dyke selves alive and sane. Scout camp, that's what.

Scout camp was the one place I'd ever seen where women ran the world. Not a very big world, but ours, and girls counted. "Scout camp was like Catholic girls' school," says my partner, an alumna of both. "Very supportive, very repressive. But at least all the role models were women."

Sometimes a vocation, Catholic or pagan, shows up early in life. When I was seven, an issue of the Girl Scout leaders' magazine came to our house with a cover photo of a Brownie scout. She wore beanie and knee socks and was kneeling by a campfire, carefully, skillfully tending the flame in that little pyramid of sticks. I saw the future. I *knew*. "That's me, isn't it, Mom?"

That's how she tells it. Mom was on the Girl Scout council and says she had never intended to be a troop leader, since as far as she could see, the only way any woman ever got out of it again was to have either a heart attack or a baby, "and I was too young for one and too old for the other." But she was always good about saying yes to what her little daughter really wanted: a jackknife, a football, a Girl Scout uniform.

Frankly, scouting didn't introduce much new to my life. Like every other troop, we mostly made little crafts for shut-ins and had potlucks. We spent endless hours making sit-upons and buddy burners (how to fry an egg in only three hours). Going to camp that one week in the summer was the main point of it for me. Even though I already had plenty of other places to run around outdoors, and did, scout camp became the focus of my summer.

Actually, our camp wasn't much, looked at with cool-eyed objectivity. No archery, no horses. No canoes, which would have been my idea of heaven— just one old Lund rowboat, and I'd already been rowing since I could lift oars. Certainly not much in nature awareness. Once there was a contest to identify flowers. I was excited, then very let down, since all the wildflowers were common ones—like goldenrod and daisies. I'd collected and pressed them all years before to earn the Wildflower Badge. I was bored; I won. I suspect no one else even entered.

Every year there was a Snipe Hunt, with little girls running through the night woods as beaters while the new girls hopefully held open pillowcases until finally the triumphant jeer, "Hahaha there's no such thing as a snipe!" But there was too such a thing. I knew. I'd earned my Bird Badge, tromping the fields alone before school on spring mornings. The snipe, or woodcock, in the bird guide even looked a lot like the "imaginary" bird they described.

I was disappointed that the adults didn't know more, but I kept that subversive knowledge to myself. At least racing around in the dark was fun.

One summer the camp director certified we'd earned the Dancer Badge. Nancy and Penny and I were indignant. We had NOT fulfilled all the requirements, we fussed. We refused to accept it, as a point of honor. (I think the scout council made us take them.) The real point was that we little tomboys did not *want* the dancer badge, a little ballet shoe. We yearned for the Pioneer Badge, wanted black kettles and bean-hole beans and three piled stones to signal danger. But no one at our camp used those wonderful trail signs or wanted us to be Pioneers.

Still, there were perfect moments. The best part of camp was The Pines, a hill where one small stand of white pines and Norways had somehow escaped the sweep of Weyerhauser and Swallow Lumber decades before. Each tree was so big two kids' arms didn't reach around it. "Virgin pines," we whispered respectfully. Toward the end of each camp week we'd all roll up our blankets and pillows and a ground cloth and carry our bundles to The Pines. We'd arrange our bedrolls around the campfire and sing. Then we'd giggle and whisper for several hours; beyond us the counselors murmuring quietly about their grown-up concerns. Firelight flickered on massive tree trunks. Stars glittered in the blackness. Eventually the voices would hush, and even the mosquitoes would leave. I'd lie there entranced, watching the embers, thinking about primeval forests and human life and eternity. Then it would start to rain, and we'd all snatch up our bedding and race back to the cabins, skidding on the slippery pine-needle path, while the counselors shouted, "Don't run!"

Camp was important to me not for what it actually *was*, but for all the things that it stood for. In a small way, it institutionalized and gave dignity to the outdoor activities I otherwise did all alone. Camp meant achievement. It meant a community of women. This was a vision worth holding on to. My camp buddy Cathy lived in the next town, only three miles away, but we never visited each other during the school year—that might have spoiled the magic. Instead we wrote letters in invisible ink. Beyond our little camp were others all over the country; somewhere Mariner Scouts were on the high seas, and somewhere girls met at Roundup. There was even Our Chalet! "High uuuuup, high on the mountain, we've founded Our Chalet!" we piped earnestly, although none of us expected ever to see it, or any real Swiss chalet, for that matter. Still, once some Swiss Girl Guides did actually visit our camp, ate our bean-hole beans and danced their folk dances for us. So there were possibilities, for girls. Beyond The Pines there were far wilder places, somewhere.

And, more tangibly, camp gave us strong, almost-adult women to look up to, women who weren't our mothers, or our friends' mothers, or our buttoned-down teachers. Counselors! Of course we knew they were just junior college or even high school girls from the next town. At home they drank cherry cokes and giggled, might even have been cheerleaders or baton twirlers. But at camp, they were stand-ins for the goddess. There's a snapshot in which I called on all my twelve-year-old art to express this. The counselor, whoever she was, Ginger or Turk or Joker, stands hand on hip, looking off into the distance, a very adult, womanly pose. Behind her, the soft branches of a white pine reach heavenward. I shot from a low angle, so her handsome head would be framed by clouds. It looks like I used a yellow filter to intensify those clouds—so maybe I was using my dad's ancient fold-out camera, the one I liked for serious photos. I should tack that photo over my desk: Portrait of the Unknown Counselor. I doubt that I had a crush on her, or not a personal one. It was the Platonic idea of Counselor that attracted me, the competent strong free woman.

"How old do you have to be to be a camp counselor?" I asked the head of our Girl Scout council, a friend of my mother. I was fifteen. Way too young, of course. But when Punkie, the camp director, arrived to find that only four counselors had been hired, she refused to stay without more staff being found. So there I was, an underage last resort. I was impressed by Punkie's insubordination and nerve, and I was in heaven, privy to that exciting adult side of camp. Skinny dipping under the shooting stars of August. A staff corn feed. That winter, a staff reunion at Punkie's condo in Minneapolis, where I learned how a career woman keeps her nylons sorted: different colored threads looped through the tops. I soaked up every crumb of information on the adult world.

I took very seriously my responsibilities as a counselor. One camp session, a mother dropped her child off and pulled the senior counselor and me aside. She suspected her child just might start her, ah, periods soon. She wanted us to be alert because she hadn't explained anything to the child. And because I was now A Counselor, I knew somehow I would figure out how to do my duty and would talk honestly with the child about periods and sex and the adult world, of which I knew almost nothing.

Later, in college, I was a camp counselor every summer, and it didn't then seem to be a very adult thing. Certainly we didn't feel like goddesses. (My photos from those years show us in cute little sailor hats and hooded sweatshirts, baby-faced bobby-soxers.) We were conscientious and hardworking, but we sensed that camp life was a privileged extension of childhood, an approved way of continuing to play, to escape some of the boredom of acting like women.

Camp was full of the rituals, lore and silly rules that make for creative play. I've always thought some of this ritual and lore was code, a key to some little rebellions, secret strengths and dykiness that camps unwittingly fostered.

I still recall the gasps of horror in the early morning if a corner of Our Beautiful Banner dangled near the ground. Bongo delighted in being flag counselor, a job most of us hated even more than latrine counselor or table counselor. She'd swap "kapers" often so she could give the cute little eight-year-olds the most gawd-awful inspirational poetry to read at flag-raising. Then she'd watch the rest of the sleepy counselors, Jiff, Yogi, and me, biting our lips, trying to suppress giggles and snorts at the summer's tenth or eleventh heartfelt singsong reading of, "If you can't be a pine on the top of the hill, be a shrub in the valley below."

Another peculiarity of camp life was the nicknames. Counselors' real names were guarded with obsessive secrecy. Accidentally calling another counselor by her given name was as unthinkable as dropping the flag. Back then I liked to expound my theory that the Girl Scouts wanted kids to think their counselors weren't real young women you'd meet on the street (although once in a while a camper did, with astonishment and delighted embarrassment). No, they wanted campers to think we lived maybe in hollow trees, emerging only for the camping season.

We laughed at this clear separation of camp and real life, but didn't question it. Timber, Skye and Max were real, the most real women we knew. Larger than life. But at the same time they were creations of camp. Strong women like that could not really exist in the Eveleth or Duluth or Minneapolis of 1960. Some of the nicknames assumed a life of their own. Twenty years later, when women from the Minneapolis lesbian coffeehouse decided to hold their own Girl Scout Roundup, I heard familiar names mentioned. "Does anyone know where Skye is?" "Oooh, yeah, Skye!" I've never met the woman, but I've had a bit of a crush on Skye myself. I've heard the way women breathe her name.

If our own camp had no living dyke goddesses on staff, there were still moments that lit up everything, moments that hinted at larger secrets. Once a friend of our director visited. She wore the most wonderfully aged denim, out at the knees, faded at the fly, long before anyone dreamed up marketing "distressed" jeans. Her hair was sun-bleached, her walk arrogant, and she signaled with authority to her little dog Plato. "Actually," she drawled, "Aristotle was the greatest of the Greek philosophers, but you can't call a dog that." I was smitten. An intellectual! A tough woman. More than that, a . . . I had no name for it, but I knew what I liked.

In the early sixties it was easy to know nothing about lesbians, but we were intensely aware of the undercurrent of crushes. There seemed to be a lot of mixed worry and amusement about crushes. It wasn't clear why, but it didn't particularly seem to be about deviance. Just liking *anyone* too much, a boy, a teacher, a counselor, would be embarrassing. Better to protect precious feelings by hiding them.

We hovered between blissful unselfconsciousness and shrewd awareness. One summer many of us on staff were pre-dykes, including me (Sam), Yogi, Jiff, and Bongo, but I think none of us knew it yet, except our director Micky and her buddy Max, the director of another Girl Scout camp nearby. The rest of us joked about Micky's frequent visits to Max, yet we couldn't have said why this embarrassed and excited us.

Then Jiff, the P.E. major who was our waterfront director, developed a huge crush on Windy, the cute college freshman who was junior counselor for the ten-year-olds. It was very embarrassing to us all. She mooned around and trailed after Windy in every spare moment, oblivious to how it looked. They shared a cabin, and Jiff spent a lot of time in Windy's bed. Just cuddling, actually. Nothing else had occurred to them. But their cabinmate Bongo went into a panic. Other things *were* occurring to her, and all the staff knew that something was terribly wrong. "Wow, Bongo's really losing it," was our analysis.

At some point a camp director has to take action. Micky did. She sent

Bongo home. Just for a short break, a little R and R between camp sessions. Get yourself together, she said. She told Jiff that on the swimming dock she had better keep her mind on the job and her eyes on the kids. Other than that, she acted like it wasn't a big deal. Which of course it wasn't. Just a sweet young crush. But in 1960 how did young Micky have the wisdom to know that, and the guts not to panic and fire the "lesbian" to cover her own tracks?

Other camps have handled this heady brew of naiveté, young lust, secret societies, idealism and yearning far worse. For two summers I was a trip counselor in Maine at a private camp for kids from wealthy families. The director was a slick New Yorker, an ex-Marine, who wore shorts, knee socks, and a pipe in a leather case at his groin. In staff meetings he would allude, very briefly, to the potential for camper crushes in a snide, knowing tone that shut down any chance of useful discussion. (I was meantime having a mad crush on the drama counselor—a very useful emotional experience.)

At other camps, lesbians or not-quite-lesbians got fired. Pat, an earnest, overachieving young counselor-in-training was kicked out of a Minnesota scout camp for being a dyke. She was, in fact, but absolutely unaware of it at the time. She was just a kid, a stocky little tomboy whose style was way too butch for the director's comfort. Years later when I met her she was still hurting and confused by the experience. And there were Barb and Lou, who met at a Maine scout camp and in the first week were both fired for being lesbians. Lou had never even heard the word. They stood out at the parking lot, stunned, two girls who hardly knew each other and did not understand what had happened. With her summer plans shot, Barb decided on the spot to go to Minnesota with Lou, who soon decided that if that's what Barb was, this lesbian idea was a pretty good one. Last time I saw them, they were still together, twenty-some years later, with a son and a house.

Nice results, in some cases, but a hell of a way to come out: ostracized, whispered about for being something you did not even know existed; guilty, of something you haven't yet even thought of. And yet somehow you knew the accusations were true.

At other camps the emotional temperature could run quite a lot higher without the staff or director getting too nervous. Perhaps the staff understood the adolescent need for excess. Jane, a decade younger than I, spent her summers at a scout camp that had developed tearful farewell campfires to an art form. They had ceremonies that did such a job of bonding that everyone was bound to come back the next summer. Every year, she reminisces, on the final night of camp, they launched wishing boats—little wooden boards, each with a little candle stuck on, set loose in fleets on the dark lake. As the tiny winking lights bobbed away, the girls clutched each other and cried over losing camp and each other. And they sang—songs like "Unchained Melody" or from *West Side Story:* "There's a Place for Us."

It would be nice to think that decade by decade camps change and girls grow up with a little more information and wisdom available to them. I can't imagine the depth of ignorance of my Girl Scout days surviving in the era of Madonna. But I suspect we're losing only innocence, not ignorance. After all, didn't the United States Surgeon General get fired not long ago because when asked point blank, she said well, masturbation is a pretty ordinary part of sexuality and yes, maybe we could mention it in sex education. We'd better hope the Girl Scouts, or someone, gets bold enough to talk to girls about bodies and spirits and sex, about lesbians, about being heterosexual, about women's lives.

As a modest first step, we could start by acknowledging that a crush can be a very nice growing experience, one that may or may not be focused on sex. It wasn't just each other we were lusting after, those of us bold enough to have our crushes. It was our selves we wanted, the selves we hoped to be, bigger, wiser, stronger. Or just bolder and sexier. Until a kid is ready to see the good qualities in herself, it's not too bad a start to recognize them—or imagine them—in someone else. What if as young staff counselors, we'd been taught how to direct that high energy of our own or the campers' crushes toward accomplishment, toward appreciation of ourselves and other women? A friend turned her junior high swimming team's crushes on her into a regional championship. Instead of all that embarrassed skulking around, you could have an army of little not-quite-ready-to-be-lovers who couldn't fail.

Mixed blessing that scout camp was, even back in my day it gave many of us glimpses of what women might be, who we could be. It provided some of us with our first possibility of imagining lesbians. We'd have come to it anyway, but it was easier away from home and school, out in the woods. Standing in line by the mess hall, Jane watched two counselors doing The Twist, giggling about doing it with their boyfriends but looking hard at each other. "I didn't know what I was seeing," she says. "But I sure knew I was seeing *something*." Lou took a closer look at the smart and funny woman, a "lesbian" they said, who had just been fired with her. I watched a cocky college philosopher in faded jeans who walked with a surer stride than a woman is supposed to.

And we all had flashes of instant recognition. "That's me, Mom, isn't it?" But there was no one to say, "Yes, dear, it is. How wonderful for you."

In time, some of us looked for ways to improve on the camp experience and get clearer about our path. "Wouldn't camp be great without the campers," the young counselors would say, and when the season was over, we'd go off together on a canoe trip. In time, a few of us got into the adventure travel business so adult women could go to camp. And now we can do it right. No kaper charts. No flag ceremony. No dancer badges, or any other kind. Just all the canoeing, hiking and play we want, for the sheer joy of it. We can do back rubs, laugh a lot, and talk about anything. And—if we just have the guts to remember this—no one has to pretend that there aren't any lesbians.

So what happens in a group of a dozen women, mostly new to each other, when we say *the L word* right out loud? The earth doesn't split open. Women aren't that easily shocked. Once the taboo word is said we can get right on with canoeing, watching sunsets and telling the stories of our lives, but without censoring. About once every three or four years we may get a client who is clinically homophobic, or simply naive enough to imagine she's never met "one of them" before. Then the leader gets to call on all her tact and skill, to be the camp counselor willing to explain some facts of life. The rest of the group just goes on being delighted with the wilderness and each other.

One of the first trips I ever guided taught me the value of being out. It was 1975. For days no one acknowledged explicitly that there were both lesbians and nonlesbians on the trip. Finally one woman couldn't stand it.

"This is weird. No one has said *the L word* even once, and it's my *life*."

"I didn't want to shock the straight women," said another. She meant sweet, naive-looking Sally. But Sally had told me that one reason she'd come on the trip was to meet lesbians. She had decided she needed to be less mystified and frightened by the idea.

That may be the best reason for saying *lesbian* out loud. It's not only for the sake of the lesbians in a group. After all, we've found some of our own truth, and we have plenty of experience in how to be ourselves, or not, in mixed company. It's also for the straight women. Not telling them the truth is insulting, demeaning. Sheltered women may have no idea how many lesbians are among the strong, courageous women of the world. Any woman with a general fear of lesbians can be frightened away from being her own strongest self, for fear of being a lesbian, or just being thought one. Any woman, lesbian or straight, needs to stop worrying about Going Too Far. Until she does, she's on a leash.

When women are frank with each other, it's more likely to create bonds than alienation. One typical scene, of dozens that I can remember: women sit on a rocky lakeshore at night, some with arms around each other's shoulders, watching lightning flash between towering clouds. "The organic light show," Emily from Brooklyn calls it. And she tells a good family story, about bringing her new love home to meet the family, introducing her only as "my friend." Grandmother, "in her 90s, and just getting sharper every day," pulled her aside and said, in Yiddish—"That's a nice girl, that Debbie."

"Yeah, Gramma." She felt very nervous, but she was cornered.

"Boys, girls, it don't make no difference to me," said Gramma, "But just don't tell your mother—it'll break her Jewish heart."

It's the straight women who most love being let in on this story. Grandma

Judith Niemi

would be having a good time here, I think, would like being part of a conspiracy of women old enough or bold enough to tell truth, to get out of line.

Girls and women get tamed by too many things; the wilderness undermines that conditioning. If lesbians can sometimes symbolize to other women the essence of women self-defined, uncontrollable by men, we also need to feel that in ourselves. How can we *not* be our most free, frank and strong when we're away from civilization? Women's power busts out and grows when we match our reflexes with fast rivers, wallow in mud baths and sit under the stars. People in the outdoor education business like to talk about this in tidy psychological terms like *self-esteem* and *empowerment*. But it's not that controllable or teachable. It's power that comes straight from the body and spirit, absorbed from the mud and skies and water. We're allied to those big forces—wind, waves, lightning, bears.

CHAPTER 12

All I Really Need to Know about Being a Lesbian I Learned at Girl Scout Camp

Terry Martin

This college English professor learned it all in the Girl Scouts.

Alll I really need to know about living and about being a lesbian I learned at Girl Scout Camp. Wisdom was there in the forest, on the trails, by the lake, around the campfire with a hundred and fifty other girls. These are the things I learned:

- The biggest fashion decision in your day should be which T-shirt to wear with which shorts.

- Get your chores done first thing in the morning so the rest of the day is yours.

- Clean up your own mess, and leave a place cleaner than you found it.

- Plan snacks into your day.

- Be a sister to every other scout.

Terry Martin, 1973

- Rest hour can change your attitude.

- When planning meals, include something munchy, something crunchy, something juicy, and something sweet.

- Don't forget to shut the lid.

- You can do anything in the rain that you can in the sun if you just add a flannel shirt and raingear.

- Exercise and fresh air are good for you.

- If you stay up all night around the campfire, you'll be cranky the next morning.

- Wear sensible shoes.

- Live a balanced life—every day, hike some and swim some and canoe some and sail some and dance some and learn some and flirt some and laugh some.

- Crushes can be time-consuming.

- When you go hiking, stay on the trails, stick together, and hold back the branches for the girl walking behind you.

- Sport a low-maintenance hairdo.

- Wash your hands.

- When the whole patrol helps plan and cook a meal, the food tastes better.

- Spend as much time as possible in and on the water.

- Respect Mother Nature. She will care for you as you care for her.

- Even the best camp counselor has a bad day from time to time.

- Apply sunscreen.

- Bring enough underwear.

- Laugh until your sides ache—it won't kill you.

- You don't have to be good at arts and crafts to do them.

- Getting mail is wonderful, and you're more likely to receive letters if you send some.

- Squirrels and birds and bears and packrats and even the little mice in your tent and in your sleeping bag die. So do we.

- Look up at the stars at night.

- Firelight and candlelight and moonlight are extremely flattering.

- "Don't ask, don't tell" may work for a while, but it's meant to be grown out of.

Terry Martin

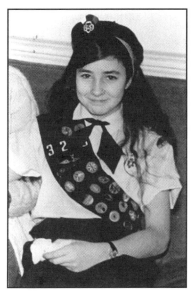

Laura L. Post, 1973

Whittington's terseness in terms of her Scottish heritage and advised us girls to obey her but not to take her sharpness personally.

Unbeknownst to me, Miss Whittington had apparently grasped that I felt isolated by the difference created by my religion as well as by my growing understanding of my sexual orientation. Perhaps she saw me fulfilling my potential separate from the troop: an eager girl whose enthusiasm was tempered by fear of other scouts. Maybe Miss Patterson had told her that I seemed comfortable taking up space with my body and uncomfortable talking about boys.

In any case, Miss Whittington invited me to be one of her four assistant scoutmasters for a late-season extended winter retreat, in upstate New York, with four troops of exuberant New York City Brownies.

I anticipated spending three days reminding forty little girls not to wear their snow-covered boots into the Big House of the retreat. I imagined doing their chores because that was easier than bugging them to carry out their assigned jobs themselves. I dreaded the looks and orders from Miss Whittington.

By the end of the first day, I found myself enjoying the juvenile hijinks, ghost stories, shadow-figures, snow-angels, and impromptu sledding. I was having my first experiences of unfettered physical fun. I felt like a youngster again: my long hair flying out of neat braids, my steaming socks leaving a moist trail across the kitchen linoleum, reddened thawing fingers held gingerly toward the heat of the snapping fire. Somehow, as I unfroze, I noticed that Miss Whittington, who seemed to notice and approve of my blending with the kids, no longer seemed so bad after all.

Finally, departure day came. I shepherded my allotted ten Brownies back down the crackling frozen trail to the buses that would drive us back into the urban jungle. I tried to guess the temperature using the Brownie rhyme I had learned: "If your nose hairs freeze, then it's below fifteen degrees." Suddenly, Brenda, a girl in another group, came running to me, babbling that her buddy Ann (we used the 1:1 system as a backup on the adults' keeping track of the campers) was missing. As I listened to the breathless story, the other girls gathered around.

I remember it as the first authentic moment of adulthood, trying to keep my rising panic under control, knowing I was responsible for the missing girl and that my young charges were looking to me for a decision.

Ann had last been sighted half a mile back, in a thicket bordering a steep grade that we had all been warned away from. The girls and I retraced our steps. Near the stand of trees, one pink mitten and a backpack were visible, sprawls of color against the drifts of clean white snow.

After cautioning the girls to stay on the road and to sit on their packs, I edged carefully down the sheer bank. I could hear muffled sounds of running water below and could feel the stares of the huddled group above me; I didn't want to fall. Finally, I saw the girl. She was half-submerged in water, at the edge of a fractured sheet of ice.

I reached the ice, stomped into the water and pulled her out. She was conscious but dusky; chilled and sluggish. I took off my coat, wrapped her in it, and half-carried, half-dragged her up the bank.

When we reached the road, I ordered the Brownies to leave their packs on the road and to follow us to the Big House. I took their silence to mean that they would obey; I counted heads again anyway.

With my ten Brownies and Brenda behind me, I carried the wet child toward the Big House, running nearly a mile to reach it. I knew that Miss Whittington would be doing the final cleaning since the other three assistant leaders had been sent ahead, each with her own ten Brownies.

When we arrived, Ann was moaning and clinging to me with damp fingers. I hardly noticed the icy rivulets trickling under the top of my long underwear where the ice on her hands had melted against my back. I was barely aware of being winded.

After counting heads again and praising the Brownies' obedience, I placed Ann near the fireplace and went looking for Miss Whittington. I put Ann's buddy, Brenda, in charge.

Ann made a complete recovery and was back at her troop meeting the next week. Miss Patterson hugged me, and Miss Whittington, who had hardly said anything to me all weekend, was unusually positive about how I had handled the emergency. She even put her hand on my shoulder in a gesture of approval. I was kind of a hero in my troop for a while. What mattered most to me, however, was the approval from Miss Patterson and Miss Whittington for being coolheaded, strong, and quick; for doing the right thing even though I was frightened and was worried about being punished for the accident.

Someone's mother told us Senior Scouts that Miss Whittington was an ex-nun and that she had been married. Another mother called Miss Whittington an "Old Maid," laughing at the label.

But the quiet love of Miss Whittington taught me everything I needed to know about finding my own inner spirit—which turned out to be a

PHOTO CREDIT: IRENE YOUNG

Laura L. Post

lesbian one. At the moment that Miss Whittington touched my shoulder, I did not feel alone or different or afraid; I felt valued and valuable.

I learned that it was okay to follow my instincts and intuition, that I could think effectively on my feet, and that my small interventions could produce large results. I am a doctor, now, and I think that the courage to pursue that training was instilled back then. Most of my medical decisions incorporate intuition about a patient, thinking on my feet, and believing that my intervention can make a difference.

At the end of that year, in the last Girl Scout year-end ceremony I would ever attend, I was allowed to read from The Gospel According to Matthew: a passage about loving one's brother and taking care of other people. Afterwards, when I reached out to accept my attendance pin from Miss Whittington, she again placed her hand on my shoulder. She said nothing, and I'm sure that few others noticed her spare "booster shot." I received it gratefully and knew that I would carry a sense of competence with me for the rest of my life.

CHAPTER 14

✳ ✳ ✳

I Know A Song
And It Wants To Be Sung

Marcia Munson

The songs this former Girl Scout sang around the campfire, to begin troop meetings, or while washing dishes at camp provided the basic elements of a belief system that has served her well throughout her adult life.

"Make New Friends"

"**M**ake new friends, but keep the old . . ." That tune comes into my head nearly every time I walk into a group of women, whether it's at a party, a music festival, or Red Dora's Bearded Lady Café in San Francisco. Just as I expected the unit of campers to include and welcome me my first summer at Girl Scout camp, so I expect every new group of lesbians to welcome me if I make an effort to be friendly. Most people want to make new friends. Greeting strangers with a smile almost always works to warm them up. "Were you ever a Girl Scout?" is a good question to get someone talking. I am rarely discouraged by a negative response—I just try to be friendly to others. It's one of the things that I learned in scouts. Sooner or later, it pays off. Someone always needs a buddy.

As Girl Scouts we learned that we were part of a worldwide sisterhood and that we could find friends wherever we traveled. That seemed true. When my family moved from California to Colorado, there was no Junior troop at

109

Mapleton Elementary. So once a week, I rode my bike to a Girl Scout meeting at another school. I was always a welcome part of the group. No one seemed to notice or care that I didn't attend Whittier Elementary.

In junior high, our Cadette troop met in the evenings, so no one wore uniforms to school. There were about thirty Girl Scouts among five hundred kids. It felt like a secret sisterhood, smiling at other scouts in the halls, sharing that bond of recognition with girls from different grades and friendship groups.

By high school, there was only one troop of Senior Girl Scouts in the whole city of Boulder. I remember asking one adventuresome, outdoorsy friend why she wasn't a Girl Scout. She said she had quit after sixth grade because it wasn't cool anymore. Being a scout certainly hadn't earned me any popularity points in junior high school, but it didn't detract from social acceptability either. Rather, Girl Scouting offered a sane alternative world. My troop meetings had been a welcome relief from the social pressure associated with appearance, hairstyles, clothing, and boys that pervaded the school environment.

The Girl Scout dream of being connected to a worldwide sisterhood seems to have come alive in my life as a lesbian. Each time I have moved to a new lesbian community—Portland, Colorado Springs, Estes Park, or Fort Collins— it has been easy to make new friends.

I've always tried to keep old friends, too. Open relationships, the idealized model of coupling among dykes I knew in the 1970s, seemed like a natural phenomenon, hardly a radical notion. When monogamy became popular among lesbians I knew in the 1980s, my Girl Scout background made me resist the practice of clinging too tightly to just one lover. When butch/ femme role-playing reappeared in the late 1980s, I often wondered, "Weren't they ever Girl Scouts?" I had learned years before to be the perfect switch, working simultaneously on my Cooking, Handywoman, Beekeeper, and First Aid badges.

"It's a Web Like a Spider's Web"

I think I got hooked on being a Girl Scout because it was one place where I was noticed and appreciated. At home I often felt ignored by my single mother who was struggling to keep the four of us fed, clothed, and out of

Marcia Munson, 1967

trouble. At school I was a quiet student who pleased the teacher by reading a novel at my desk after I finished my work. Girl Scouts was different—I was encouraged to do things, not just sit quietly. Whether we were weaving newspaper sit-upons, designing pine cone Santas, or dancing the Hora, the leaders always made sure everyone participated. My Girl Scout meetings were the two hours each week when I was entwined in the web of action, instead of waiting on the sidelines. The activities were always varied and noncompetitive. I never got labeled as clumsy or quick, as I did at school. I learned to value scouting activity and to devalue school. This has carried over into my adult life as an affinity for community volunteer work and long vacations. I have almost no interest in furthering a "career," which I equate with the boredom of school.

"Have Fun, Our Motto Is"

This song has provided a purpose more often than the official Girl Scout motto of "Be Prepared." Yes, I'm usually prepared for a blizzard or an earthquake, but I'm always prepared for a hike or a picnic. As an adult, the fun of being outdoors and escaping routine has been the guiding force in all my employment choices. Girl Scout memories have shaped and inspired many projects.

One of my early career projects was to develop a Minimum Impact Camping Techniques slide show for the Yosemite Institute, based on camping skills I had learned in the Girl Scouts. (It was a very progressive concept at the time.) Today, I try to live a Minimum Impact life in the city as well as in the wilderness, using public transportation, recycling, and resisting the culture of overconsumption.

My first job after college was an extension of my career as a summer Girl Scout camp counselor. I taught science for a sixth grade environmental education program in the foothills of Mt. Hood. Next I worked as a wilderness guide. In 1977, I started the Women's Wilderness Institute Northwest with my lover Linda, whom I had met years before at Girl Scout camp. When I changed careers, it was the active outdoor element that led me to fighting forest fires in the summer and weatherizing houses in the winter. Even when I sought a year-round steady job, it was the freedom of walking all around town that led me to being a mail carrier. Now, the white-collar bureaucratic job I have with the federal government can rarely be called fun—except that the government has allowed me to stay a seasonal worker. My two-to-six month layoffs each year allow plenty of time for world travel, backpacking, and other Girl Scoutish pursuits.

"Firm Be the Bonds that Bind Us Fast"

I came to love my Girl Scout uniform, which meant not having to worry about what to wear. As scouts, we complained when the leaders insisted we wear those constricting, ugly dresses, but then jumped into our troop activities without being distracted by fashion consciousness.

When I applied to attend a National Conference on the Inner City in 1967, part of the selection process involved attending an afternoon tea with other applicants. I was nervous about the tea, and when I called to check on details, inquired, "I suppose we are required to wear our uniforms to this event?" The Senior Scout on the other end of the line replied, "It's not absolutely necessary, but it would be better if you wore your uniform." I breathed a sigh of relief. At least I didn't have to figure out what to wear!

About half of the dozen girls, and most of the adults, were in uniform on the appointed afternoon. The reassurance of those green outfits helped me relax . . . enough to be chosen to attend the conference.

Several years ago I bought an antique Girl Scout uniform—the long-sleeved style the older sisters of my troopmates wore—at a Goodwill store. It has become my favorite Halloween costume. Now and then I like to wear the uniform when I present sexuality workshops at women's events. It represents my Girl Scoutish attitude towards lesbian safer sex, which is similar to my attitude toward ticks, lightning, and poison ivy. I think it's a good idea to deal with even the minimal risks of sexually transmitted disease (STD) transmission in woman-to-woman sex, but we should never let excessive caution keep us from having fun. Wearing my uniform makes me feel more confident, and I think it reassures my audience, too.

"Dewey Love Each Other? I Should Say We Do!"

I was twelve the first summer I attended Girl Scout camp, and I felt like I'd reached Nirvana. "Going to camp" became my reason for living for fifty weeks each year, from seventh through twelfth grade. My only career goal was to become a camp counselor—to create the challenging, serene, safe, fun, female mountain environment I so loved. My college years are a blur, but I recall vividly the two months each summer I spent as a counselor at Camp Quidnunc, Camp Klahanee, and Camp Arrowhead. I can hardly picture my college boyfriend, but when I think of late nights around the campfire with Sinker or Dusty, I long to be poking those embers and laughing with my female flames.

I wasn't even aware of lesbians or homophobia in those days. When my camp director Sappy told me she had been hired to "clean out the queers" at the camp, I asked her how she could tell someone was "queer." I wondered what kind of queerness was unacceptable. She never explained.

The next summer, at a different camp, I walked in on two naked counselors embracing early one morning in the staff house double bed. I simply thought, "How nice, snuggling together." It didn't even occur to me that Sappy's queer-hunt the summer before was related to this event. (I found out, a few years later, that at least half the staff, including the director, were lesbians that summer. Some were speculating on when I would come out.)

Looking back on my scouting days, I can see a few subtle instances of homophobia. Anne and Sue, two older girls in my Senior troop, were often referred to as being "too good of friends." I was baffled. I didn't know how anyone could be critical of their lively warmth and focused enjoyment of each other.

As early as Brownie days, I remember being encouraged to "switch buddies" periodically. I always thought the leaders were concerned about cliques. Now I suspect, at least when we were older, some of this pressure to change our friendship ties stemmed from the leaders' fears of homosexuality.

Yes, I learned to make new friends but keep the old. I've usually been in open relationships as a lesbian, and a few friendships have flowed in and out of sexual phases over the years. Three years ago, I planned an anniversary party with my friend Martha, another ex-Girl Scout. More than one hundred of our friends and lovers helped us celebrate twenty-one years of open love, uncommitted sex, firm friendship, and wild adventures.

"This Land Is Your Land, This Land Is My Land"

Nearly everyone in my second grade class in Long Beach, California in 1957 was a Brownie, Cub Scout, or Blue Bird. Even the kids of fundamentalist Christian families had a scout-type club complete with uniforms and neckerchiefs that they wore one day a week.

Those in uniform got to stand at the front of the class and lead the Pledge of Allegiance. I felt lucky that my day was Wednesday because there were no Cub Scouts in uniform, only Brownies. We girls did a fine job of leading our classmates in the morning ritual.

Then at recess, we would sometimes go outside and shinny up the thirty-foot flagpole and slide down. By tucking our Brownie uniforms just so between our legs, we could get the perfect ride! I remember melting in ecstasy in the sand at the bottom of the flagpole, with a great big Brownie smile.

Leading the whole class in the Pledge seemed like a natural thing for a few girls to do. I had observed in first grade that girls were smarter than boys. My view of girls as competent, strong, independent, and ambitious was shaped by my years as a Girl Scout.

I loved flag ceremonies in Girl Scouts, especially the ones we planned. One summer at camp, our patrol choreographed a flag raising, complete with marching-in-step like we had learned in school band practice. We felt very radical, ignoring the Pledge of Allegiance, and replacing it with a favorite Woody Guthrie song.

Years ago, our troop leader encouraged us to write letters to protest the building of the Glen Canyon Dam on the Colorado River in Arizona. Our efforts failed. Later, no adults ever found out about our secret burning of survey stakes in a National Forest area we hoped would remain undeveloped. Those efforts were successful. Girl Scout lessons taught me the value of maneuvering both inside and outside the established political system.

I've always seen the flag as mine to fly and defend. I was proud to carry the American flag at the head of the Colorado contingent in the 1987 National March on Washington for Lesbian and Gay Rights. While I worked to pass domestic-partner legislation in San Francisco a few years ago, I flew a tiny rainbow flag beside an American flag on my desk at work. When I worked with five other women to pass a gay rights ordinance in Boulder, Colorado, in 1987, I saw the project as my patriotic duty.

One way my Girl Scout upbringing has set me apart from other lesbians is that I firmly believe in a patrol or camp-council organizational style. The "collective process" and "leaderless groups" that have been popular among dykes for the last twenty years have seemed absurd to me. I know that someone will emerge as a leader, even if you don't elect her. The only way to have a rotation of power, the only way to let each person develop her leadership skills, is to elect new officers periodically, like we did in Girl Scouts. The only way to hold a person accountable for her actions is to recognize that she is the president, or treasurer, or secretary, or whatever position she holds. The efficiency of voting allows a group to accomplish more tasks and plan more activities, thus increasing the possibility that the minority will soon have their turn.

This is a concept I've tried to teach many women's organizations over the years, with limited success. I'm sure that the Women's Cultural Center, Who Farm, and my NOW chapter would have been more successful had they been open to learning some of the participatory democracy practices I learned as a Girl Scout. The Boulder Lesbian Connection and the Equal Protection Coalition were willing to try bits of scout-style structure, with tremendous improvements in their organizational effectiveness.

"High Up, High on a Mountain"

Backpacking was a rite of passage I looked forward to for years. Only Senior Scouts were allowed to strap heavy frame packs on their backs, load up their sleeping bags and food for a week, and head off on the Big Circle, a fifty-mile trip in the Lost Creek Wilderness Area of central Colorado. The summer I was fifteen I signed up for the three-week backpacking session at Flying G Ranch. During the first week of daily conditioning hikes, it became obvious that I was the slowest in the group. One afternoon as I was trailing the others, Cazoo asked me if I was sure I wanted to go along on the five-day trek into Lost Park, over Bison Peak and Witches' Ridge, through the Garden of the Selfish Giant and down Goose Creek. I nodded yes, not wanting to waste the breath required to speak.

Marcia Munson

It was determination, not ability, that decided who remained in the backpacking group. I was one of eight girls and two counselors who headed up a fading trail, map and compass ready. Nine times during the first few miles our trail crossed a stream; at five of those crossings I slipped from the rocks or log bridge, and fell in.

That trip taught me the art of mind/body separation. My feet and back ached unbearably, so my brain learned to fly in the clouds as the miles went by underfoot.

Years later, when I dabbled in SM, I thought it was mildly entertaining, but no substitute for a good backpacking trip. I never understood how anyone could settle for a reward less spectacular than the red rock/blue sky/billowing cloud vistas of the mountains around South Tarryall Peak.

The peaks behind my favorite Girl Scout camp are the home that I return to, year after year.

Girl Scouting wasn't just a part of my life. It was the core of my existence from the ages of seven to twenty-two. I learned all the useful life skills (other than reading and arithmetic) that I've needed to survive and flourish in my work life, in my personal life, and in community service. Hardly a day goes by that I don't hum a Girl Scout tune to ease the emotional edge of some incident, or silently recite a Girl Scout law to give me some direction when I find myself in a dilemma.

I learned snow camping, library research skills, cooking, wilderness ethics, bicycle repair, map reading, interpersonal communication, goal-setting, knot tying, supervision, fire building, and political organizing in the Girl Scouts. I learned to appreciate and defend wilderness areas. Most of all, I learned to love and admire women.

CHAPTER 15

The Ship

Jamie Anderson

This professional Arizona musician with several albums to her credit began her career by playing the guitar for Girl Scout sing-alongs and by following her heart into a mariner-oriented troop.

I sat next to Beth (pseudonym) in a tenth grade science class. Although we belonged to different troops, we quickly discovered that we were both Girl Scouts.

My troop leader, Mrs. O'Hara (pseudonym), had been involved in scouting for years as a leader, camp nurse, and camp director. Her authoritarian manner scared some people, but she was strong and knowledgeable. (And now that I think of it, her always-short steel grey hair and casual tailored clothing made her seem pretty butch for a married lady.) I was in her Senior Girl Scout troop simply because it was the only troop in our Phoenix suburb.

Beth belonged to a troop in nearby Mesa. Affectionately called the Ship (because it was mariner-oriented), this troop was much larger than my own. Beth often came to class with stories about the latest event they were planning or how much fun they'd had at the last meeting. There were also stories of the Ship before Beth had joined. One time, they challenged a Sea Scout troop of Boy Scouts to a mariner competition and kicked their butts. Another time, they participated in a regatta with other Girl Scout troops. The Ship held its own even though the other troops thought it was funny that a troop from the desert would even compete.

My troop, run by the iron hand of Mrs. O'Hara , didn't get to make many of our own decisions about activities. We didn't go on exciting trips and we didn't socialize much. There were no stories of past glory.

Beth often talked about members of the Ship. The one she mentioned most was a senior named Lois, a poet who drove a restored orange Model A Ford. Beth had lots of stories about Lois' lead-foot driving and the Model A's peculiar habit of losing parts as they were driving down the street. Lois would just pop out of the car, stick the part back on, hop in, and roar off.

One day, just after science class had ended, a barefoot woman in jeans and a T-shirt came into the classroom. With an elfish grin, Lois introduced herself to me. My brain was moving at high speed, but all that came out was, "Oh, hi." She and Beth swept out the door. I was left like a failed runner at the starting gate, my heart still racing.

Beth started talking about the big trip that her troop was going to take through California, Oregon, Washington, and Canada. The scouts were planning the trip; their leaders only offered guidance.

I couldn't stand it. I had to join the Ship. Terrified to approach Mrs. O'Hara, I thought about leaving her troop without saying anything. But, she'd only find me—she knew were I lived—and I decided to get it over with. She accused me of defecting to the Ship simply because of the trip they were planning. She was wrong, of course. How could I explain the Ship's lure of power and companionship?

I joyfully attended my first meeting, with Beth by my side to introduce me to everyone. I was greeted with big smiles and hugs. Many of the girls were born-again Christians; they often touched each other. I wasn't a Christian but I didn't mind the hand-holding and other affectionate touches.

Lois was at that meeting. By this time, her father had sold the Model A. She had a brand new red Maverick with an 8-cylinder engine, and it MOVED. I always tried to get in her car if we went out after meetings. I loved being in the seat beside her as she beat out the high school boys at every light.

Lois and I started spending time together outside of Girl Scouts. She would pick me up from school to go shopping or to a movie. I felt so independent.

Jamie Anderson, 1964

Our time together began to include overnights. I was absolutely smitten with her, and it led to more and more physical contact, always done under the pretense of friendship. But there was something else. Something we couldn't name. I just knew that lying next to her at night filled me with an electric current. One night, I rolled over and kissed her. She kissed me back.

We became lovers although it wasn't a word we used. I felt connected to her in ways I'd never felt with anyone else. I thought about her all of the time. She wrote me poetry, and I made her laugh. I spent so much time at her house that her parents jokingly adopted me.

Not long after Lois and I became lovers, our Girl Scout troop left on the Big Trip. Twenty or thirty scouts and four escorts hit the road in an old school bus.

Late one night, with the bus rolling across the California desert, Lois sat close to me on the front steps, and by the light of the dashboard, she quietly sang old country songs in my ear. (She loved ballads with a moral.) The intimacy of that moment is the strongest image from the trip. That and Beth's anger. In my naiveté, I didn't know that Beth was in love with Lois and resented my relationship with her. On the trip, Beth's attention-drawing antics included nightmares that kept Lois awake, trying to comfort her. One night, Lois woke up to find a switch blade at her throat. Beth crouched above her with the knife in her hand, mumbling incoherently. Lois talked her into putting the blade away.

Soon after the trip, Lois graduated out of the Ship. Beth and I remained friends, in spite of her sometimes peculiar behavior.

The next couple of years with the Ship were wonderful ones. We went sailing and canoeing, and I learned to handle a sailboat by myself. I remember races across the lake, going so fast that the sails nearly dipped into the water. I was never good at racing, but Beth was. She used to show off, holding the main sheet (the line that holds the main sail) in her teeth.

I also learned to play the guitar, and I often accompanied campout sing-alongs. The music brought me great joy, and one of our leaders lovingly told me that I'd brought music to the Ship.

One Ship ritual that I loved occurred on campouts after we had bedded down for the night. One of the other girls would give out goodnight kisses—the chocolate kind, but such a big deal was made about them! The one handing out kisses would jump from sleeping bag to sleeping bag, doling out her treats. Our advisors never said a thing.

Lois and I remained close. After I graduated from high school, I moved in with her. She took me to my first lesbian bar, where I saw my first all-woman band. I was hooked. At midnight, on January 1, 1976, I looked around at all those happy women and thought, I belong here. I'm a lesbian.

Even though I'd thought about being a camp counselor or leader, I never went back to scouting. Stories about counselors who had been fired for becoming "much more than friends" frightened me. I didn't want to suffer that humiliation.

A few years later, at the 1979 Michigan festival (my first women's music festival), I heard familiar music. When I found the source, it was a group of women sitting under a tree singing Girl Scout songs! I joined them immediately. We were from all over the U.S. and we knew the same songs (with slightly different lyrics, but who cares). We didn't get to talk much, but the music started me thinking about how Girl Scouts had shaped my life.

A few years later at the West Coast Women's Music and Cultural Festival, I organized a workshop for scouts and about sixty women came. We shared wonderful stories. Some had met their first lovers at Girl Scout camp. One couple was still together several years later. A few women were currently in scouting. Some served in council positions and one woman was a camp director. She offered all of us a job. And of course, we sang songs.

A few years ago, I helped organize a Ship reunion. We camped out at a lake. The turnout was great, and it was good to see everyone after ten years, but I didn't feel as if I belonged. Even when I pulled out my guitar to sing the old songs, that feeling didn't change. Most of these women now had husbands and kids. I was an out-lesbian with three cats. The other lesbians (there were about five of them) didn't come out—not even the one who brought her girlfriend.

Beth was there. In her mid-twenties, she already had four children and a husband. Beth smiled a lot, but her eyes were sad as she talked about her kids and the struggle to pay the bills.

I'd stayed in contact with Lois over the years but couldn't convince her to come to the reunion. Maybe she didn't want to be out. Maybe she thought she couldn't measure up to all those freshly scrubbed Christian families.

I'm a professional musician now, and I sing a song about my coming out experience in Girl Scouts. I joke that I found women's community early. I did. What a difference it made!

We spent the night at each other's house
She was a poet, we were both Girl Scouts
She taught me bravada and I made her laugh
*One night I kissed her and she kissed me back**

— from "I Don't Know About the Night" words and music by Jamie Anderson

Jamie Anderson

* ©1991 Linda Su Owns the World Music

CHAPTER 16

✳ ✳ ✳

Twist Me And Turn Me

Susan Rothbaum

Girl Scouting can have a profound and longlasting impact even on those who were involved for only a brief time. Looking back, this writer finds new meaning in her Brownie Scout initiation.

I was determined not to tell that psychiatrist anything. My parents were making me see him, but that didn't mean I had to talk. So I didn't. Except when he asked what I wanted to be when I grew up. I said, "Either a private detective or a Marine."

Five years earlier, when I started grade school, my hair was curly and short. People asked, "Are you a boy or a girl?" I said, "A girl." Or, "A tomboy."

I played touch football with boys from my class. I rolled down the lawn in a Whamm-o Tank, a camouflage-covered cardboard cylinder. When Ricky and I got benched at recess for talking in class, I drew pictures on pink paper of naked ladies: two circles with dots in the center, over an upside down triangle. I'm not sure I knew what I was drawing, but I knew Ricky liked it.

One morning on the playground, all the girls clustered around Ricky.

"Ricky, would you marry me?"

"Uhh...sure."

Susan Rothbaum, c. 1958

The tallest girl in our class scrunched down to his height, hands clasped at her knees. I had dreamed one night of the bathroom in her house. The walls were covered with breasts. Now she smiled winningly.

"Would you marry *me?*"

At nine years old, he tossed back his black forelock, shuffled and shrugged like Marlon Brando.

"Yeah, okay."

I hung around the edge of the circle, then took the plunge:

"Ricky, would you marry *me?*"

"YUCK!"

That moment was a dividing line. I wouldn't call up boys to play rough games with me anymore, and I was flunking being a girl. On the playground, I sat out games whenever I could. If the teacher let me, I sat on the lunch benches, book in hand. Ever since I had learned to read, I had lost myself in books. Now they were the only open door that I saw.

At home, I read a book or two each night. Books about dogs and men in the frozen north. Boys cast adrift at sea. Boys cutting their way through the jungle. Books by Armstrong Sperry. Arm Strong and his boy heroes: Chad, Wade, Judd. Thud.

I read about adventurous boys and men, and I read the *Girl Scout Handbook*. At my grandparents' house I read the old edition my mother had used, with the story of Juliette Low and pictures of scout uniforms through the decades. Scouts in bloomers—once considered a cross-dressing costume.

I read the updated 1950s edition. I wanted to earn and wear a sashful of badges. Bibliophile, Journalist, and Minstrel would come naturally, and as for the daring ones—I could start with Back-Yard Camper then work my way step-by-step up to Adventurer and Explorer.

I was inspired by the Girl Scout Laws and the picture they painted of a community of girls.

- **A Girl Scout is courteous.**

"Oh, excuse me. I got so excited I forgot it wasn't my turn to speak."[1]

Could I learn to do that? Could I learn to be as good as I wanted to be? And would the other Scouts treat *me* that way?

- **A Girl Scout's duty is to be useful and to help others.**

"Here, let me give you a hand with your bedroll. I'll teach you how to make a bowline and then we can tie it."[2]

Imagine . . . just imagine that.

When the time came, I got my pale green uniform and dark green beret. I wonder now if I was surprised when the girls who teased me all day in school teased me at troop meetings in the church basement. I don't remember, but I soon dropped out.

Jump ahead three decades. I'm forty-two years old. My partner and I are on vacation at Lake Superior. I have a *Girl Scout Handbook* that I found at a used-book store. *I still want those badges.* I still want someone to help me learn outdoor skills step-by-step and award me a badge to prove it.

For the rest of our vacation I earn badges. Driver's Assistant (read the map and don't tell the driver what to do). Creek Crosser. Insect Helper (we move a storm-beaten dragonfly away from the waves to a sheltering bush). Hiker. Dream Reader. Storyteller.

One day, when I was an adult but not yet middle-aged, I went to have a massage. As Irene moved her hands on my back, I remembered what I had dreamed that morning. *A group of women. A ritual we were doing together.*

I told Irene, "I have such a hunger for that."

As I turned over on the table, a phrase jumped into my mind.

"Turn me around... That's not quite it. Turn me and turn me..."

I remembered being seven years old, a Brownie Scout. I remembered the Initiation. A mirror on the patio, surrounded by leafy branches. The circle of girls. A blindfold loosely tied over my eyes. Hands turning me in circles, three times around.

> *Twist me and turn me*
> *And show me the elf.*
> *I looked in the water*
> *And saw myself.*

Susan Rothbaum

[1] Girl Scout Handbook: Intermediate Program, (New York: GSUSA, 1953), p. 9.
[2] Ibid. p. 6.

CHAPTER 17

✳ ✳ ✳

We Loved Fiercely

Donna Tsuyuko Tanigawa

A college teacher and fiber doll artist from Hawaii received her early training as an entrepreneur in her Girl Scout troop.

Without any knowledge of mainland lesbian-feminism in the 1970s, the girls in Girl Scout Troop 446 embodied its values. We formed a sisterhood, and we were powerful. We were proud. Without a political vocabulary, we believed that all girls were created equal, and we fought for a female-centered context in our lives. Like our older lesbian-feminist sisters, we lived by codified rules and practices. Our recreational activities, creative expressions, and friendships separated us from the other school girls (and all boys). We developed a culture around Girl Scouting. We were *ohana* (family). Our troop met us where we were in life and took care of us. Like a dependable suspension system, scouting absorbed the shocks of our fragile girlhood—*divorces, family alcoholism, child abuse*—and preserved our young spirits. Scouting gave us confidence and taught us skills.

Troop 446 consisted of thirty girls and three adult leaders. We lived in Waipahu, once a sugar plantation community, twenty miles from Honolulu.

Girl Scouting was my first teacher of multiculturalism. Some of us were third-
or fourth-generation descendants of Asian and European ancestors, others
recent immigrants. We were Japanese, Filipino, Portuguese, Chinese,
Hawaiian, Korean, African-American, Polynesian, *haole* (white), and "mixed
plate." We came from all parts of town. We lived in middle-class
neighborhoods and welfare housing. Our family structures included nuclear
families, single-parent families, and extended families.

I believe that many of us were closeted lesbian-girls. We loved fiercely.
While other girls giggled and acted coy around boys, we played, worked, and
laughed with each other. We enjoyed girl company. Scouting gave us the
confidence to love and care for girls.

I was a Brownie and a Junior during elementary school. My mother was an
adult leader. I believe that our relationship grew and developed though
scouting. It gave Mom and me a safe place to enjoy ourselves. Because my
mother worked part-time, she was able to devote much of her free time to
Girl Scouts, and she and I spent many afternoons working on official scout
business.

Although I learned to cook and sew in Girl Scouts, I never felt that I was
being trained in domestic heterosexuality. Rather, I was learning valuable
life skills. My favorite dish was fried eggs cooked on the bottom of an empty
coffee can. We prepared "coil burners" by filling tuna cans with corrugated
paper, household wax, and charcoal bits. Spam and fried eggs tasted best at
Camp Paumalu, the official Girl Scout campgrounds located in the Ko'olau
Mountains overlooking the North Shore.

My first sewing project was a denim bag for my mess kit. I remember my
clumsy fingers trying to manipulate the needle and thread. My mother taught
us how to paint and draw. I remember sitting with a canvas and brush at Ewa
Beach. There were thirty girls sketching one-foot waves that day. We did
arts and crafts. For Christmas we made pressed *ogo* (seaweed) greeting cards
for a retirement home. I believe empty egg cartons and glue, which made
charming bikini tops for my Drowsy dolls, guided me toward art. Today I am
an accomplished fiber doll artist. The ethnic dolls I create under my trademark
"Dolls by Donna" have their roots in Girl Scouting.

We were separatists. I remember standing near a ledge at Camp Paumalu
overlooking the Boy Scout camp a mile away. We heckled their bugle call
and fired spit balls in their direction to pledge our solidarity. I made a vow

Donna Tsuyuko Tanigawa, 1974

never to concede to boys.

We wore our official Girl Scout uniform to school every Wednesday. I had my school photos taken in my brown, and later in my green outfit. Some of us were decorated with badges. These embroidered patches were our medals as we trooped through life.

Girl Scouting, with its initiation and award ceremonies, had a spiritual dimension. I remember walking across a *ti* leaf-covered bridge from Brownies to Juniors at the school cafeteria. I wept as we lighted our candles. We were joined in unity. There were celebrations and festivities. There were pledges, ". . . and I promise to live by the Girl Scout laws." I studied my official handbook to better understand those laws.

We felt a sense of Girl Scout Pride. I remember marching down Kalakaua Avenue in Waikiki at the annual Girl Scout Council of the Pacific Parade. The crowd cheered. People waved. Female admirers took Polaroid snapshots. There was the annual "*Lei* Around Diamond Head." Hundreds of scouts joined miles of freshly sewn *leis* (flower wreaths) around the perimeter of Diamond Head. These *leis* symbolized the unity of all Girl Scouts throughout our state and nation.

We were entrepreneurs. Each year we devised better ways to sell Girl Scout cookies. People enjoyed free samples and were more likely to buy our products after tasting them. A card table parked near the entrance of a supermarket around dinner worked well. When I added, ". . . and you can freeze them, too," a customer would often buy additional boxes. We learned how to handle and manage money. We were fund raisers, not capitalists.

Many of my friendships grew in the context of Girl Scouting. We saw each other during recess, after school, and on weekends. My best friend was a Girl Scout. Our troop had slumber parties where each adult leader hosted ten girls. I enjoyed baking *bibinka* (Filipino rice cake) at the home of one of our leaders.

I was an active recruiter. I befriended a girl in my fourth grade class whose mother had died several years before. She played alone. One day in art class, we were making vases for Mother's Day. She and I decided to make her vase for the school janitor, an older single woman. That afternoon she came with me to our troop meeting.

Girl Scouting taught me how to build relationships. There were inevitably bruised feelings, gossip, and cliques. We worked out our problems. I grimaced

Donna Tsuyuko Tanigawa, day of commitment ceremony with Lee-Ann Matsumoto, 1992

the first time my leader paired me off with a tomboy. *There's dirt under her fingernails*, I thought. We sat together on the bus ride to Camp Paumalu. She held my hand on the hike to catch me when I fell. By the end of the day we were friends. We giggled. She was a precursor of the butch woman I "married."

I learned to overcome many of my fears. I remember the first time I had stage fright. Our group was assigned a skit. We wrote the dialogue. We rehearsed. I was unsure whether I could remember my lines. A few seconds before we went on stage my stomach did a *huli-huli* (complete turn) on me. I felt sick. My leader whispered, "Believe in yourself, sweetie." I delivered my lines.

The girls from my troop have long since grown up, their uniforms and sashes relegated to boxes in attics and closets. Perhaps some of them have little girls of their own. My partner Lee-Ann and I hope to band a Girl Scout troop of our own some day, and we will equip these girls with the vocabulary to say that all girls are created equal. Perhaps they'll love as fiercely as the girls of Troop 446 did.

CHAPTER 18

✳ ✳ ✳

I Will Do My Best:
To Be Honest

(Excerpt from the Girl Scout Law)

Holli Van Nest

The "troop" this Boston woman discovered at Girl Scout camp recently supported one of its members while she was dying of cancer.

My first year at Girl Scout camp, I noticed two counselors who seemed very fond of each other. I remember them laughing, hugging, singing, wrestling, and dancing. Their relationship created a joyful atmosphere in our unit. It was my first experience of people openly expressing their love for each other. I left camp determined to keep this extraordinary place a part of my life.

Girl Scout camp became my anchor. I went back as a camper for the next six summers and as a counselor for five summers after that. Camp was the place where I could be free, could be Tig (my camp name). I learned to tie knots, build a campfire, paddle a canoe, find my way in the woods, lash a table, and use a saw. I learned that women could be strong and capable. I learned that friendships were a blessing. Most importantly, I learned that there was no shame in loving women.

At camp, we lived and worked together twenty-four hours a day, singing,

132

Holli Van Nest, 1967

hiking, biking, singing, canoeing, sailing, singing, swimming, cooking out, eating, singing, talking, laughing, and singing. I began to think of my life as a Broadway musical. (My fifteen- year-old niece finds pleasure and embarrassment in my ability to find a song in just about any situation.) Even though we are spread across the country, many of the friends I made twenty years ago remain close friends today. Girl Scouting gave that to us.

I was sixteen when I began working at camp, first in the camp kitchen and later as an apprentice counselor. I was in heaven, living in the woods with magnificent women. I fell in love with Deirdre (pseudonym). I spent a lot of that summer experiencing ups and downs I had never felt before. I was not alone. Many of my friends were on the same ride. We didn't use the words "lesbian," "gay," or "homosexual," but we talked at length about how much we loved these women.

By the end of the summer, Deirdre returned my love. For the next three years, camp was the backdrop for our relationship. We lived apart during the school year, staying connected through letters and long distance phone calls. Thoughts of Deirdre consumed my every waking moment—what she had said, how she walked, and how she had touched me. She was intense, pensive, smart, funny, immensely capable, and emotionally distant. My goal in life became to reach her, to have her love me the way I loved her. Our relationship was passionate and tempestuous. It probably wasn't much different from many first loves. Sometimes Deirdre wanted me, sometimes she didn't. I always wanted her, in a way that I know now was overwhelming and needy. I saw her as my way out of my emotionally barren family (interesting, since she herself was so distant) and away from my abusive father. No wonder she wanted to run. But she kept coming back, wanting the love I held out to her. Three years of up and down, up and down. It was torment. It was bliss.

Then one day, a friend told me that she thought Deirdre was gay. I was stunned. Our relationship had been more emotional than physical, but it had also been physical. Nevertheless, it hadn't occurred to me that I was gay, and it had never occurred to me that Deirdre was gay.

"Deirdre couldn't be gay," I protested. "I would know. I'm her best friend!"

Even though the idea came as a shock, on some level I recognized its truth, and within a few days, I had accepted it. I wrote to Deirdre, who was living in another state, and asked if she thought that meant I was gay too.

Deirdre wrote back. She was enraged that Judy was spreading vicious rumors. She was sorry she had gotten involved with me. That letter ended our relationship.

Many years later, I found out that Deirdre had become involved with another woman from Girl Scout camp that summer. Within two months of my receiving her letter, she had made plans to move so they could live together. In retrospect, I understand that Deirdre used my question as an excuse to leave me. At the time, I didn't know how I would survive losing her.

What helped me survive was learning to be more true to myself. One lesson in honesty had actually happened the year before my breakup with Deirdre. It was the end of camp, and I was looking for another counselor so I could put my things in her car. I had seen Peg walking down toward one of the units and went there looking for her. All the tent flaps were down, and I walked through the unit, calling her name. I heard some women laughing in one of the tents and started toward it. Peg came out, pulling her shirt on over her head, smiling broadly. I thought she had been in there smoking dope. (I was aware of some things that went on.)

Peg said, "Tig, there's something I have to tell you. I'm gay."

"Okay," I said. "I was just looking for the key to your car."

Peg told me where the key was, and I left. While her coming out style may not be the one either of us would use today, it did teach me a lot about being direct.

While honesty was greatly valued in Girl Scouting, Peg was a rare exception to the unwritten rule of silence and dishonesty regarding love relationships. As I thought about my relationship with Deirdre, I began to look more closely at the other counselors. I saw that for some of them, the women they loved were more than friends, too. We had few coming-out conversations, but gradually, that is exactly what we became—out to each other. Breaking the taboo eventually created a supportive and loving lesbian community at Girl Scout camp.

Camp came to epitomize the lesbian community I have since searched for, and sometimes found, every place I have lived as an adult. While not all the counselors were lesbians, many of us were. (My partner Lisa gets a kick out of my showing her old Girl Scout staff pictures and pointing to woman after woman, saying, "dyke, dyke, dyke, dyke, dyke.")

I have always felt blessed by Girl Scout camp. All around me I saw women loving women. I had a strong sense that something so wonderful could not be wrong.

Many of us—lesbian, straight and bisexual—have stayed connected since working together at Girl Scout camp. That connection was strengthened six years ago when one of our camp friends, Laurie, developed breast cancer. Laurie had worked at two Girl Scout camps and had been a professional Girl Scout. When her father disowned her because she was a lesbian, she turned to her Girl Scout friends to create a new family. While she later reconciled with her family, her network of Girl Scout friends continued to provide support throughout the years she struggled against cancer.

In the spring of 1995, her cancer spread, and it became clear that Laurie was losing the fight. Her Girl Scout friends began to gather round her, literally and figuratively. The ongoing support she had been receiving increased, and Girl Scout friends came from all over the country to visit her. They called and sent letters filled with loving thoughts. Throughout the summer, as Laurie began to say good-bye to this life and all the people in it whom she had loved and been loved by, she continually recalled the strength and joy she had received from Girl Scouting.

Three weeks before she died, two other Girl Scout friends and I went to stay with her. Throughout those three weeks, Girl Scout friends called or came to see Laurie. It didn't matter who was lesbian or who was straight. What mattered was the attachment we had all formed so long ago as Girl Scouts.

Laurie's one wish for her death was that her last days be filled with laughter and love and song. One week before she died, we gathered in her living room for a last campfire and spent the evening laughing and singing, granting Laurie her wish.

At our reunion in the summer of 1996, we gathered without our dear friend. We laughed and reminisced and sang together. At the Scouts' Own for Laurie, we were reminded of the love we share, regardless of our sexual orientation. We became new friends when we were young, but I know now, more than ever, that we will be old friends forever.

Holli Van Nest

CHAPTER 19

What We Let Ourselves Become

Henri Bensussen

From the freedom and strength of her Girl Scout days, through the restrictions of marriage and motherhood, to an imagined future in a wheelchair, this California writer illustrates the pain of having one's potential crippled.

A Girl Scout Birthday Party was held a few years ago at Stanford University, where I work. The Scouts were celebrating their eightieth year. About sixty of us met in the rotunda of the Hoover Tower, with its solidly-engineered cement spire pointing toward the heavens. The two oldest women in attendance, in their seventies and eighties, both wore their uniforms. One of them said she missed that wonderful belt made of green webbing with a brass buckle that you could cinch tight around your waist. Others wore their badge sashes. It hadn't occurred to me to look for mine. If I still had it, it would be buried in an old box deep in a dusty cupboard.

Each of us was given a green and white pin that said "Once A Girl Scout . . . Always A Girl Scout!" Song sheets had been printed up for us to prime our memories. We began with the Brownie smile song, then did "Girl Scouts Forever." I could feel myself about to break into tears as the sound of our voices echoed around the marble enclosure.

A sudden memory transported me back at Girl Scout camp in the San Bernardino mountains near Los Angeles. It was 1955, my second year as a Counselor-in-Training and my last year of scouting. We were gathered at the campfire circle—staff, CITs, the young campers—listening as the last notes of "Day Is Done" faded into the darkness of an August night.

I left the Stanford party early with the excuse that I had a train to catch. I had to keep moving or I would have started to cry for the girl I had been forty years ago. That girl took big stretched-out steps hiking in the mountains, breathed deep, laughed with the other girls, sang about the open road or a bucolic ash grove.

Now I sing the songs while driving alone at night with the windows up. I still hike, but my steps aren't nearly as wide because my left hip hurts and my knees creak. My body's internal structure shows the effects of age like a plaster wall full of cracks. The tissue between bones wears away, breaks down from misuse and accidents, leaves the vertebrae of my spine bare as old, broken piano keys.

That girl. Always striving toward the wrong reward. Rote learning and good grades, but too shy to ask questions. Marriage instead of college because

Henri Bensussen

it was easier for everyone. Denying her interest in one special girl met at camp because she was unwilling to take that leap of imagination out of heterosexualized culture. No risks for her; she was too practical and responsible.

Now divorced and out as a lesbian since 1983, I fantasize retirement in a wheelchair-accessible house, my degenerating spine cushioned from jolts. But who is in the wheelchair? Is it the girl I used to be, stuffed into a vault at eighteen, almost silent from her confinement? Maybe it's she who cries when she hears a sentimental song from a past she wishes might have been lived differently. Those days when almost anything was possible, and Scouts believed they could survive in the wilderness with a jackknife, a cotton bandana, the knowledge culled from the *Girl Scout Handbook*, and their own experiences of camping. We testify to truth in what we let our selves become.

Disillusionment

Disillusionment

Not everyone experiences Girl Scouting as consistently empowering or fulfilling. The gap between the professed values of the organization and the actual practice can be painfully wide. Part III show how Girl Scouts have dealt with fear, dishonesty, racism, and homophobia within the organization. It ends with the inspiring story of a woman who turned the heartbreak of losing her job and her home in Girl Scouting into a legislative victory.

CHAPTER 20

✳ ✳ ✳

Beneath One Roof

Rachel Wetherill

A mail carrier in rural Virginia lost her Girl Scout troop and her dream of going to Our Chalet because of a bizarre accusation by a disturbed child and the homophobia of the local Girl Scout Council. (The names of some people and locations have been changed to protect identities.)

It was 78 degrees outside at 6 a.m., so I knew it would be a three-quart day. Three quarts of water and six trays of ice would see me through the fifty-nine miles of delivering mail. It was the seventeenth year of my career as a rural carrier. Some of my customers were the descendants of farm workers brought up from the Tennessee-Virginia border to work on the horse farms of Loudoun County, Virginia, while others were urbanites escaping the hectic life of Washington, D.C.

I had been sorting mail for three hours when the window clerk called, "Rachel! A hold order."

I approached the counter to greet 315 Main Street, also known as Catherine Horton. I had known Catherine since moving to Virginia nineteen years earlier. We had co-led a junior Girl Scout troop before I'd been asked to leave.

"I guess you're going on vacation," I said. "Where to this time?"

145

"Switzerland, with six Senior Girl Scouts. We're going to Our Chalet."

I had dreamed of going to Our Chalet since childhood. I bit my inner lip. "Send me a postcard."

As I turned away past the sorting cases, I heard Catherine call, "Postcards are too expensive, but I'll take your spirit."

I reached the gray door of the bathroom and collapsed on the seat, my stomach twisting. The pain of my dismissal and the yearning for Our Chalet came rushing over me.

After a minute, the window clerk called, "Box 373 is looking for a package." I dried my tears, and went out to do my job.

In a town of five hundred, the most widely known people are the store owner and the mail carrier. My partner Yvette ran the general store while I delivered the mail. We were not exactly closeted. A young man had broken into our apartment above the store and had seen a copy of the *Lesbian Tide* on our coffee table. Word spread quickly, but it was never discussed in our presence.

Hearing Catherine talk about Our Chalet brought back memories, reminding me of how entwined my life was with Girl Scouting.

The Beginnings

As a child, I loved the female community of Girl Scouts. It gave me the opportunity to explore myself and become an independent person. At school I always felt like an imposter. When I was away at camp, I could be who I really was.

My family had moved to California when I was nine, into a neighborhood on the fringe of Beverly Hills. The first day at my new school was a nightmare with the kids ridiculing my clothes and laughing because I didn't know how to play handball. Then I was invited to join the Brownie troop, and my life changed. At first what I liked best was the uniform. On Wednesdays I proudly put on my brown dress and was part of a group of girls with a higher purpose than being fashionable.

The troop was scheduled to fly up to Intermediates soon (the equivalent of today's Junior and Cadette Scouts), and I had to cram to learn all the laws and practices. But it was worth it, because the new uniform was even better: green with a beret, badge sash, and tie. With the new uniform I could envision

Rachel Wetherill, 1961

myself as a WAC or a WAVE in training. I fantasized that if a national emergency were to befall the country, I would be one of the persons called on to help. This fantasy was not that farfetched. It was the year of the Cuban Missile Crisis, and our troop leader said if a nuclear attack occurred, we might be asked to help evacuate the school and render simple first aid. However ludicrous this scenario seems today, it made me feel important and allowed me to think of myself as a leader.

During that year, troop meetings were cut short so that we could rush home to watch President Kennedy's weekly press conferences. Even an eleven-year-old was expected to have a knowledge of world politics. With that came a desire to work for world peace.

That's what Our Chalet was all about. High up, high on the mountain in Adelboden, Switzerland, was a building where scouts and guides from all over the world could learn to know each other. If President Kennedy and Premier Khrushchev had such a place, I thought, the world wouldn't be so dangerous. I made myself a vow that one day I would get to Our Chalet.

To achieve my goal of getting to Our Chalet, I had to advance in scouting, and I did so fanatically. I took every opportunity to earn proficiency badges, and when the cookie sales drive came around, I decided, with my mother's encouragement, to sell more than anyone else in my troop. Every day from 3:30 p.m. until dark, I was posted at the corner of Wilshire and Westwood. In full uniform complete with green ribbons on my pigtails, I would stand asking passersby, "Would you like to buy a box of Girl Scout cookies? We have Trefoils which are good for infants and the elderly, and Mints which are everybody's favorite, or maybe you would like to try something new, Savannahs, a delicious peanut butter sandwich cookie." For a usually shy girl it was quite a spiel. When the sales results were in, I had finished with 409 boxes. Not only was this more than anyone in the troop, but it was more than any other Intermediate Scout in Los Angeles. I got my picture in the *Los Angeles Times* and was very, very proud.

Graduating from sixth grade marked the end of innocence in my Girl Scout career. Whereas in elementary school most every girl participated at some level, in junior high school many girls dropped out. Others stayed in only because their parents made them. Where were the girls who wanted to be Girl Scouts? The number was dwindling fast. Some of the girls complained about having to wear their uniforms to school, so the uniform requirement was abolished. Girls told me never to mention scouting in front of non-scout schoolmates as it was embarrassing to be known as a Girl Scout. The final blow came when my cohorts from elementary school scouting told me they didn't want me eating lunch with them anymore as boys wouldn't talk to them with me around. Girl Scouting was no longer mainstream or normal. Those who remained were a part of a secret underground society. I had no idea at the time how deep and dark that closet would become.

On the surface I tried to fit in with junior high school life and pretend that I was interested in boys and clothes. But I was really terrible at it, and to complicate matters, I was developing crushes on my gym teacher and on older girls. I had no friends and basically stopped talking to everyone save my baby sister. Troop meetings continued, but we were doing things that didn't interest me, like planning a fashion show. I focused on the summer and going away to camp.

My first camping experience had been at Camp Lakota, a Girl Scout camp which inadvertently had been overbooked. There were not enough sheltered beds, so some girls had to sleep out in the open. I was the first to volunteer.

The second night it began to rain and when I awoke, a counselor was putting me in a storage closet to sleep. I thought this was wimpy. Juliette Low would not have slept in a closet to avoid the rain. By morning I had wandered back to my soaked cot.

Annual summer trips to Girl Scout camp were important from then on. I usually went not knowing any of the others who would be there. This delighted me because it meant the other campers did not have any knowledge of my awkward and mute personality. I could be myself and excel at the things I loved without being thought of as odd. I made friends easily. We would joke about stealing a canoe late at night and paddling over to the Boy Scout camp in the next cove. I could participate in this fantasy despite the fact that I wasn't interested in the boys. The thought of a secret moonlight canoe trip with my bunkmates entranced me.

During the summer of 1966 at Camp Catalina, my crushes on counselors escalated. "Scat," one of the leaders of the Molokai unit, seemed to take a special interest in me. I followed her everywhere, and on her day off, I was grief stricken with the thought that she was off meeting a young man in town. I wore my hair in a long braid down my back, and one afternoon she offered to comb out my wet hair. As I sat on her bunk with her breasts against my back, I was in a nervous sort of ecstasy. The last day of that session she signed her real name to the back of my camp picture. I cried silently on the bus ride home and vowed to myself that I would find her again. I knew that she liked to bowl, so I spent every day for the rest of the summer staking out the bowling alley at the UCLA Student Union. Finally one day she appeared. I thought I would faint. She said hello and gave me a hug. I was so nervous I could hardly speak, and then she was gone. Not to be deterred, I posted notices on the local bulletin boards. "Looking for an old friend, Sherry Van Liere, please leave address." I did get her address this way and wrote several letters to her, but I never mailed them.

Although things were wonderful at camp, troop life was difficult. There was a move afoot to allow boys to participate in Senior Scout activities. In addition, some of the troop members got involved with a Synanon-style encounter group designed to prevent drug abuse. We were scheduled to go see the film *The Killing of Sister George* and then have an all-night marathon encounter session. Before the film started, a short-haired, wiry woman approached my scouting friend, Jan. The woman said she was glad to see Jan at this movie and asked if she would like to meet afterwards. Jan looked uncomfortable and said she had other plans.

This 1968 film was the first public acknowledgment of lesbianism I had seen. Despite its stereotypical characters, I could for the first time imagine women living together in a loving relationship.

But Jan was a nervous wreck. Afterward in the car she said, "Did you see what happened to me? Where were you when I needed support? That woman is a lesbian."

"I thought you knew her from Girl Scouts." I replied.

"Yes, but she's graduated from Girl Scouts and is still hanging around."

I was memorizing the scratches on the glove box lid, unable to look at Jan. The next twenty minutes were filled with silence.

We arrived at the house for the discussion. After ranting about the unnaturalness of homosexuality, the group asked if I had anything to say. I felt tears coming, but said nothing. They asked me to leave; voyeurs were not appreciated. I sat in the car until morning, contemplating the railroad tracks, the realization of who I was slipping from the unconscious to the conscious part of my brain. I needed to find women like me, and Girl Scouts wasn't the place to look.

It took almost a year from that night to find the community of lesbians I was seeking. After my first year in college, I wandered around the country in my Volkswagen van, ending up in a women's commune in Washington D.C. Like scouting, it was an up-and-down life, but I did meet Yvette there. We were friends for five years before we became lovers and she moved in with me.

Troop Leader

Yvette and I had been living in Virginia for three years, when Catherine asked me to be a Girl Scout troop co-leader. Catherine had been a leader of the Junior Scout troop, but she wanted to move on to the Cadette troop. When she asked me to co-lead that year and take over the troop the next year, I couldn't stop smiling. There was nothing I wanted more than to be back in scouting.

Yvette had never been a scout and did not understand my delight when I told her, but with a kind of hesitation in her eyes, she urged me to go for it.

Six months of co-leading with Catherine went well. At most of our meetings we planned for the troop's first camping adventure: two nights at Camp Potomac Woods. I taught the troop to make an emergency candle, sew a dunk bag, and build a campfire. The girls were ready and excited about their first camping experience, and I was exhilarated.

We got to Potomac Woods late Friday night. There were sixteen girls in three platform tents. Catherine and I shared a fourth canvas tent with another leader, Lydia.

It was a damp morning for oatmeal and French toast, but it tasted good. The sun came out, and I took the troop on a search for fallen wood for the evening campfire. Around noon I noticed that Catherine and one of the campers, Daisy, were missing. I figured that they must be off working on a badge. Deep in my gut I felt a twang, but my brain said *relax, you are being paranoid*. We fixed a dinner of grilled cheese sandwiches and tomato soup. By the time Catherine and Daisy appeared, the troop had assembled for grace and said they wanted to sing a song dedicated to me.

It was my favorite song, "High up, high on the mountain / We've founded our Chalet." Sung in my honor, it made me grin from ear to ear. As the girls reached the last line, "Each race, each creed, each nation / Beneath its roof are one," a voice in my head said *maybe one day they will add sexual orientation to that pledge*.

It was late when we bedded down in the leaders' tent. I wanted nothing more than to dream of Adelboden, Switzerland, and a whole universe of Girl Scouts.

"I need to talk with you before you go to sleep," Catherine said.

She probably wants me to plan the Scout's Own for tomorrow.

"Daisy was upset this afternoon," Catherine continued. "She says that you pay to have sex with her mother."

My head and stomach spiraled into space. "That's absurd," I heard my out-of-body voice reply. "Some people do pay to have sex with her mother, but certainly not me."

Lydia said, "We know, Rachel, that you are, uh, uh, gay. We had you checked out before we asked you to co-lead the troop. One of the teachers at the elementary school said you live with another woman in, uh, a relationship, but that you are a fine person. The girls' parents have warned them never to be alone with you," Catherine added.

My mind was still high up on the mountain. This wasn't really happening. I turned over in my bag and said, "I need to go to sleep now."

I thought about Daisy, the girl who had made the accusation. She lived in substandard housing on a street formally known as Victoria Avenue. The locals called it Vietnam Street because the fighting there was worse, the veterans said, than the action they had seen in Southeast Asia. The street dead-ended at Daisy's house. Daisy was thirteen and in the fifth grade. She shared the house with her mother, her mother's boyfriend, her mother's husband, seven siblings and their spouses, numerous nieces and nephews, and some unrelated male farm workers.

The next day, numb and teary eyed, I made it through breakfast and Scout's Own. When I dropped the last girl off at home, I broke down and cried. I knew the local Girl Scout council members wouldn't let me lead a troop once they got wind of the rumor. There was only one more scouting event before summer vacation: the Court of Awards.

I will fight them, I vowed to myself. *Tomorrow morning I will call Linda* (the lesbian mother of Ashley, one of my scouts). *Linda will be outraged, and she will call other mothers, and they will demand that I remain as troop leader.*

The next morning I went by Linda's house. We sat on the wide Victorian porch sipping tea.

"What did Ashley say about the camping trip?" I asked.

"Not much. Only that she was tired and dirty."

It sounded like my reports to my mother after I had returned home from camping. I told Linda what had happened, waiting for her to blow up. Instead she said, "I don't know why you wanted to become involved anyway. Why would you want to spend your weekends at a dirty campground with a bunch of whiny pubescent girls? If I had that much free time, I'd go to the District to visit art museums or see a play."

"But I like Girl Scouting."

"Well, it's best if you drop it right now," she said. "There's no hope that they will want you back."

I made my scheduled appearance at the Court of Awards. Clean pressed blouses and well-combed hair surrounded me. Catherine read off the names of the recipients while I pinned them. Giggles abounded. Catherine had stated that recipients should place their hand underneath their blouse to prevent the pinner from accidentally sticking them. *Or*, I thought, *to keep the dyke from copping a feel of a nubile breast.* Catherine presented me with my ten-year pin. An inner voice said, *This is the last award that you will ever get from Girl Scouts.* I bit my lip and said good-bye to the organization I loved.

The End

Two months later was Linda's fortieth birthday. A party with most of the town invited was held at her house. I was glad to see Ashley again and Linda's girlfriend Deb. Then I noticed an out-of-towner, Lydia, the co-leader from the camping trip.

"What is she doing here?" I asked Linda.

She said Lydia had come because she wanted to talk with me.

A fine way to spoil a great evening, I thought. *But maybe she wants to apologize for the accusations.*

Lydia asked if we could speak alone. I nodded, and she led me into Linda's bedroom. We sat on the bed as she told me that she and Catherine had met with the council chair, Sue Palmer.

"What happened?" I asked. I was feeling that dark spiraling feeling again, so I laid my head down on Linda's pillow. *How dare they have a meeting about me without even notifying me.*

"Well," Lydia continued as she mirrored my position by resting her head on the other pillow, "Sue heard the whole story. She says that there are two kinds of lesbians in this world: the kind that attacks children and the kind that doesn't attack children. As far as she can tell, you are the kind that doesn't attack, but you can't be too sure. The council just can't take the chance on having you as a leader."

My first thought was, *what are you doing lying on a bed with me, a known lesbian who may be prone to violent attacks on unsuspecting innocents?*

"I'm sorry about the way this has turned out," Lydia concluded.

I got up, walked out of the room, and put Girl Scouting behind me.

Postscript

Since that night, the only contact I have had with Girl Scouts has been at the Michigan Women's Music Festival. Usually there is a huge reunion of former scouts. From discussions there, I find my censure was atypical. In many areas, lesbian scouts and leaders exist under a kind of *don't ask, don't tell* policy. Although I'm bitter about what happened, I have forgiven my friend Linda for her lack of support and myself for my lack of assertiveness. My biggest regret is not to have understood Daisy's call for help. In hindsight I am convinced that she was experiencing sexual abuse in her home.

If ever the organization becomes less homophobic, I would gladly rejoin Girl Scouts as an older, wiser, open lesbian. In the meantime I am content to buy a dozen boxes of cookies from any Girl Scout who asks.

And I dream that one day, I will get to Our Chalet, and that each race, each creed, each nation, *and each sexual orientation*, will be welcome beneath its roof as one.

Rachel Wetherill

CHAPTER 21

Lesbians in the Girl Scouts: "You Don't Bring Your Lover to a Troop Meeting"

Jorjet Harper

Chicago writer Jorjet Harper published this landmark piece of journalism in New York City's now defunct OutWeek *magazine (November 26, 1989), the first and, until this book, the only analysis of lesbian Girl Scouts to appear in print.*

"**M**any, many girls fall in love with their counselors," says Sheila Zelenski, who has directed Girl Scout camps in Illinois and Wisconsin. "The reason is that the camp environment allows you to experience things outside of yourself. When you go to camp you've left your everyday life behind."

"Lots of dykes get into the scouts as campers or staff, and work their way up in the organization," notes Nina Berger (pseudonym[1]), a 26-year-old Midwestern lesbian Girl Scout camp director, who, like all of the women quoted in this article who are still involved with the Scouts, spoke only on condition of strict anonymity. "Most of the women I know who are lesbians and work as professional Girl Scouts are from camp, and move up the ladder from there."

Zelenski, who left her job with the Girl Scouts to work for another service organization, cautions that this isn't always the case. "There's a perception that camp is so dyky, so butch. Right away a lot of people who are homophobic think, 'girls learn it there—it's all those camp people.' But there are lesbians in all phases of Girl Scouting, whether in outdoor programs, urban programs, training leaders, at the national staff level and the council level. Every single area has lesbians in it."

Up the Ladder

Girl Scouts of the U.S.A. has about 750,000 adult members, almost all of them women. About one percent is paid professional staff, and the rest—troop leaders and local level administrators—are volunteers. The organization's national headquarters is in New York City; 334 local councils cover every geographic area of the country.

While there is no way to verify how many lesbians participate in the organization, Karen Gotzler, a Milwaukee businesswoman who worked as an administrator at a Midwestern Girl Scout council for four years, says that among the Girl Scouts' paid professional staff, the percentage of lesbians is much higher than the ten percent estimated in the general population.

The lower down in the Girl Scout hierarchy toward the level of troop leader and local volunteer, Gotzler observes, the more one is likely to find heterosexual mothers, "whereas if you're talking about the professional staff, the percentage of lesbians is much higher. I'd say probably—let me give you a rough estimate—I'd say at least 30 percent. I'm trying to be fair. My first instinct is to say more than half, but keep in mind that I was more likely to seek out those lesbians. So there probably weren't as many as I like to believe."

Pat Reddeman, who worked for two different Girl Scout councils in the late 1970s and early 1980s, agrees with Gotzler's observations. "I'd say there's a very very high percentage of lesbians who are hired as professional Girl Scouts, and for obvious reasons: most lesbians are single or supporting themselves or dependent on their own income and therefore need careers; it's a great organization to work for, because you're working predominantly with women; and lesbians—or let's just say unmarried women—are a lot more mobile, so they can advance to a higher position in another council more easily than a married woman who has a family and is tied to a town because of her husband's job."

Barbara Dane (pseudonym), a 40-year-old lesbian from California, has been involved in the scouts since she herself was a Brownie. "Professionally speaking," she says, "I think what's drawn women to the Girl Scouts for years is that it's given women the chance to be a professional in a field that had more opportunity. In the Girl Scouts there really aren't many men to deal with, as there are in teaching, for example, where principals, typically, are men. But in the Girl Scouts, it's wide open for women, and the top positions are held by women. It's a very feminist philosophy—as much as any of them will not admit that it is. And that's one reason, certainly, that I loved the Girl Scouts: it was teaching girls to be independent."

Dane, who worked for a number of years at the National Headquarters office in New York, also agrees with the roughly one-in-three figure Gotzler proposes. Girl Scout headquarters has a staff of 500.

"At the national office there are a lot of older lesbians who wouldn't in a million years come out," says Dane. "They may not even be lesbians sexually, but they are woman-identified from Day One, and have lived with other women their whole lives."

Zelenski thinks the 30 percent estimate is about right, and seconds Gotzler's view that they are clustered in the administrative jobs. "I think there's a fraction of volunteers and troop leaders who are gay, but the majority are straight moms. But I also feel that some of those volunteer moms who are married and in the heterosexual schtick are lesbians who are frustrated, and the companionship and camaraderie and the feelings they get when they interact with other leaders is their way of fulfilling that part of their being."

Caroline Jones (pseudonym), a lesbian working in a Southwestern state, estimates that in her council the percentage of lesbian paid professional staff is much higher than that, "maybe 70 or 80 percent." But another lesbian, Mary Abernathy (pseudonym), says that she worked in a council office with sixteen employees, and there were only "three of us."

There are definitely lesbian troop leaders, too. Ann Johnson became a leader, as is often the case, when her daughters became old enough to be Girl Scouts. She was a troop leader for six years in a Midwestern blue collar community. "I didn't hide the fact that I'm a lesbian, but I didn't advertise it, either," she says. "You don't bring your lover with you to a troop meeting, for instance. But I know that if most of these parents had known I was a lesbian they would have pulled their girls out of my troop." She adds: "If anyone had point blank asked me, I would never lie to them. But surprisingly enough, nobody ever asked."

Johnson knew three other troop leaders in her council at the time she was a leader who were also lesbians. She says they all believed that if the parents—particularly the fathers—found out, the parents would have removed their kids from the troop. "We try so hard to come away from those old myths, but they still exist—that fear that the children will be harassed," she says.

"I love working with kids. I always have. They're easier to communicate with sometimes than adults. It's the parents who have the prejudices." Johnson, now a grandmother, raised two natural children and 12 foster children—most of whom were troubled teenage boys when they arrived at her home. All of her children know that she's a lesbian, and, she says, "They all come home for Christmas."

Helen MacDonald (pseudonym), a troop leader in Texas who has been with the scouts for forty years, agreed with Johnson that she would lose her troop if parents found out. She too, has never been asked. "In their heads some of them may know, but as long as it's not brought up, they can live with it," she says.

Check

How do lesbians in the Girl Scouts find each other? The same way they do everywhere else. They meet in concerts and at bars, they wear some kind of pin or symbol and see who comments on it, they "throw around telling innuendos." And especially, they meet through other lesbians.

"When I first took the week-long training in 1975," says Gertrude Hulbert (pseudonym), who worked in the scouts for ten years, "we picked up the roster of who was there—about 30 or 40 of us—and we'd start checking off people who were gay. Then every time we'd go to an association of Girl Scout executives staff or to the national conference, we'd get the roster and do check marks." With typical Girl Scout pluckiness, it became an activity that involved more and more players. "We began calling it 'the checks,' and if you walked by someone and said 'check,' that meant you knew they were gay.

"We had an elaborate scheme. To be a check you had to be for sure. We had slash marks for people we thought were but we didn't know. Then we

Patsy Lynch,
self portrait, OutWeek
(November 26,1989),
in which this article first
appeared.

had X's: people we thought were, but *they* didn't know. And zeros, for people we wished were, but weren't. We used to go to the national conventions—six or seven thousand women—and do this, and laugh and hoot and bring people in from all over the U.S. and just have a great game of it," said Hulbert.

"Sort of a sad game, though, because it was the underground game."

A Closet Full of Cookies

Lesbians in the Girl Scouts work in a paradoxical closet: even though there are more of them than in most work environments, many of them feel that fact creates added pressure to stay hidden. One woman told me that if all the lesbians quit, the organization could not go on. On the other hand, many lesbian Girl Scouts say they believe that if they came out, the organization would become thought of as lesbian-run, and lose all its funding. "It's not like the Catholic Church, which will still have plenty of money even if all the lesbian nuns come out," says another.

Consequently there is a very high level of homophobia within the organization itself, despite its large lesbian population.

"Nobody's really open; they're all fearful for their jobs," Zelenski says, "and of the homophobic people in the community. In my region, to even suggest that there may be gay people in the organization is scary for a lot of people. It's a shame, but that's the way it is."

"There's no way that the board would tolerate an awareness that there were lesbians on the staff, because the people in the communities would not accept that. It's the same as if they found out a teacher was a lesbian," says Delanna Wells (pseudonym), 31, who works for an East Coast Girl Scout Council. "A lot of people have an image of what Girl Scouting is and what it stands for, who would never in their minds think that a professional Girl Scout could be a lesbian."

For lesbians in the Girl Scouts to stay in the closet is "totally understandable," says Wells, "because of the 'child sensitive' thing. People who are in child sensitive professions—like teaching—tend to get hit more with the general public's fear of the stereotype that homosexuals are going after the kids, and all that bullshit."

"I am of two minds about being closeted," says Dane. "I felt we needed to protect the Girl Scouts. We need to be sure lesbians are in there, and to do that we have to hide them. They are the strongest women around teaching girls to be independent. They have the strongest feminist values within themselves personally. I think uncovering them would shut it all down. You have to remember who the supporters of the Girl Scouts are—the churches who give the meeting space, and the conservatives. Ultimately, I think the issue is the funding sources. When you really look at who funds the Girl Scouts, you realize you need to be careful."

"They are very scared, afraid they'd lose their funding, donations—big time donations—and that they'd lose their membership," agrees MacDonald.

Ten-year veteran Hulbert is the only one who disagrees with this scenario. "I don't think Girl Scouting would fall apart if it were to recognize that some Girl Scouts are lesbians. I think to a lot of people that's fairly well known—at camp, anyway."

But make no mistake about it—these women are scared. Not a single woman I spoke with in researching this article who is currently employed by the organization (or who hopes to one day work for it again) felt she could risk using her real name in print. "It's sickening for me that I can't use my real name, but if I ever wanted to get a job in the Girl Scouts again, they wouldn't hire me," Hulbert says.

Lina Bartell (pseudonym) is a current Girl Scout employee, and her position is typical: "I need to tell you that I'm real sensitive about this. We're talking about my career here and the way I feed my family." Bartell asked me to be as vague about her identity as possible, and report only that she works for a Girl Scout council in "a western state." To do something to "expose the Girl Scouts in conjunction with lesbianism," she says, "is like slitting my own throat. Nobody would hire me in this country, and that's really the bottom line. I have witnessed incidents in my area where a rumor can literally destroy a family in Girl Scouting. So the danger of talking about sexual orientation is extreme."

I called Girl Scouts of America National Headquarters in New York to see if they could offer any help or comments on the subject of lesbians in scouting. I was directed to Deborah Mason, manager of media relations there. After listening to my explanation of the article I was researching, Ms. Mason said she could not put me in touch with any out lesbian Girl Scout staff who would be willing to talk about their experiences.

"That's one of the things we would never know, because we don't ask," said Mason. "We really have only two spokespersons. One is our national director and the other is our national president. And they certainly couldn't speak to the question you're asking. They wouldn't know."

I told her that in speaking with former and present Girl Scout professionals around the country, there was general agreement among them that the percentage of paid professional staff in the Girl Scouts is around 30 percent, including at headquarters. "I don't know how they would come to that figure," she said. "I don't know how they would know that, because no one is ever asked about what their sexual preference or lifestyle is. As part of the hiring practice, that question would never be asked."

I observed that while no one may ask, lesbians do find each other. Mason said only, "I couldn't comment on that."

Nevertheless, the degree of openness possible appears to vary from council to council. "There are councils where a lesbian will have her lover's picture openly on her desk, and others where the lesbians go out of their way to wear heavy makeup and such just to disguise any hint of being dykes," says another current Girl Scout council employee who asked not to be identified. Toni Gonzalez (pseudonym), a 25-year-old camp counselor from upstate New York, says she knew one lesbian camp director who wore a wedding ring and talked about her fiancé to deflect suspicion.

Gotzler's experience was less extreme. "My boss, who was the executive director of the council, was aware that I was a lesbian, although we didn't talk about it at any great length. Her position to volunteers was: I hired this woman to do a particular job, and she does it well, and what she does outside of this office has no bearing on her job performance, therefore I don't know anything about her personal life. She knew—but she was very careful not to ask me any questions and I didn't offer anything. I certainly didn't wear a scarlet L on my shirt. But I also didn't make any bones about it. I didn't make up stories about fictitious boyfriends, and if I were ever approached about it directly, I never lied about it. And I think for the most part that's the most common posture for somebody who's a lesbian and a professional Girl Scout.

"The higher up you go the more paranoid people get," Gotzler adds. "But I think that's gradually changing as younger people move higher up the responsibility ranks, because they're a little more likely to be out." In fact, says Gotzler, "there are some councils where nearly *all* the professional staff are lesbians. That would be more typical when you have an executive director who's a lesbian herself or where she's very comfortable hiring lesbians and it's not a concern to her. The problem is the same as with any minority group: when there's a problem with any employee who's a lesbian, typically they blame her lesbianism and not what the actual problem is."

Wells says she knows of a case in which a lesbian was accused of sexual harassment by another council employee simply because she talked openly about her sexuality. "The other lesbians on the staff were floored, and didn't know exactly what to do. It was a really lousy situation."

Reddeman quit a Girl Scout job because she was about to be fired for being a lesbian, but was later hired at another council. There she became the supervisor of a camp director. "We had a problem at the camp that summer. The camp ranger—a man who I supervised who lived on the property—

discovered that there were a couple of lesbians on staff and was horrified. He tried to make trouble for them, calling the executive director of the council, saying he didn't want his wife and his son anywhere around lesbians. I sat him down and said, 'Listen, you have nothing to say about this. They're my staff and they're doing fine.' They didn't get fired or asked to leave. We dealt with it. And he just shut up, after that. I called the women in, too, because they needed to know what people were saying about them and what was going on."

Some councils—each of which operates more or less autonomously—are reportedly considering revisions in their affirmative action statements to include sexual orientation. But most of the lesbian Girl Scouts I interviewed see no likelihood that they will be able to be more out in the foreseeable future. Many of them believe that the situation can change "only as society changes."

"Remember," says Wells, "we're talking about Apple Pie, the Flag, and Scouting! It's going to take a long time. I don't think you can realistically believe it's going to be any quicker to change than the rest of the world. On the contrary—it's going to be slower."

PHOTO: TONI ARMSTRONG, JR.

Jorjet Harper

[1] *All names that have been changed were done so to respect interviewees' requests for anonymity.* –JH

CHAPTER 22

✳ ✳ ✳

Dear Nancy

From a Concerned Girl Scout

A graduate student and assistant camp director who had planned to write a piece about her wonderful memories of lesbian role models and friends in Girl Scouting gave permission to publish this letter.

March 2, 1995

Dear Nancy,

I am writing with some unfortunate and disturbing news. I won't be able to contribute to your book on lesbians in Girl Scouting. After talking with you, I got excited about this project, wanting to share some childhood and adolescent experiences which involved my most influential role models— the majority of whom I met through scouting and many of whom were lesbians. I feel that it's important for people to see the positive contributions that lesbians have made and are still making to the field of Girl Scouting.

After talking with a current professional Girl Scout who is both my former and future summer employer, however, I've had to make the tough and unfair choice between doing what I feel is morally right or protecting my friends.

In addition to other concerns, I'm leery of the possible political

164

ramifications that my contributing to your book might have. In January 1994, Connie Chung aired an *Eye to Eye* investigative piece criticizing Girl Scout fundraising practices. Cookie sales dropped dramatically during that year, which hurt Girl Scouts at the council level since councils depend on cookie proceeds to pick up where the United Way leaves off; at the troop level, since they had less money to spend on activities; and at the level of individual girls. Even I paid for many summers of resident camp with my cookie credits.

I am concerned that a book on lesbians in the Girl Scouts might have a similar chilling effect. The organization has enough trouble with internal homophobia without needing any help from a book or TV show. A few years ago, for example, one southern California council conducted a lesbian witch-hunt, which led to a large percentage of the council staff being fired. It will take this council over a decade to repair the resulting financial damage.

My home town council in the Southeast also experienced a homophobic scare, during which several churches, without any investigation into the sexual orientation of troop leaders, announced that troops could no longer meet in their facilities. The financial burden of having to pay for a meeting location could easily destroy smaller and less affluent troops. While I am certain that your intentions are not to harm the Girl Scout organization, I fear that the book could produce the same sort of public response Connie Chung's report did.

Although this is a lesser concern, my supervisor also made it clear that if I contributed to your book, I would not only no longer be employable by that council, but I would likely be blackballed by Girl Scouts of the U.S.A. from volunteering even at the local level. While it would be unfortunate for me to be excluded from an organization I've grown up in and for which I have a high regard, I have never had trouble finding summer jobs or organizations in need of good volunteers. Thus, such a decision would not end my career.

My personal employment and volunteer considerations aside, however, regardless of how positive my intentions might be for writing about my influential lesbian friends and role models in Girl Scouting, I would have no control over how my writing for your publication might affect the people whom I care about who are still actively involved in Girl Scouting either as girls, professionals, or committed volunteers. I know from working in the field of literature that the people who most often censor books are those who haven't read them. Hence, I suspect I'd be "preaching to the converted" and not talking at all to those who really need to hear what I'd like to say.

This hasn't been an easy decision, and I find that I'm really angry that mainstream America is still too blind to embrace difference. Thus, in spite of how positively I feel about my particular experiences with lesbians in scouting, I care too much about the people whom this book could hurt to contribute to it. But I do feel honored to have been asked. Thank you.

Sincerely,

A Concerned Girl Scout

CHAPTER 23

* * *

Lessons in
Green and Brown

Cara L. Vaughn

In addition to learning wholesome camping skills and the lesson that girls don't need boys, Cara Vaughn experienced an awful silence surrounding incidents of racism in the Girl Scouts.

A few years back, I got a letter out of the blue from my third grade Girl Scout leader, Ruby. I remembered her as tall and skinny with dark hair. She was married to this kind of loud, happy, slightly chubby guy named Harry. They were pretty poor, poorer than just about anyone in the troop. "Poor" meant *poor* in our rural town of 5,000 with no blue bloods and just enough upper middle class to count on two hands. It's a wonder to me now how such a poor woman with kids of her own could volunteer to lead a scout troop. Therein lies the best lesson she ever taught us: helping people does not require that you be standing on a base of cash or things.

Ruby wrote me because she'd heard I had cancer. In one of life's grand gestures, she was now a rich widowed psychologist. Seems Harry had won a million dollars in a contest, had lived long enough to enjoy some of it, but then fought his own battle with cancer. She told me about Harry and sent encouragement and prayers. She gave me a boost in energy and spirit, and a line to my Girl Scout past.

Our troop met at Ruby's house. I remember looking at her stove and being disgusted because it had dried-up spaghetti on top. (Now I look at my own stove and laugh at how my standards have changed.) Ruby and Harry, who pitched in sometimes, taught us to march. Every year the Girl Scouts participated in the town's Memorial Day parade. I always looked forward to this day because it's my birthday (or it was until Congress got ahold of the holidays in 1971). I got a day off from school and sometimes was in the parade. My friends and I would pretend the parade was for me. Some years we made a float out of a helpful farmer's flat-bed truck; some years we marched. And some years we did both.

I enjoy people engaged in a group activity that requires precision, whether it's the Rockettes or Sweet Honey or the women in my family cooking together. We scouts, however, weren't trying for precision, we were just trying not to run into each other. During practice, Harry yelled out at me to stop worrying about my arm movements. He said if my feet were doing the right thing, my arms would follow naturally. It worked. I became a great marcher, and in one parade I had the honor of carrying the flag at the front of our Girl Scout procession.

What a terrible job that turned out to be. I was informed that the correct way to hold the flag pole was with my arms held out in front of me, elbows bent breast high (and no, they did not say *breast*; they just showed me), forearms parallel to the ground, palms outward, hands wrapped around the pole. I hurt like hell just a quarter of the way through the parade. My arm muscles hurt. The leather flagpole holder pressed hard into the top of my shoulder. I had to balance this heavy pole *and* watch my feet. When you're in front, you're the one who has to watch for horse manure on the parade route; when you're in the back, you can just follow the girl in front of you, go with the slight bow that has suddenly appeared in the marching line. I never did that flag job again.

Ruby was the first scout leader I remember clearly. After her came Olivia. This was the time when my mom was an assistant leader. Fortunately, I was young enough so that Mom's being around was not a problem. Olivia had a daughter, Karen, who was also in the troop. One time Karen and I were discussing our mothers. She said her mom was twenty-nine. I was just appalled. I exclaimed, "Really?!" and she nodded. I was silent a few moments so I

Cara L. Vaughn, 1963

wouldn't say anything bad. I had very skewed ideas about ages. My mother had me, the oldest of three kids, when she was thirty-three. So being nine and having a twenty-nine-year-old mom just struck me as ludicrous. She asked me how old my mother was. I said, "Forty-one." She couldn't believe it; forty-one was so . . . old. We just stopped the conversation right there because we didn't know where else to go with the topic and still be polite. I told my mother later how old Olivia was, and she said, "Yes, she's very young." I felt vindicated.

Olivia taught us to camp and hike. Well, actually, it was more like walking down a country road in a straight line, but we called it hiking. And then we'd go into the woods and set up camp. We made little camp stoves out of coffee cans. (I do not remember how this was done exactly, but they seem remarkably similar to the eight dollar, no chemicals needed, charcoal starter I just bought.) Whether it was cooking over our little stoves or building a campfire, all scouts were sent out to collect prodigious amounts of kindling. One try was never enough. "It has to be smaller. Those sticks are too big. You need more, go get some more." This got really old, really fast. We were usually starving, but those were the days when kids were obedient, so we trudged back into the woods with sighs and grumbles as big as the great outdoors. And when we finally got enough, and had prepared, cooked and eaten dinner, then we could finally get to the best thing about Girl Scout camping: s'mores.

Oh, what a ritual. Find the perfect stick. Of course, this took nearly as long as collecting kindling, but who cared; this was *important*. Select a properly round, not crushed, marshmallow. Carefully toast it to perfection, not too burned, not too raw. Just melted hot and golden brown. Place that baby on a square of Hershey's chocolate broken perfectly along the lines and nestled between two graham cracker halves, similarly broken. And proceed to burn the hell out of the inside of your mouth. No matter. It was sugar, it was chocolate, it was legal, and it defined Girl Scout camping. Today I live in the San Francisco Bay Area, and s'mores out here would probably have to be Godiva chocolate, stone ground whole wheat graham crackers, and health-food marshmallows. Well, I suppose that's okay. As long as they get their own kindling.

Other than s'mores, there was one other thing that defined Girl Scout camping for me, especially summertime sleep-over camp—singing. Girl Scouts *always* sang. And I quickly fell in love with the sound of girls' and women's voices joined together in song. We sang to raise the flag, to say grace before meals, to hike, and to be together around the campfire. I thought it was wonderful. It was also a great lesson in how no one individual has to be outstanding for the whole to be absolutely beautiful.

The best thing I ever learned in Girl Scouts was that you don't need boys. Even though this lesson was never articulated, I inhaled it as easily as I did air. It was clear that women were in charge and could be effective, inspiring leaders. Nowhere else in my life did I have that understanding or example. School, church, home, even stores were all run by men and filled with attention-getting boys. There is no better lesson in life for a girl than that she can find her way in the world in the company of women: men are an option.

In scouts, women taught me how to walk in the forest, set up a tent, collect wood, build a fire, make a float, and create presents from everyday objects. The Girl Scouts taught me some of the same things boys learn through sports. I learned teamwork and resources allocation by working with the troop to build a parade float on a $3.50 budget. I learned persistence when it took me three hours to set up the mosquito netting over my tent at summer camp. The counselors made me get it right because it was Jersey in July, when mosquitoes are designated the state vampire.

A few things I got from Girl Scouts weren't lessons, but experiences which brought to sharp consciousness lessons I had learned elsewhere about race and class in America. One of those experiences was in summer camp. I was the victim of a practical joke perpetrated by some of my bunkmates. The joke was not unkind or anything out of the ordinary for ten year olds. I don't even remember exactly what it was. I think something unusual may have ended up in my bed, or perhaps I was short-sheeted. Anyway, I was coming into the tent from the back and I saw the four girls run out. I knew something was up. I checked my things and found their joke. I remember thinking it wasn't very creative, but I also felt left out and hurt. Two of the jokers were friends I had grown up with. I wondered why they had picked me. Were my friends being influenced by these bunkmates we never had met before? Was it because I was the only Black girl in the tent? I didn't know. The question just hung in the center of my head. I wanted to respond with a practical joke of my own. Unfortunately I couldn't think of much to do. And I knew, I was positive, that if I went even a little too far, I would be punished. And I knew the punishment would be more severe because I was Black. I knew those things because I was an African American who had lived ten years in America. It's a lesson we learn very early. So I did nothing, a lesson I learned watching my elders. And my bunkmates got no response from me about their joke. Finally, one of my friends asked me if I had figured it out. I said yes, and she shrugged without surprise, as if to say that she had known from the beginning that it wouldn't work. The whole thing died a quiet death, except for that unanswered question, which still hangs in the middle of my head.

Another reverberating experience came five years later when I was a Cadette. Our weekly meeting had just ended, and many of us girls were standing outside the building waiting for our rides home. An old Black man rode by on a bicycle. One of the girls asked our troop leader, Carol, who he was. In this small town, none of us had ever seen him before. The leader said, "I don't know his name. We just call him 'ol' nigger Joe'."

I felt slapped hard. She had unconcernedly but deliberately poured ice water on my guts to make sure that I understood the current reality. I thought

Joe was just a worker riding home at the end of the day. But something about him reminded me of my older relatives who had endured hardships and worked hard so that my dad could wear a suit. Joe seemed to be among the group I called "sir" and "ma'am" and ran willingly to do favors for, among those whose determination and strength of character I admired and aspired to, among those nearly invisible to my leader, publicly deemed unworthy of respect and consideration. To me Joe felt close. I thought we were basically the same.

My dad soon arrived to pick me up, and two troopmates and I climbed in the car. We went home. Neither my friends nor my troop leader ever said a word to me about the comment. They could have. We all went to the same church.

That was 1968, my last year in scouting. Martin Luther King had been assassinated. The Vietnam War was hot. Racial tensions were high in my small country high school. I had been a Girl Scout for nearly ten years. Most of my childhood was spent wearing some form of brown or green and going to meetings. (Sounds like perfect training for the U.S. Army.) I was sick of

PHOTO: TEE A. CORINNE

pipe cleaners, crepe paper, merit badges and wearing berets. I had different, more important, things to think about and to do. The good lessons and experiences of scouting were fewer the older I became. Though scouting had helped lead me to this point, I had to move on. I was preparing to take my place in the world as an adult, and it was now clear to me that Girl Scouts was for kids.

Cara L. Vaughn

CHAPTER 24

✳ ✳ ✳

Lies! Lies!

Krysta Sutterfield

A camp counselor describes going out of her way to avoid touching campers or other counselors in order to preclude any suspicion of wrongdoing, a degree of circumspection not unusual for a lesbian in Girl Scouting.

During my twenty years in Girl Scouting, I have often wondered why Girl Scout handbooks and other materials are exclusively heterosexual. Why do they always say, "your mother and father," "your boyfriend," or "Senior Scouts might enjoy including boys in some of their activities." I've thought about starting a special-interest Senior Girl Scout troop or campaigning to add sexual sensitivity training to current materials. But I must be careful. Not only is my own position at stake, but I must consider my mother, who works at the local Girl Scout office and is well-known.

Girl Scouts of the U.S.A. official policy is one of non-discrimination, but we all know how far official policy goes.

When I worked as a camp counselor in 1995, I was extremely careful not to touch campers or other counselors, but I hated myself for being *so* guarded. One camp song had the mandatory ending of everyone being hugged by someone, and I would go so far as to step out of the way to avoid even a hint of anything wrong. One woman noticed and asked why. I gave her the lame answer, "I'm not a very huggable person." (Lies! Lies!)

I've never seen a conflict between my feelings for women and the Girl Scout Promise or Law, but trying to compensate for others' prejudices can be hard. I always wonder if I should actively educate people or just go on being the best person I can and let them come around on their own. I'm usually a wimp when it comes to confronting prejudice.

I prefer to be a good example—a helpful, kind, humanitarian, upstanding citizen—so that when people make rude remarks about homosexuals ("Damn dyke," or "They're sick"), I can look at them and say, "I never knew you felt that way about me" or "But I don't molest kids." Of course this only works well if the bigot knows me.

I wish GSUSA would take some official action to recognize lesbians in the organization and protect us from bigoted Girl Scout leaders, counselors, and staff. I wish I didn't have to tell any more lies.

Krysta Sutterfield

CHAPTER 25

✳ ✳ ✳

My Other
Dysfunctional Family

Kim Messner

A computer specialist found Girl Scouting as dysfunctional as her family of origin. She is not a volunteer today because the necessity that she and other lesbians remain silent about their sexual orientation sends the message to girls that it is wrong to be gay.

When I was thirteen, my parents became worried about my sexuality. Up until that point, I had been Dad's helper. I held the flashlight while he worked on the cars; I found the screws he misplaced; I questioned him endlessly about how things worked. All this suddenly came to an end. Dad started going off and doing projects on his own. Mom and Dad became more affectionate with each other in front of us kids. I got the message that it wasn't okay to have crushes on my girlfriends anymore.

Although I began to keep my crushes a secret, I discovered that one way to remain close to women/girls was through Girl Scouting. Through Girl Scouting I learned that I could be anything I wanted to be and do anything I wanted to do. I could be myself.

Girl Scout resident camp was my saving grace. Every summer from the late 1960s until the late 1970s, I spent at least two weeks at Camp Wood Haven in Pine Grove, Pennsylvania. We did all the camp chores, jobs that required the use of saws, hatchets and other tools that girls typically did not handle. One of my favorite chores was the lanterns. We took them apart, cleaned them, and put them together again. I have always had a natural curiosity about how things work, and at camp this curiosity was encouraged.

Camp also taught me patience and persistence, even when I wasn't particularly interested in the project. I learned that once something was started, it was not always possible to quit in the middle of it. This lesson aided me tremendously in my adult life, especially when I worked in nontraditional jobs. Without my Girl Scout training, I do not think I could have worked as long as I did in some of the jobs I've had. I also learned that I could survive on my own without a husband or boyfriend to do the "man's" work.

Girl Scouting provided many strong female role models for me. One of the most influential was Tina, the director of Camp Wood Haven for most of the years I attended and my boss when I started working there as an aide. I respected Tina because she personified the qualities that I thought a good camp director should possess: warmth, understanding, love, and the ability to get the job done. She allowed me to be me.

In 1976, when I arrived ready to work as a kitchen aide, my face and arms were covered with poison ivy. I was not allowed to work in the kitchen and wound up trading places with the arts and crafts aide. After several days of hearing the arts and crafts aide protesting her misfortune, Tina informed me that I needed to get that poison ivy healed or go home. I would have done anything to stay at the camp, the only place where I could find love and happiness and not have to act straight. Someone had told me that Ivy Dry was a good remedy. I scratched my blisters open and drowned them in Ivy Dry. It worked! They disappeared almost overnight (although I wouldn't recommend that you try this), and I went to work in the kitchen.

Two years later I became a unit assistant. This meant I lived and worked at the camp for nine weeks and learned how to be a leader. I designed and ran programs for the girls. I learned how to get up in front of people and lead them through activities or songs. All this helped prepare me for jobs I held later in my life.

By then, I had known for three years (since I was thirteen) that I was gay. Although I had no proof, I was fairly sure that other lesbians worked at camp. In fact, we heard rumors that some parents had complained that their daughters had come home talking about their gay counselors. I never witnessed anyone being gay in front of the campers. I believe some of the girls misunderstood hugging or putting an arm around another as a sign of homosexuality. Nevertheless, these rumors forced me deeper into the closet. For a long time, I resisted touching anyone for, as Meg Christian states in her song "Rosalind", "Touches blow your cover, only touch the one you know to be your lover."

During my last year at Wood Haven, we had a new camp director, and she and I didn't get along. The camp felt different. Issues were not discussed. Tension filled the air. For me, this was too familiar. This was how I grew up. For camp to feel like home was the kiss of death. After that summer, I figured I was done with Girl Scout camp for good.

But four years later, I found myself working as a Unit Leader at Camp Hidden Falls in the Pocono Mountains of Pennsylvania. That summer, I became friends with the camp director's sister, Sara (pseudonym). When I came out to Sara, she was very accepting of me even though she said she was straight. On our nights off, sometimes we would go to dinner or the movies. One night, I took Sara to the Rainbow Mountain Resort, where there was a gay bar and disco. We had a great time.

The next day, the camp director came looking for me in her pickup truck. She found me walking across a field carrying a typewriter on my way to deliver it to Sara. The camp director slammed on the brakes, jumped out and charged across the field. I put down the typewriter and watched her approach me. Smoke poured out of her nostrils! When she reached me, she launched into a tirade, accusing me of corrupting her sister. I remained quiet. When she was through, I picked up my typewriter and turned back towards my unit. I intended to pack up my stuff and leave the camp. The camp director stormed back to her pickup truck and drove across the field toward me. I wondered if she was going to run me over. Instead, she asked me to get in so we could talk.

Her complaint involved my taking her sister to a gay bar. The camp director and assistant camp director were dating, and they feared that if I continued to take Sara to gay bars, we would run into each other. The camp director did not want me to "out" her to her sister. I assured her that outing her was not my intention. I felt fairly sure that Sara knew about her but didn't say so. I couldn't promise not to take Sara to the gay bars, but I did respect the camp director's fear of being discovered. I said if at all possible, I'd let her know if I was going to go to the bar with Sara. This seemed to pacify her. And I got a ride over to Sara's tent so I didn't have to lug that typewriter across the camp!

Homophobia ran deep at all the camps I worked at, but this was the first time I had been confronted with it. At my exit interview from Camp Hidden Falls, I had to sit down with the camp director and her assistant for an oral evaluation. They said that they wouldn't hire me back because "I intimidated my staff." What a joke! Up to that point in my life, I don't think I was capable of intimidating anything! I believe that I was ousted because of the director's fear of being outed.

I was completely disillusioned by the Girl Scouts. I wanted nothing more to do with them. Girl Scout camp and the Girl Scouts in general appeared just as homophobic and dysfunctional as the family in which I grew up.

Twelve years later, I still toy occasionally with the idea of volunteering for the Girl Scouts. Even though I now live in Maine and have had no dealings with them here, I am reluctant to call. Young lesbians who are growing up in the Girl Scouts need to know that they are okay. They need positive role models. By denying my sexuality, I would be saying it is not okay for you or me to be gay. I am tired of hiding my sexuality, and I fear that I would be required to do that if I were involved with Girl Scouting again.

Kim Messner

CHAPTER 26

＊ ＊ ＊

Testimony

Kristen Renn

When an Assistant Dean at Brown University lost her summer job with the Girl Scouts in 1992, she had no legal recourse. For the next three years, she testified before the Rhode Island state legislature in favor of a bill banning discrimination on the basis of sexual orientation. In May of 1995, the bill passed, with one senator crediting Kristen Renn with opening his eyes to the existence of "this kind of discrimination."

> **On my honor, I will try . . .**
> **to be honest . . .**
> **to be fair . . .**
> (from the Girl Scout Promise and the Law)

Honor. Honesty. Fairness. When I first memorized the Girl Scout Promise and Law I had no idea how much these values would shape my life. I also didn't know that these values would be set aside by some members of the very organization that had taught me their importance. I joined the Girl Scouts in 1971 and continued as an active member until 1993, when the council in which I was volunteering discovered that I was a lesbian. With a remarkable lack of honor, honesty, and fairness, a handful of executive Girl Scouts pushed me out of the family of scouting. The Girl Scouts had been for me a spiritual and emotional home. I grew up in the organization, and in it I developed my identity first as a girl, then as a woman, then as a lesbian. This is my story of being rejected by the Girl Scouts of Rhode Island, of coping with the apparent hypocrisy of their actions, and of making Rhode Island a safer place for all people to live honestly and in fairness.

> *"Twist me and turn me and show me the elf,*
> *I looked in the water and saw MYSELF!"*
> (from the Brownie Investiture Ceremony)

So began my twenty-two years in the Girl Scouts. A second grade Brownie Scout, with an energetic and creative mom as a troop leader, I was so proud in my uniform—beanie and all. Then I moved to Connecticut, flew up, and entered the ranks of the *real* Girl Scouts—the Juniors, with their moss green uniforms, gold flashes on green wool knee socks, and, most important, badge sashes. My mom continued as my troop leader through three years of Juniors, complete with cookie sales, camping trips, badge requirements, and annual drives to the wilds of central Connecticut to deposit me at summer camp.

Formerly a stay-at-home mom, my mother heard the call of feminism and got a part-time paid job with the Girl Scout council when I was in sixth grade. My involvement in the organization was then not only my own experience, but also a chance to see the "insiders' view" of the organization that was becoming my spiritual home. Through the Girl Scouts I grew in my sense of myself as a girl-child capable of doing anything anyone else could do, and I saw my mother growing, too. The Girl Scout Promise represented not only our commitment to live with honor in service to God and community; it also represented the promise of a world where all people could live free of prejudice and discrimination based on gender, race, or religion. I felt at home with these "family values" and with the sister-friends who shared them.

My identification with the Girl Scouts as a supplemental family grew when my parents separated. I was eleven and had just come home from camp when my parents announced that my father was moving out. I immediately asked to return to camp and did. When my father left, the Girl Scouts became not only a psychological home for me, but also the primary source of our family's income. In agreeing to put my mother into a full-time position, the council's executive director, a lesbian, supplied what would become our family motto:

"Make it into a positive learning experience." Compassionate, fair, and unrelentingly tough-minded, she became my mother's mentor and a model of the potential of Girl Scouting at its best.

Meanwhile, I was busy earning leadership awards and badges, going camping with my troop, doing career-exploration projects, and generally enjoying all the activities Girl Scouting had to offer. Several of us in my troop went on Wider Opportunities, and a handful earned Girl Scout religious medals. When the Gold Award was created late in our Senior Scout careers, we dedicated ourselves to working together in pursuit of this high honor. We each earned the award in our last year together as a troop. My mother, still my troop leader after all these years, stood beside me in her uniform as the small gold trefoil was pinned on my sash. We were proud of ourselves and each other.

> *"I know the woods, I know the stars, I know myself as well,*
> *For this I thank you, friend of mine, I thank you Camp Laurel"*
> (from the Camp Laurel song)

Though my troop was the center of my Girl Scout family during the school year, it was my annual summer trips to Camp Laurel that formed the core of my identity as a scout and as a woman. Under the pines, oaks, and maples of Laurel's woods I found bliss—tents full of girls like me under the leadership of women I hoped to be like when I matured. I found lifelong friends who attended the same sessions I did every year, many of whom, it turns out, are also lesbians. And the counselors! These were our idols. We developed crushes on a few every summer and desperately hoped they would notice us. We tried to be best at everything to make ourselves stand out. We played the role of Suzy Girl Scout—lashing fallen limbs together with twine to make flagpoles, swamping and righting canoes, cleaning latrines like we were in the military—anything to get the attention of that year's objects of affection. For two weeks every summer I didn't have to pretend I liked boys, even though at that time I didn't know that I would never like them in *that* way.

The summer my parents separated and I asked to be returned to camp was the summer I transferred my familial allegiance to the Girl Scouts. Things were lousy at home, but back at Camp Laurel things were, as always, paradise. The songs were the same, the dining hall was still too small, and the campfires still burned bright. My counselors knew about my home situation and took special care of me. I even got a hug from the most standoffish of the counselors on whom I had a crush. The other girls were jealous when they saw it. I lost my heart to her. She probably didn't notice.

Several years later, when I had my first job as a counselor at a Girl Scout camp in another council, I was still getting crushes on the counselors. This time, though, I was eighteen and had just finished my first year in college. And this time, another counselor seemed to feel the same way. I sent her notes and gave her backrubs and asked her to walk me back to my tent through the dark places in the woods along the way. We never did anything more than hold hands that summer, but I wondered in my journal if my feelings for her meant I was a lesbian. The following summer when we worked together at another Girl Scout camp and initiated a physical relationship, I knew I was.

By then, I was also becoming aware of the larger context of the lesbian world—especially within the Girl Scout family—in which I lived. I had a name for my childhood feelings of adoration for counselors. I could identify the Dyke Idols of my summers at Camp Laurel. I speculated about which of my mother's colleagues at the council office might be lesbians. I discovered that a number of my best camp buddies from childhood were also identifying as lesbians. I found role models in older lesbians in the organization and I found, more than ever, a home. When I came out to my mother after my junior year in college, she said she was not surprised and told me that several of her professional friends and colleagues were also gay. She made sure that I knew she would continue to love and support me, and she gave me the gift of knowing I was not alone as a lesbian Girl Scout.

"To show respect for myself and others through my words and actions"
(from the Girl Scout Law)

I was not naive. I knew there were plenty of people who thought lesbians and gay men should not be allowed to work with children. I knew that within the Girl Scout organization there were many people who would like to drum us out. As I began to live my life more and more as an out-lesbian I talked with my mother about what risks I might be taking professionally, personally, and within the organization. In the mid-eighties, I understood the GSUSA

Kristen Renn, 1972

stance on lesbians to be the original *don't ask, don't tell*. Councils were advised not to ask about sexual orientation so long as members didn't make an issue of their orientation (never mind the thousands of heterosexual adult volunteers whose family life was integral to the leadership of many a troop where fathers and mothers worked together on cookie campaigns, camping trips, and service projects). A number of progressive councils added sexual orientation to their nondiscrimination policies, but in most places a lesbian could be deemed an inappropriate role model and thereby ineligible for volunteer or paid positions with girls in the organization. So as an out-lesbian dedicated to the Promise and the Law—including living with honesty, honor, and fairness—I risked being asked to leave the organization/family that taught me those tenets. This dilemma was never covered in the Junior Girl Scout Handbook.

> *"Day is done, gone the sun, from the lakes,*
> *from the hills, from the sky..."*
> (from "Taps")

After leaving camp administration in 1989 to work full time in higher education, I found myself missing my Girl Scout family. I contacted a Rhode Island council, and we decided that I should be an adult volunteer with older-girl programming. In my time as a volunteer, no one asked my sexual orientation, and it never came up in my work with adults or girls. Anxious to return to a resident camp setting, I jumped at the opportunity to work as the Counselor-In-Training (CIT) director in the summer of 1991. We had a successful program, the council leadership reviewed my work positively, and I looked forward to being involved the following summer. During the following fall and winter, I continued as a volunteer with older-girl programs. I was getting to know other volunteers in my new council and enjoyed my interactions with them. I felt at home again.

In December 1991, I met with the council's executive director and assistant executive director about a pending opening in the outdoor program staff at the council. I mentioned that my mother was a Girl Scout executive director and asked if either of them knew her. They did not, but they had known the executive director in Connecticut who was my mom's mentor. The conversation was casual, and the executive director asked me about my home life. I responded that I had a partner. She asked if this was "a gentleman." I said no, it was a woman. Since this executive director and her assistant shared a house, I wasn't surprised that they did not appear shocked by my choice of partner. In fact, I thought it was clear at this point that I had come out. We met again in January and discussed my leadership of the CIT program for the following summer. We agreed on dates for the program, I scheduled my vacation to coincide with it, and the council began to advertise for participants. It was clear that we had an agreement that I would work for the council as the 1992 CIT director. I expected that, as the year before, I would sign my summer employment contract in the spring.

In March 1992, an article appeared in the *Providence Journal-Bulletin* about lesbians and gay men on college campuses. Since I had been appointed the Liaison for Lesbian/Gay/Bisexual Concerns at Brown University, I agreed to be interviewed for the article. I was quoted near the end of the piece about being one of the first out-lesbian administrators on campus and about being a role model for students and colleagues. I stressed the importance of living openly, honestly, and with self-respect. I did not mention my work with the Girl Scouts or other community organizations.

We were having a busy spring on campus and I was new to my job. I was somewhat relieved when a late-March Girl Scout program I was supposed to lead was canceled "due to lack of interest." But by early May, the school year was beginning to settle down, and having not yet signed my summer contract with the Girl Scout council, I called the office. After a long wait on hold, I was informed by a staff member that I would not be working as the CIT director. I asked why that was. She responded that she thought I knew why. I said that I didn't know. We went back and forth a number of times, she said she couldn't tell me, and I hung up the phone in tears. Beginning to suspect what I later learned was the truth, I was devastated, confused, and angry.

I spoke to a friend who worked at the council and she told me the whole story. Another staff member brought in the newspaper article, the executive director called a meeting, and a handful of staff discussed my situation. They are said to have talked about what kind of role model this made me, whether I was obeying the Girl Scout Promise, and even whether they could figure out if I treated my partner according to the Girl Scout Law! To their credit, not everyone involved in the meetings opposed my continuing to serve the council, but even these allies complied with the executive director's swift decision to terminate my involvement. They had immediately cancelled the day-long program I was supposed to run in March, not because of lack of interest, as they told me, but because of the decision to curtail my activities with the council. They never asked me about the article or about my sexual orientation. They never even bothered to tell me about their decision to keep me out of council activities. They waited for me to call them.

At great risk to her own job with the council, my friend spoke with me off and on through the spring and summer about the on-going scramble to replace me as CIT director. Even though it was fully subscribed by aspiring camp counselors, the council considered canceling the program. They would apparently have rather turned away young women from a Girl Scout program than have a *lesbian* in charge.

I spoke with an attorney who does civil rights work. She contacted the council. They denied that my sexual orientation was involved in their decision not to continue my involvement, claiming instead that because they hadn't heard from me sooner, they figured I wasn't interested. They would not release any statement about their policy/guidelines dealing with sexual orientation of volunteers or employed staff. I knew through my mother that some councils had adopted nondiscrimination clauses including sexual orientation and that Girl Scouts U.S.A. advocated the *don't ask, don't tell* position, but the Rhode Island Girl Scouts would not divulge any information. Because there were no state or local laws prohibiting discrimination based on sexual orientation, I had no legal recourse, no place to take my case for a fair hearing. My attorney and I eventually decided to drop the issue so that I could get on with my life.

"On my honor I will try,
There's a duty to be done and I say I,
There's a reason here for a reason above,
My honor is to try and my duty is love."
(chorus of "On My Honor"[1])

At the time of this event, lesbian and gay activists in Rhode Island had been trying for eight years to get state lawmakers to pass civil rights legislation. A colleague at Brown was very involved in the Rhode Island Alliance for Lesbian and Gay Rights (The Alliance), and he knew my story with the Girl Scouts. When the bill came up in legislative committee the following spring, Jim asked if I would testify. He said that one of the biggest obstacles facing the bill was that a number of legislators did not believe that discrimination was actually taking place. Of course, in a state with no civil rights protection—and in a small state, where many people who are born here stay for their entire lives—victims of discrimination were understandably hard to persuade to testify publicly. Furthermore, organizations like the Rhode Island Girl Scouts had testified against the bill in the past, claiming that they should not be required to hire people who violated their sense of values. The Alliance, Jim said, needed me to testify.

It had been a hard year for me since learning of the Girl Scouts' decision. I had struggled to recover from the rejection and loss their decision meant for me. I felt ambivalent about taking my story public. I was angry at the Rhode Island council, but the Girl Scout family was still my own. I did not want to expose the Girl Scouts to that kind of publicity or public controversy. I still hoped for an amicable resolution. Also, there was my mother to consider. She had at this point achieved her professional goal of becoming the executive director of a major council. She was relatively new to her job and, though we had different last names, I was afraid that my making waves could affect her negatively, but when we discussed the issue, we decided that I should do what the Girl Scouts had always taught me to do—to act with honor and honesty, to tell the truth when the truth badly needed to be heard.

In the spring of 1993, I testified before the Rhode Island House and Senate committees considering the bill. Reading from my carefully and painfully written testimony, I told my story of discrimination, but I decided not to reveal the name of the agency that had discriminated. There were few others who could testify to actual discrimination, and the bill was defeated. In 1994, with my mother in the hearing room to watch her daughter acting on our shared principles, I returned to tell my story again. It was the same story, plainly spoken, with a little more distance from the event, but the same result: the bill was defeated.

When Jim approached me in the spring of 1995, I told him that the legislators must be weary of hearing my tired old story by now, and since it hadn't seemed to influence anyone anyway, I wondered whether it was still important for me to go. He gave me the good news that the bill was being sent through a different, and allegedly friendly, committee, that the (Republican) governor had promised to sign it into law if both houses passed the bill, and though he was quite guarded, he was optimistic. I agreed to testify again. An illness kept me from the House of Representative's Special Legislation Committee hearings, but even without my story, the bill passed. There was talk of adding an amendment that would exempt youth service agencies from the prohibition against discrimination, but the amendment failed. In discussions, this youth service exemption came to be called the "Boy Scout Amendment," since it was the Boy Scouts who were most vocal in their support for the amendment. Shortly after the bill passed in committee, it passed on the full floor, unamended. We were halfway there.

"Learning our motto, living our creed..."
(from "Girl Scouts Together")

On Monday morning, May 15, 1995, Jim asked if I would testify that afternoon at the Senate Special Legislation Committee hearing on the civil rights bill. I cleared my schedule and dusted off my testimony. When I arrived at the State House, the hearing was already underway. The hearing room was packed to capacity and the overflow crowd was watching the hearing on closed-circuit television in the hallway. I put my name on the list to testify; I was about number 100 on the list.

To the credit of the committee chair and the legislators, they made a commitment that everyone who had come to testify would be heard. A two-minute limit was set for testimony, and the chair kept everyone to that time. She took witnesses in order, alternating between supporters and opposition. Witnesses on either side quoted the Bible, attested to the moral indecency of passing or not passing the bill, claimed the history of Rhode Island as a state founded for religious and personal freedom, and spoke of the effect that passage or defeat of the bill would have on them and their family. Lesbian and gay youth spoke about their alienation and isolation. Rhode Island's Teacher of the Year came out publicly during the hearing. But few witnesses could tell of being personally discriminated against because of their sexual orientation.

As I stood in the hallway, surrounded by men and women I had come to recognize from these annual hearing rituals and from events around Rhode Island, I listened to a representative of the Boy Scouts of America speak in favor of a youth services exemption. To my utter amazement, a response to him included quotations from the Girl Scouts that they, in fact, did not discriminate on the basis of sexual orientation and that the local council did not seek or support passage of the Boy Scout Amendment. I was shocked. Was this the same council that had treated me so badly? The executive director had changed since my incident had occurred, but this seemed too great a reversal to attribute to one personnel change. Hoping to underscore the importance of *not* exempting youth service agencies, I had planned finally to name the Girl Scouts in my testimony but changed my mind before testifying because it would be counter-productive to do so after the Girl Scouts had been held up as an example of an agency that did not condone discrimination.

Testimony began in the late afternoon and continued into the evening. By 11:30 p.m. the opposition witnesses had all spoken, and only we supporters of the bill were left to testify. Everyone was exhausted. The room was hot and still. I was hungry, I had a headache, and I was missing the last night of my sister's visit to New England. I was cranky. I considered just going home. Guessing that the committee was in about the same mood I was, I decided not to read my prepared statement and wrote an abbreviated version while I waited my turn to speak. At 11:45 my name was called. I moved to the stand and this is what I said:

> I'm here tonight because I lost my job with a youth service agency on the basis of their perception of my sexual orientation.

The details are contained in the written testimony you will be getting. The basics of my case are:

1) I had worked with the agency for a number of years and they thought I was a good volunteer—they had told me so.

2) my name was in the *Providence Journal* in association with an article about gay and lesbian students, of which I was not one.

3) they terminated my employment.

This happened in 1992. It was devastating, painful, awful. The worst part was that I had nowhere to take my case for a fair hearing.

In the three years since, I've gotten on with my life, worked on the grief and pain and anger. I'm doing okay now—I have a job at a school that has chosen to include sexual orientation in its nondiscrimination clause. But what still hurts and makes me angry and keeps me up some nights is the fact that I never got a chance to argue my case, to present my side, to seek a just resolution.

Please pass this bill as received, and send it to the floor unamended. Create a mechanism for justice to be served.

I left the hearing satisfied that I had done my best. I had been honorable and fair, and above all, honest. The values, skills, and leadership opportunities I gained through my years in the Girl Scout family are what compelled me to go to the State House and tell my story. The love, care, and support of my friends and family made it possible for me to act on my values.

On Wednesday, May 17, the committee voted. They passed the bill, unamended. We were one step closer, but there had been other years when we had been this close and still lost the final vote. The Alliance had decided that if the Boy Scout Amendment was attached on the Senate floor, they would ask the bill's sponsor to withdraw the motion. They would rather not have the bill pass if it reified the notion that lesbians and gay men should not be allowed to work with children. I agreed.

On Friday, May 19, the bill came to the Senate floor. I decided not to be present for the full vote, but I made sure that someone would call me when the vote had taken place. There was much debate about the Boy Scout Amendment. Rhetoric on both sides was passionate, with at least one senator saying that the Boy Scout organization he remembered from his youth would not have embraced discrimination. In the end, the amendment failed and the civil rights bill passed.

"All is well, safely rest . . ."
(from "Taps")

The following Monday was the bill-signing ceremony. Though the ceremony was open to the public anyway, the Alliance asked Jim to specially invite me to attend. I was surprised because I always felt a little guilty that all I'd ever done in support of the Alliance's efforts to pass the bill was to trundle down to the State House every spring and read my testimony. Jim explained that my involvement had been important to the Alliance, and he told me that my name had even been mentioned on the Senate floor during the debate about the bill. One senator had said that though he hadn't believed that this kind of discrimination had been happening in Rhode Island, he'd left the committee hearing with the stories of real people—and here he said my name and another—who had experienced real discrimination. When Jim relayed this story to me, a sense of release went through me, and a weight

Kristen Renn

I hadn't known I was carrying lifted. I had been heard, and I had been believed.

I do not believe that everything happens for a reason. I do not believe that every cloud has a silver lining. And I do not believe that I was made to go through tremendous rejection and pain and loss because someday I would make a difference to one senator in Rhode Island. I do believe in turning struggles into "positive learning experiences," and I do believe that living with honor, honesty, and fairness is the right way to live. I believe that the women who raised me, those at home and in my troop and especially at summer camps, live the Promise and the Law. They instilled these values in me, and these values are the source of the integrity with which I live.

I have also finally come to believe that it was not the Girl Scout family that rejected me. It was a few small-minded individuals within the family. I am sad and angry that they were able so effectively to separate me from my home, but I am hopeful that the Girl Scout family I love—and whose voice I heard speak out against the "Boy Scout Amendment"—will nurture all girls and women, regardless of sexual orientation, but particularly its lesbian daughters, in an environment of honor, honesty, and fairness.

[1] *Cindy Dasch, "On My Honor," written in 1971, copyright 1981.*

PART IV

Acceptance
and
Integration

Acceptance and Integration

Lesbians in Girl Scouting have stayed hidden in deference to public prejudice as well as in compliance with organizational practice. They have hesitated to jeopardize not only their positions and effectiveness, but also Girl Scouting's accessibility to all girls, especially those from conservative families. Although an understandable attempt to keep the doors of Girl Scouting as wide open as possible, hiding reinforces homophobia. In addition, it deprives members of the community and of the organization—gay and straight—of opportunities to unlearn stereotypes and accept genuine diversity. The organization is already committed to ethnic diversity. It's time for the Girl Scouts to openly accept and integrate its lesbian members as well.

In Part IV, seven Girl Scouts describe various levels of acceptance by the organization. The section begins with an American and a Norwegian who were tacitly acknowledged as a committed couple at Our Chalet in Switzerland. It continues with three accounts of Girl Scouts more openly addressing the issue at a camp, in a troop, and in a council office.

This section concludes with essays by current professional Girl Scouts. Jill Kennedy, from a conservative part of the country, wonders if by not using a pseudonym, she is risking her career with the Girl Scouts. In contrast, Beth Toolan, "can't imagine" being in the closet. She treasures the opportunity to integrate her family life with her work life, a privilege most straight people take for granted. The successful acceptance by her Girl Scout council points to an era when anti-gay prejudice will be regarded not only as unwise and unfair, but as antithetical to fundamental American values: liberty and justice for all.

CHAPTER 27

* * *

High Up, High
on the Mountain

Roberta Garr and Maike Haaland

*An American and a Norwegian met while working at the
Girl Guide/Girl Scout World Center in the Swiss Alps. The
friendship they started there crossed national boundaries and
challenged social conventions, but the couple found a measure
of acceptance at Our Chalet.*

When the World Association of Girl Guides and Girl Scouts met in
1929, the idea of a world center was born, a place where Girl Guides and
Girl Scouts from all over the world could come together to forge friendships
and learn about each others' lives across national, social, and ethnic
boundaries. Helen Storrow, a Girl Scout from Boston, generously offered to
donate the center, on the condition that it be built in Switzerland.

In the summer of 1976, American Roberta Garr and Norwegian Maike
Haaland met at Our Chalet in Adelboden, Switzerland. The village of
Adelboden had grown since Falk, the first Guider-in-charge, showed Helen
Storrow the property in 1931. Hotels had sprouted up in all parts of the
valley, and the village street had gained many more shops. But the view over
the majestic Bernese Oberland mountains and the superb opportunities for
skiing and hiking remained the same.

Maike first went to the Chalet in 1969 as a sixteen-year-old Girl Scout.

197

Her visit was a dream come true. She loved the long hikes that left her exhausted but exhilarated; the fun of getting to know girls from the United States, Holland, South Africa, Germany, Brazil, and Switzerland; the beauty of the mountain slopes covered in alpine flowers and dotted with tall pine trees; and the evenings in the big room filled with girls and women singing together. In 1976, she returned for ten days as a leader for a troop of fourteen Norwegian Girl Scouts and met Roberta, who was working as a volunteer.

Roberta first visited the Chalet in September 1975 for a nine-day session. She had been working as a volunteer at Olave House, the Girl Guide/Girl Scout world center in London and extended her time in Europe, taking a boat across the English Channel to France and a train to Switzerland. Roberta's journey to Our Chalet, like Maike's, was a dream come true. As a Cadette Scout, she had seen slides of the Chalet and had hoped that, one day, she would get there.

When she arrived, Roberta was awestruck by the grandeur of the mountains and the rugged steepness of the paths. During her first hike to a towering mountain peak, with aching legs and gasping breath, she wondered why on earth she was putting herself through such torture. The exhilaration she felt at the top, however, as she scanned the incredible shapes and sizes of the surrounding mountains, inspired her to hike again the following day. By the end of her stay, her legs and lungs had become strong, and she was not ready to leave those mountains behind forever. She asked Inge Lyck, the Guider-in-charge, if there was any chance she could work the following summer. It turned out that there was a very good chance, and she returned in June 1976 as a volunteer.

During that summer of 1976, Roberta immersed herself in outdoor activities and the magic of being part of an international community. Impressed that women alone were capable of managing all aspects of running the Chalet, she developed a growing respect for the abilities of her gender. She found it exciting to meet women from all over the world. Every ten days, the faces changed and, although by the end of her five-month stint, many were forgotten, she did not forget Maike. The ease and excitement of their conversations left a lasting impression. She was happy to hear that Maike had applied to work the following summer as Roberta was also returning to work for another five months.

Meanwhile, Maike thought Roberta was unlike any other American she

Our Chalet, 1980

had met. She was strong and somehow unsettling, very unconventional with her patched clothing and funny red felt hat. She seemed like a person who could do whatever she put her mind to.

They got to know each other more closely during the summer of 1977. They led hikes in the mountains, organized evening programs with the guests, and helped maintain and clean the buildings. They showed visitors around the house, pointing out the bedrooms' different themes and decorations. They told the story of the *Baby Chalet*, perched on a grassy hillside, which Helen Storrow had built for herself. The miniature chalet was so small that the bathtub was hoisted to the second floor before the walls were built.

Maike shared a room with three other helpers in "Squirrel House," a separate house with staff quarters on the second floor. Roberta lived in "Egypt," one of the single rooms in the main building.

They had fun together that summer with the guests as well as the staff. The long hikes were challenging, and yet the choices were simple. Would they hike to Schwandfeld or Bonderspitz? What was the physical condition of the guests? How was the weather? In the evenings, they would watch the sun paint the snow-peaked mountains pink and then gather inside to sing. They sang about working toward a better world, about love and friendship: "Sing for joy, sing for love, sing for peace, sing for happiness, sing as you journey along"; "Love of my life I am crying, I am not dying, I am dancing,

dancing along in the madness, there is no sadness, only a song of the soul"; and "This is people loving people in a very special way. . . ."

They sometimes wondered if Helen Storrow had planned for this simple life to be so seductive and had known how close women could get while living together in this way. She must have known about women loving women, but did she know about loving the way that they did? Sometimes Maike would find herself pausing on the path at the sight of Roberta's strong calf muscle, covered with soft hair. Or, while contemplating the gentle curve of Roberta's breast, she would miss the volleyball completely. Roberta, in turn, would feel her heart race and her laughter come easily when Maike sat down to talk with her.

But girlfriends were supposed to be different than boyfriends; there was no sex involved. Maike started questioning this logic as she felt small waves of desire roll over her when they walked at night holding hands. The whole subject seemed taboo. Could this be what the assistant Guider-in-charge had meant when she and Maike were waltzing together one night:

"If we were dancing like this in Norway, people would talk."

Maike had nodded, but did not really want to think about what those words meant. It seemed as if knowing more would interrupt the wonderful time she was having.

Roberta had also been warned against "special friendships."

"It just isn't a good thing," the staff person said. "It will cause problems." She went on to share how she once had a special friendship that led to hurt and complications. "So you shouldn't spend a lot of time exclusively with Maike."

Roberta and Maike did not think that they were exclusive; they often invited others to join them. But being alone together was special, and they cherished those moments. To create this time, they stayed up later and later at the kitchen table. They talked until two or three in the morning, sharing everything in their lives, giggling and staring at each other. They never, however, talked about what was happening between them.

Maike finished her working stint first that summer and left for Norway. Roberta joined her six weeks later. They continued their long, intense conversations. They also went to the swimming pool and sauna, washed each other's hair, walked in the snow, and exchanged back rubs. Maike's breath would catch when Roberta sat close to her, and one day she wrote in her journal, "Maybe I am a lesbian?" She never said anything to Roberta. Her feelings still seemed too far beyond the international friendship that Girl Scouting promoted.

They left Norway together in December, perhaps remaining together because they could not speak of the pain of parting. The traveled to Spain, and there, they let the sparks between them light a strong and passionate fire. They were in love, in lust and finally, ready to act. They let passion be their guide.

A week later, they were traveling through Switzerland and, of course, they stopped at the Chalet. The staff members were preparing for the winter guests and were happy when Roberta and Maike volunteered to help for a few days. They were put up in the attic of the big house, a place usually filled with the noise and bustle of thirty girls. They lay on mattresses on newly polished pine boards, inhaling the fragrant scent of soft soap and wax, the breathtaking mountains silhouetted through the windows.

They started to talk about what was happening between them and to be more playful in their lovemaking. They pretended that they were other Girl Scouts making love and collapsed in laughter at the thought. They invented advertisements for the Chalet, complete with jingles and one-act skits, such as "Girl Scouts Coming Out at The Chalet" or "Feast on Friendship at the Chalet."

They sometimes pretended that Helen Storrow were in the house and wished they could have asked what she thought of the turn their international friendship had taken. Their togetherness seemed like the most natural and simple thing in the world, and they felt that their love was blessed by all the women who had traveled through the Chalet.

After a few days, they had to part company, each leaving behind not only the other, but also the magical world of the Chalet. Maike went home to Norway and Roberta returned to the U.S. It was hard to pick up life where they had left it. They were not the same any more, and they missed each other and the simple life of the Chalet immensely. Not knowing if and when they would ever meet again, they wrote long letters every other day.

A year and a half later, in 1979, Roberta accepted a full-time position at Our Chalet. She and Maike were both excited and a little nervous about continuing their relationship on the same continent. They had started on a new path in Spain and wondered if they could continue on this path at the

Chalet. Could they explore the meaning of the love they felt and the multitude of ways of expressing this love? Would their joy, pleasure, and happiness with each other spill over and nourish the Girl Guide/Girl Scout community?

During the next few years, they were able to spend several months together each year. Maike, in school at the time, continued her volunteer work at the Chalet, and they took their vacations together. Although they didn't get encouragement for their relationship, no one at the Chalet did anything to stop it. No one said anything about the times they disappeared into the shower for hours or the long mornings they spent together in Roberta's room on their days off. They usually slept in Roberta's narrow single bed. No one barged in to wake them up in the mornings or questioned Maike's absence from her bed in her room.

After the World Conference in 1980 in France, the Chalet had an unusually large number of guests. At the breakfast table one morning, a staff person suggested that Maike's bed could be used for a guest. "She never sleeps in it anyway!" This was the closest to a public statement recognizing their relationship, and it left Roberta and Maike breathless and silent.

They had some inkling that other "special friendships" had existed within the Chalet's walls. They combed through their experiences, looking for clues that would give them role models or at least confirm the existence of love between women. They had noticed sparkling, meaningful looks exchanged by other women and heard unspoken words of connection. There was little talk of husbands and boyfriends, and it was as if everyone was happy to be in an all-female atmosphere.

Roberta and Maike were good at following the rules, both the spoken and unspoken. They were never physically affectionate in public—well, almost never. On one hike up Albristhorn with a group of volunteers, they ended up at the rear and, as the path wound in and out along the mountainside, managed to sneak little kisses when the others were out of sight. They made love very quietly. They spent time with others and made sure there was nothing exclusive about their behavior.

One summer, a Girl Scout from Boston joined the staff. The three women were cleaning bathrooms when Nan ran to her room for some music to inspire their work. Soon, Meg Christian was singing "Ode to a Gym Teacher." As soon as she found some time alone with Nan, Maike eagerly brought up the subject of lesbianism and her relationship with Roberta. She finally could talk openly with another lesbian Girl Scout. Nan brought with her an unfamiliar piece of the outside world, the budding lesbian cultural scene, and an affirmation of their love.

Maike found it difficult to be silent about their relationship. Not liking secrets, she spoke with the other Scandinavian volunteer helpers and any others who she felt could handle the information. Roberta didn't feel the same need, but she did share her thoughts and feelings with a couple of lesbian guests.

In general, feminism and lesbianism were taboo topics at the Chalet. Despite this, Roberta and Maike loved the Chalet. They were happy there was a place they could be together, working, living, having fun, and feeling some degree of acceptance.

The Chalet supported them after they left. When they had to supply proof that their relationship had lasted at least three years in order for Roberta to obtain a residence visa in Norway, Chalet committee members wrote a letter attesting to the fact that "even though Roberta and Maike remained discreet about their relationship, there was no doubt that they were a couple,

Roberta Garr (l) and Maike Haaland (r), 1996

and we are not surprised that they want to establish a common household." The two women were happy there was a legal way for them to be together in Norway since no such possibility existed in the United States.

Thanks to the Chalet, Roberta and Maike developed an international network of lesbian Girl Guide/Girl Scout friends. They even have thought of starting an organization: LEGGGS, Lesbian Girl Guides and Girl Scouts. They have visited two of the other three Girl Guide/Girl Scout world centers: Sangam in Poona, India, and Pax Lodge (formerly Olave House) in London, England. They haven't yet made it to Our Cabaña in Cuernavaca, Mexico.

The Chalet has a special place in their hearts because the friendship they started there not only crossed national and ethnic boundaries; it also crossed boundaries of convention and expectations from both their cultural backgrounds. They wonder if their presence at the Chalet has made any difference to other lesbians. Has their energy been left behind in the air, the walls, and the showers? Have they become part of the unspoken message that lets women know they can love other women within the Chalet's walls and Switzerland's mountains?

They hope so.

✳ ✳ ✳

CHAPTER 28

Rocky Mountain High

Rosemary Le Page

At one Girl Scout camp, sexual orientation was not a taboo topic. In fact, thanks to a perceptive administration team, the issue was addressed openly during the initial training session, setting the tone for an exhilarating summer.

Girl Scout Camp Star Ridge sat at ten thousand feet above sea level in the Colorado Rocky Mountains. There was an ideal lake for sailing. A 1937 Conservation Corps log lodge had two majestic fireplaces, one at each end of the fifty-foot long main room. Girls practiced rock climbing on the stone chimneys, and hours of wonderful singing filled the high rafters. The aspen woods, lake, and meadows created an outdoor wonderland where campers learned about flora and fauna, outdoor survival, and skills for community living. It was a magical place that inspired some of the best Girl Scout camp programs I have ever experienced.

In 1974, I was on the summer camp administrative team for Camp Star Ridge. It was the age of personal growth and self-awareness. Werner Erhardt was teaching people to confront their personal demons, and *Time* magazine had declared, "God is Dead." The feminist movement had begun, the impact of the gay rights uprising at Stonewall was spreading across the country, and standard American values were being challenged. In a time when we grown-ups hardly knew what to believe, how could we know what values to model for children? At Star Ridge, we turned to reliable standards such as kindness, respect for the environment, self-worth, and self-sufficiency. We sang John Denver songs with all the enthusiasm of "Rocky Mountain High!" We believed in platonic love and innocently accepted the admonition to "love the one you're with."

We wanted to provide campers with a highly professional and well-conceived program of arts and outdoor education. We wanted wonderful music, fairy tale magic, and personal challenges. The administrative team consisted of a professional Girl Scout, an artist, and me, a psychologist. We were all lesbian. We had a great camp site, good equipment, and support from the organization. We hired twenty people with the talents and skills needed to run the place, and while they were mostly women (some lesbian) there were also a few men.

The administrative team knew from experience that falling in love is to be expected in high mountain meadows on moonlit summer nights. We did not want our staff to be unprepared for that powerful emotion. So we discussed this matter in the precamp training. We asked the staff to anticipate falling in love and to talk about what that experience might mean in the context of their work performance. This may not have been an unusual topic for the heterosexual members of the staff, but it was an amazing conversation for all of us who had never talked openly about same-sex love.

The majority of our staff were young adults who were just beginning to understand sex. Advice on how to respond to physical attractions would normally have been relegated to private late night talks with a best friend. It was still socially taboo or at least impolite to discuss sex openly. Our message to the staff was direct and clear: We would not diminish the children's experience of camp because of staff being distracted by personal problems or by the impact of being newly in love with each other. We challenged them to design some rules for themselves that would meet our requirement.

The work sessions on this topic caused intense emotional responses. Just finding the courage to offer ideas and express feelings was enormously difficult. Some staff members offered what they had learned in their religious education. Others proposed a call to a higher purpose—serving the campers. Some of the staff were allowing themselves to consciously confront their sexuality for

Rosemary Le Page, 1973

the first time. Such personal struggles are normal for young adults. What was different at Camp Star Ridge were the open sharing of the experience in a work context and designing rules of behavior to which we would hold each other accountable. Usually sexual issues were left unclear and staff members were assumed to have the same standard.

I discovered that others had the same fears and concerns about homosexuality as I had. Are you born gay or do you become gay? Is homosexuality normal? What if you are attracted to both men and women? What did God intend? What does the Bible really say? What do you do with your feelings if you do fall in love with a woman? The negative images of homosexuality did not match with the character and personality of any lesbian staff member, and that fact contributed to the confusion about being gay.

Amazingly, our work sessions became part of the solution to the anticipated dilemmas. We fell in love with Camp Star Ridge itself. We became a strong community through our precamp work on values, standards, and program planning. Our affection for one another became such a source of emotional support that it diminished the risk of inappropriate behavior arising from emotional neediness. Anyone with a problem knew how to get immediate support. This freed the staff from over-attention to personal issues and allowed them to focus on the program activities and the well-being of the campers. We made some specific agreements about social conduct. We agreed that we would take regular assigned personal time off to prevent burnout. We agreed that any intimate relationships were not community business and that the administration would support couples who wanted the same day off so that they could be together away from camp and prevent their relationship from becoming a focus of camper attention.

Almost all of our campers came from very conservative, religious, even fundamentalist homes. Given the staff's progressive philosophy, our greatest fear was of damaging the reputation of Camp Star Ridge and the local Girl Scout council. We knew that we were working for a community that would react negatively if they knew that all three camp administrators and some of the staff were lesbians. However, during that whole magical summer, the only complaints involved a couple of "California" staff who did not shave their legs or wear bras!

The Rocky Mountain High that summer of 1974 emerged from an absence of oppression and from the celebration of our diversity. We were lesbians, bisexuals, and heterosexuals together in close heartfelt relationships. The possibility of trusting ourselves and rejecting the overwhelming negative judgments of the greater society was the reality we would ultimately choose for life.

In 1980, Girl Scouts of the U.S.A. took a stand in its personnel policies: the organization would not involve itself in what it viewed as a personal matter, including sexual orientation. Rather, it would focus its policies on standards of conduct. That was a bold stand, but not a risky one. National and local professional Girl Scout staff knew from experience that lesbians are not a threat to the organization. In each Girl Scout office around the country, there are dedicated lesbian staff—moral, psychologically normal, good people. Professional scouts know that the myths and stereotypes about lesbians are just that—myths and stereotypes.

Employing lesbians would not be a concern to the Girl Scouts if it were not for people who hold distorted views that cast a negative image on any organization that does not condemn homosexuality. This is a threat to any nonprofit that relies on a positive public image to gain funding. So Girl Scout councils around the country stay very quiet about their lesbian employees, and most of the lesbian employees stay closeted in order to protect the organization. At present, with so much ignorance and intolerance, I think it is wise for the Girl Scouts of the U.S.A. to remain silent on this issue. Speaking out about homosexuality would mean stepping into the arena of sexual politics and would take away energy and resources from what the Girl Scouts quietly and steadily do best—help girls grow into healthy, responsible adults. I am proud of the focus on standards of behavior rather than on sexual orientation. I view the Girl Scout organization as acting on a higher principle of tolerance and respect.

Rosemary Le Page

CHAPTER 29

"It Was the Girl Scouts!"

Janet de Vries

Although she has witnessed homophobic incidents, Janet de Vries' adult experiences with Girl Scouting have been mostly positive. Janet and her partner Leanne co-lead Cadette and Senior troops in Wyoming, and Janet has been a Girl Scout Council board member and vice president.

I was twenty-two years old when I came out to my mother. It was a rainy spring Saturday night in the Midwest. Dad had gone to bed early. Mom was working in the kitchen. I was in the living room trying to muster the courage to talk to her. Finally I walked into kitchen and told her.

"It was the Girl Scouts!" she exclaimed

"No, Mom," I replied, "the Girl Scouts did not cause me to become a lesbian."

My active participation in the Girl Scouts for more than twenty-five years, however, has given me something equally important: high moral standards, a strong work ethic, leadership ability, and concern for others. My longest and strongest friendships, with both straight women and lesbians, are with former and current Girl Scouts. When I meet new women who were long-time Girl Scouts, there is an instant bond. All of my lovers, including Leanne, my partner of fifteen years, have been Girl Scouts. (Leanne and I are both

Life Members.)

I've been in scouting since I joined the Brownies in third grade. My mother (ironically, in light of her later suspicions about the cause of my sexual orientation), was a co-leader of my troop for many years. I attended resident camp every summer and started working in the camp kitchen as soon as I was old enough. In 1972, I camped at Girl Scout National Center West in Ten Sleep, Wyoming, the only scout camp operated by the national organization. My council had selected thirty-five Cadette and Senior Scouts for this three-week adventure. This trip profoundly shaped my adult life in that it influenced where I would live, what I would study in college, and my career as a geologist.

My earliest recollection of Girl Scout homophobia was in ninth grade. The mother of one of my friends said she should not associate with four of our older Girl Scout friends because they were lesbians. Her father believed that he could tell from their hats! Five years later I learned that two were lesbians, one was bisexual, and the other was straight.

In 1974, when I was seventeen, I worked in the kitchen of my council's resident camp. The new camp director instigated a witch-hunt to rid the camp of lesbian staff. Two longtime, well-loved counselors resigned without admitting their sexual orientation. I did not understand why the director wanted to fire these women. I only knew we were losing dedicated and respected camp counselors. Ironically, nineteen years later, one of those women was hired as the director of that same camp.

During my first year of college, I was active in Campus Scouts and served as a council board member. When I met Claire, another Campus Scout, we developed a close friendship which gradually became romantic and physical. Since neither of us had any previous sexual relationship, we didn't know what to do and spent most of our passion just kissing. Once when I asked Claire if she thought we were lesbians, she cried, and we never discussed it again. But for me, a light bulb had been turned on—I knew I was a lesbian. At the end of the school year, we got jobs at different Girl Scout camps, and our relationship ended.

I returned to Girl Scout National Center West during the summer of 1976 as the first female handiperson. Although sexual orientation was not discussed openly, I became aware of other lesbians at camp who seemed confident and proud of themselves. I realized I was not the only one. I became involved with another staff member and discovered more about sex in one

Janet de Vries, 1966

summer than I had learned in a year of kissing.

Unfortunately, a friend from my home council discovered my relationship. She avoided me for a day, then asked what I would tell people at home. Fearing I was the only lesbian in my Midwestern hometown of 275,000 people, I said I wasn't going to tell anyone. She agreed this was best, but when I arrived home a week after she had, I discovered that she had told our mutual Girl Scout friends. As it turned out, most of those friends were lesbians. Several others realized they were lesbians as well within the next few years—including the one who couldn't keep my secret.

I met my life partner, Leanne, at a Girl Scout camp in Michigan in 1977. Two years later, when our relationship developed, our Girl Scout background was a binding force, providing a common foundation in friendship, volunteerism, honesty, communication, and commitment.

Because of my good experiences at National Center West, I decided when I graduated from college to move from the Midwest to the Rocky Mountains. Leanne and I have been active in our local Girl Scout council as Cadette and Senior co-leaders for five years, and we have served on many committees. Also, I have been a council board member and first vice president. We do not normally mention our sexual orientation, and no one asks.

I did confide in one of my co-leaders, by letter, on the day she was moving out of state. I hadn't shared this significant part of my life before, fearing she would reject me and the council would expel me. I was wrong. She responded with great openness and considered it an honor that I had shared this important part of my life with her.

In 1991 Leanne and I accompanied our Senior troop to California during spring break. We learned later that the girls had discussed our sexual orientation during the trip. One girl apparently called home upset, but wouldn't say why. Her mother guessed the problem and said something like, "Oh, you finally figured out about Janet and Leanne." Other parents were aware of our sexual orientation before the trip, but no one mentioned it to us.

Janet de Vries

Some of the parents had discussed it with their daughters, we learned from one of our former troop members who came out to us in 1995.

Recently, my mother told me that she thinks sexual orientation is genetic and there is nothing wrong with me. She's probably forgotten her original theory that, "It was the Girl Scouts!"

✳ ✳ ✳

Editor's note:

When Janet's piece was accepted for publication, she came out to her Girl Scout executive director and to her council president. The director said she had known for years, having heard about the California trip. "I figured if girls were old enough to travel to California, they were old enough to discuss sexual orientation." (Janet says that actually she and Leanne never discussed this subject with their troop.)

The council president said, "We have more important issues to worry about. In fact, I wish you lived in our town so you could be my daughter's leader."

Janet says she was amused to discover that the executive director and president were relieved that she wanted to talk with them about being gay, not to complain about a recent board decision.

CHAPTER 30

Getting Real:
Girl Scout Policies in the
Age of Diversity

An Interview with Dawn Ace

Dawn Ace is the mother of two children whom she is raising with her partner, Phoebe Rosebear. She worked professionally with the Girl Scouts for eight years and found the organization very accepting of her as a lesbian. She is a graduate of the University of Wisconsin Law School and practices law in Madison, Wisconsin.

"**I** admire the Girl Scouts' policy of not firing people on the basis of their sexual orientation as the Boy Scouts are reported to do," says thirty-seven-year old Dawn Ace. Her telephone voice is clear and warm.

"Some Girl Scout councils' personnel policies, which cover areas like family leave for funerals or the birth of a child, are very forward-looking, applying to employees' partners as well as their spouses. I don't believe the Girl Scouts would ever openly use sexual orientation as a reason to fire anyone although there are probably a few homophobic executive directors out there who would find another excuse."

"Was your sexual orientation ever an issue when you were employed by the Girl Scouts?" I ask.

"I didn't have any problems with that," Dawn says. "It's not so much that I was OUT as that I refused to lie. When I had my first child, Nicholas, my partner would bring him to the Girl Scout council office, and I would talk with my coworkers about what Phoebe and I had done on the weekend. I didn't discuss being a lesbian and neither did anyone else. I was simply myself."

Not surprisingly, some people surmised the nature of their relationship. For example, after working with Girl Scout volunteers in Minnesota for six years, Dawn announced that she was leaving Minnesota and hoped to get a job with the Girl Scouts in San Francisco. One of her colleagues was surprised.

"Oh my gosh," she said, "what about Phoebe?"

"Phoebe's the reason I'm moving," Dawn replied. "She's going to graduate school in Berkeley."

"Oh, well, that's okay then," said the volunteer.

Dawn got a job with the San Francisco Bay Area Girl Scouts as a program training specialist. She helped establish Girl Scout programs in East Palo Alto and other areas of mostly immigrant and working-class families. People there worked two or three jobs, so it was almost impossible to find parents with the time to lead a troop. The Girl Scouts provided grants to hire adults to serve as leaders in these areas.

Dawn also helped to start Spanish-speaking troops in Half Moon Bay, south of Palo Alto, using the many materials published in Spanish by the National Girl Scout office. She applauds the organization for trying to provide programs for at-risk youth in areas like these.

Dawn noticed that lesbian Girl Scout professionals and volunteers in the Bay Area felt less pressure to hide or lie about their sexual orientation. The Girl Scout council there has published a booklet[1] to help troop leaders deal accurately and openly with sensitive issues like body image, menstruation, eating disorders, abstinence, and sexuality. If a leader is uncomfortable with or uninformed about a subject like sexual orientation, and parental approval has been obtained, she can seek help from community agencies or resource publications.

"How does the national Girl Scout office regard that booklet?" I asked.

"I don't know, but I wish something like that had existed when I was fifteen."

That's when Dawn realized she was a lesbian. "Luckily," she says, "I was able to talk to a favorite Girl Scout camp counselor. That woman went out on a limb for me. We corresponded for a year, and she gave me wonderful moral support. I am eternally grateful that I had someone to talk to. Most girls don't."

Dawn Ace, 1977

Dawn realizes now that the counselor could have been fired just for writing to a camper about sexual orientation. "However, nothing could have talked me into or out of my identity."

"Was the counselor a lesbian?"

"Eventually," Dawn says, "she acknowledged that she herself was gay. I am glad she took that risk. However, most of the time, self-disclosure is not necessary. It might be more appropriate to just let the girl talk about her concerns and give her guidance and support for making the best decisions. You also have to consider whether the kid can be trusted. Not every teenager—or adult—can be counted on to be discreet."

Dawn thinks that, much as the Girl Scouts might like to, they can't hide from sexual orientation. "Kids have so many questions. We do them a disservice if we say, 'I'm sorry, I can't discuss this; go home and talk to your mother and father.' Mothers and fathers are often the last people teenagers are comfortable confiding in. It's like telling a girl who's pregnant to talk to her parents instead of giving her support and referrals. This is not to say that girls should not talk to their parents, but sometimes it's just not realistic. I know one eighteen-year old who told her family she was a lesbian only to be beaten up by her brother and kicked out of the house by her mother. She had been afraid to tell them—afraid of their reactions. She was right!"

Dawn agrees with the Girl Scouts' policy of requiring appropriate behavior and language from adults, whether heterosexual or homosexual. One of Dawn's co-workers, a camp administrator, made that expectation explicit by announcing to her staff, "No sex. I don't care if you are married, if it's a man or a woman. There's not much privacy here at camp. So no sex, period."

"The point is," Dawn says, "what's appropriate? The Girl Scouts shouldn't encourage or discourage any particular sexual orientation but should be clear about appropriate behavior for everyone."

"Is there anything else the organization should do about the lesbian issue?" I ask.

"I believe the Girl Scouts should take a strong stand against any form of discrimination, including prejudice against lesbian staff and volunteers. If every lesbian vanished for a day, the organization wouldn't collapse, but the rest of the staff would certainly be surprised, not only about how many people had vanished, but also about who they were. The Girl Scouts are not unique in this respect—just about every workplace would have a similar experience."

Did she agree with the conjecture that thirty percent of professional Girl Scouts are lesbians?[2]

"That doesn't fit my experience as a professional Girl Scout. We are in Girl Scouting just as we are in all walks of life and probably in about the same numbers. I would hate to have that thirty percent idea become a popular rumor out in the general population. It would encourage anyone with a prejudicial bent to think that Girl Scouting is a breeding ground for lesbians. The religious right would have an alarmist fit over that idea, and funding sources could dry up. Parents, out of ignorance or bigotry, might also refuse to let their daughters belong. It would end up being a disservice to the organization and to the girls it serves."

Of course, Dawn notes, funding is already affected by discrimination. When she worked in Duluth, the United Way gave the local Boy Scouts far more money than it gave the local Girl Scouts. In Dawn's opinion, the United Way's justifications for this disparity just didn't hold up. "I have no idea how the United Way allocates funding now—I certainly hope they've eliminated the disparity."

As we concluded our telephone interview, Dawn, then eight months pregnant with their second child, stressed how good Girl Scouting is for kids.

"The extra self-esteem pays off during those difficult adolescent years when a girl's self-image takes such a battering, especially if, on top of everything else, she is dealing with a difficult issue like sexual orientation. With the suicide rate so high among gay and lesbian teenagers, and teens in general having so many complicated issues to face," Dawn concludes, "the Girl Scouts of the U.S.A. has a special opportunity and a special responsibility to offer young people adult guidance and role models. I'm not even talking about openly lesbian role models for young lesbians. I'm talking about role models who are kind, competent, self-confident individuals, regardless of orientation. The Girl Scouts need to let *all* girls know that here is one place where they are accepted as they are."

L to R, Annie Rosebear-Ace, Phoebe Rosebear,
Nicholas Rosebear-Ace, Dawn Ace, 1995

[1] *The San Francisco Bay Area Girl Scout Council's 1988 booklet*
Girls Are Great *is a forty-five page publication written for local
Girl Scout leaders. More thorough and frank than the GSUSA
booklet by the same name, it lists guidelines for helping girl
members cope with social pressures and sensitive issues. The two-
page section called "homosexuality" acknowledges that this "is*

often an uncomfortable subject because of religious and moral values." It stipulates that "Parental approval must be obtained before the issue is discussed." The booklet explains common myths and stereotypes about homosexuality, attempts to provide accurate information, and lists books like Young, Gay, and Proud, *which leaders can consult for more understanding of the subject. Girl Scouts of the USA's Girls Are Great twenty-page booklet, published in 1987 for Girl Scout leaders throughout the nation, contains no references to sexual orientation.*

[2] *See Jorjet Harper's article "Lesbian Girl Scouts: You Don't Bring Your Lover to a Troop Meeting," Chapter 21.*

CHAPTER 31

The Cookie Closet

Jill Kennedy

A professional Girl Scout wrestled with using her name in this book and explains why she finally decided to take that risk.

I've been working professionally for the Girl Scouts for two and a half years. I'm not out to anyone in this council. I'm still in the cookie closet. I hate it, I hate it, I hate it. Why haven't I come out? Like everyone else in here, whether they'll admit it or not, I've been afraid. At this point in my life (I'm twenty-six, this is my first real job), I think I want to be a part of the Girl Scouts for a long time, maybe even a lifelong career. I love Girl Scouting. We often hear, "The Girl Scouting movement is the largest voluntary organization for girls and women in the world." I'm idealistic enough to think that's neat. I love working in a nearly all-woman environment. The incredible amount of work and effort given for girls by the volunteers touches me. I have met a lot of really cool people (both adults and children). I LOVE Girl Scout camp. At resident camp especially I get a sense of success, community and belonging that I savor for the rest of the year. Most of my friends are people I have met at Girl Scout camp. I've grown up to be exactly what I always wanted to be. How many people get to do that fresh out of college?

I love Girl Scouting.

I hate the closet.

When I started this job I agonized over how I should come out. I am not an in-your-face kind of person; I have no desire to wear pink triangle shirts to work. But I don't want to dissemble either. I don't want to worry about mentioning my girlfriend's name too many times, or saying that I went to a women's music concert when asked how I spent the weekend, or being blindsided by someone outing me unexpectedly.

Because my job involves working with children, I felt I needed to establish some credibility before I began to be open. I decided to wait until my first written performance review. I asked myself if I was taking the coward's way out. After all, there are many people who've put a lot more than their jobs on the line to battle the dragons of homophobia. Still, as a young, lesbian dwarf with no reputation and no credibility, would I be fighting a dragon or tilting at a wind mill?

I decided it would be tilting at a wind mill, so I waited. Time goes by fast. I received my work reviews, and they were positive. I've established credibility and a reputation as a reliable, creative, honest, hard worker. Now it's time to see if I meant what I said, or if I was just stalling and rationalizing. That's where *On My Honor: Lesbians Reflect on Their Scouting Experience* came into the picture.

I talked with a friend, a very closeted school teacher, about contributing to the book. When I discussed using my real name, she made it politely clear that she thought I was nuts, that I was committing professional suicide (she can be a little dramatic). Still, she asked good questions.

What more would I be contributing by using my name as opposed to a pseudonym?

Unless I hide the fact that I am a dwarf, I might as well use my name. The Girl Scout organization is huge but there aren't that many Little People (about 1 in 10,000 births). I don't know of a single other professional Girl Scout who is a dwarf.

To come out in a public way is scary for everyone, because it is irreversible. If it causes more trouble than you're willing to put up with, you can't say "Never mind, I was just kidding." For anyone with a visible physical difference, this is even more true. It's a bit of a joke in the dwarf community that one of the neatest things about being a dwarf is that everyone remembers you, and one of the worst things is that everyone remembers you.

Why do I even have to specifically name my physical difference at all? I could simply say I'm different and leave it at that.

Yes I could, but I don't want to leave that out. I am neither proud of nor embarrassed by the fact that I was born a dwarf; it was the luck of the draw, the hand I was dealt from the genetic deck. I am, however, fiercely proud of how I have withstood the extra challenges of being a Little Person. I feel the same way about being lesbian. There is nothing special in being gay, but I am proud that I have not become resentful, self-pitying, or ashamed as some people do in the face of homophobia. I like being different. I like being a dwarf and a lesbian and wouldn't change either of those things. I love both of these rich cultures of which I get to be a part. Being different has provided some of the greatest joy and learning in my life.

My weight lifting coaches say that the reward for lifting more weight is—more weight. When you have withstood one tough challenge you are stronger and can withstand even more. (I could do without the challenge of finding business clothes and shoes in my size though. Finding clothes in youth large sizes NOT covered with the latest Disney characters is not one of my greatest sources of joy.)

Finally my pal said, "Putting aside all the altruistic (place your own profanity here), what's in it for you? Why is it important to write a piece for this book using your own name?"

As I worked on this project, whether or not any of what I wrote was accepted became secondary to whether or not to identify myself. I can't answer why that decision became so important without some of that "altruistic" stuff because I like to think that I live for more than just myself. I hope I help others along the way.

Another reason for signing my name has to do with my favorite Girl Scout Law: "On my honor: I will try to be honest." To me, dishonesty is more than just telling someone a bald-faced lie. It's doing anything that leads people to believe untruths, including leaving out facts for the purpose of deceiving. If I judge myself by my own standards, letting people believe that I'm straight is a form of dishonesty.

Something else related to dishonesty is the hypocrisy I feel because of being closeted. Girl Scouts at both the National and Council levels are committed to promoting diversity and acceptance. We spend a lot of time and money training troop leaders, producing materials, and doing programs to encourage inclusiveness. In promoting pluralism while hiding my sexual orientation in fear of rejection, am I not talking out of both corners of my mouth? Am I not demonstrating that the Girl Scout organization (which includes me) would not welcome in everyone?

While we're on the Girl Scout Laws, my second favorite one is "On my honor: I will try to be fair." All the heterosexuals get to safely let me know they are straight, but I don't get to safely let them know I'm not. That is not fair.

It's important to me to try to make things better. (This bears a sneaking resemblance to another Girl Scout Law, "On my honor: I will try to protect and improve the world around me.") Every time someone comes out, she makes it easier for others to do the same. I look at the relative ease with which I exist as a lesbian in today's world compared to what gay life was like twenty years ago, and I am amazed. I am grateful. We all contribute to perpetuating the old rules or making the new ones. I want to be a part of the "we" who changes the rules, eliminates the need to "come out," and allows young people to be who they are from the beginning.

Have you seen the latest edition of the Senior Girl Scout handbook? It's really neat. Very contemporary with good graphics. It's a wonderful resource for Senior Girl Scouts (tenth to twelfth graders). It is candid about a lot of sensitive issues that teenage girls face. It contains, for example, information on breast self-examinations (with illustrations), AIDS, and avoiding date rape.

But as I sat in my office and looked at this neat book with plain talk, I cried just a little. I didn't find any mention of lesbians or homosexuality. I was not surprised. Still, I mourned for all the young gay women who are of the age when they are grappling with their orientation. I was pained for all the young straight women who have friends, parents, or family members who are gay. Those girls, gay or straight, will get no guidance from this book. They could have.

I think coming out is a trial-by-fire, an acid test of Girl Scouts' tolerance. As much as I would miss Girl Scout camping and the whole organization if I were asked to leave, it's still not worth living in the closet.

Homophobia is a tower of bricks. Each person who comes out into the sun removes a brick. When enough of us remove ourselves from the tower, the structure of hate and ignorance will collapse.

I'm not sure this will happen in my life time. It may never happen within Girl Scouting. But even in the six years that I have been aware of the lesbian/ gay community, I see a change. Our subculture is coming closer to the surface. And it's not scaring anyone as badly as many thought it would.

I really like the last Girl Scout Law, "On my honor: I will try to show respect for myself and others through my words and actions." I am proud of who I am. If I say that I have nothing to hide while standing behind the door with my face in shadows, I am showing that I think there is something to hide. I can not be heard if my words are muffled from speaking them through a closed door. Actions speak louder than words.

These words are my thoughts and feelings on lesbianism and Girl Scouting. Submitting them under my name is my action.

CHAPTER 32

What Acceptance Looks Like

Beth Toolan

In May 1997, Beth Toolan sent a note to IndgoGS, the Internet discussion list on lesbians in Girl Scouting, saying, "I can't imagine having to be closeted at work, particularly since Girl Scouting is so much of who I am." Her piece indicates the level of integrity possible when a lesbian tells the truth and an organization accepts that truth.

Sometimes, I am a Girl Scout who is a lesbian. At other times, I am a lesbian who is a Girl Scout. I have been a Girl Scout for sixteen years, and a lesbian for thirty three. I am also a parent, a committed life partner, a Unitarian Universalist with Quaker tendencies, and a budding violinist. I like classical music, plants, and canoeing. This is who I am. This is who I am happy to be.

My Girl Scout experience began when I was six, watching my mother and sister get ready for Brownie meetings. Sometimes I was allowed to tag along. What I remember most was the cool little coin purse for dues that attached to my sister's brown elastic belt.

My mother was my troop leader from Brownies through Cadettes, and I learned a lot from her about camping and fund raising, along with ten thousand things to do with marshmallows, glitter, and worn-out pantyhose.

I also found a niche for myself: the enthusiastic, hard worker, always the first to volunteer, even for latrine duty, always eager for the praise of my troop leaders. I remember being compulsive about picking up litter at day camp. I remember proudly posting the colors on opening day. I remember preparing for our first camping trip, back in the days when sleeping bags—tightly rolled and tied with a complicated configuration of half hitches and square knots—were about as big as a Volkswagen. I remember, particularly on our frequent camping trips, feeling that I belonged, a sensation I didn't often have at other times. It wasn't that I'd always known there was something different about me; it's more that I was at my best then, a very good feeling.

I did not make a conscious decision to pursue a career in Girl Scouting. I was looking for a job and saw the ad. I left the interview both wanting the job and feeling confident that I would receive an offer. The day after my interview, I was contacted by the woman for whose position I was applying. She had not been in the office that day before. We chatted about what she liked best and least about the job. Then she asked me something about my husband. I remember taking a deep breath and saying, "Well, my husband is a wife . . . ." After a moment of uncomfortable silence, she apologized for making an assumption, and then the conversation, and my breathing, returned to normal.

I learned later that this poor woman had rushed to her supervisor, terrified that if I wasn't hired, I could sue. We laughed about it, later, after we had become friends, when she told me. It turned out to be a moot point; I was offered the position the next day and was welcomed several weeks later.

I also learned later that I was the talk of the office, among both staff and volunteers, for several weeks before I started the job. Many people were curious; I think that for some, I was the first lesbian they were aware of knowing. If they had reservations they didn't show them because I felt that I was greeted with the same friendliness and interest as other new staff. Some people did ask me questions about my personal life. But I felt that they were appropriate and based on genuine interest rather than prurient curiosity. Although I did, and do, talk about my life and family openly, my family's difference was never the topic. I was hired for my skills and experience, and am liked and respected by my colleagues because I am friendly, competent, and can laugh at myself.

I'm glad that people had those discussions. I am glad that many of them happened before I began work. I would not want to work in an office where I had to dissemble or deflect. I have been through that, the half truths about weekend plans, the offers to introduce me to eligible men, the friends who no longer want to be my friends, the hugs no longer welcomed, the uncomfortable silences when I enter a room. Acceptance, even before most people had even met me, was and is one of the greatest benefits my partner, our seven-year old son Julian, and I have received from my Girl Scout colleagues.

I am glad I did not know when I was hired that there were some negative responses from several volunteers. They expressed concern about my appropriateness as a role model, the stability of my relationship, and other stereotypes. I have recently been in a position to work closely with one of the volunteers who was actively uncomfortable then, when I was just a name and a label. She has shared with me and others that she is uncomfortable with lesbians in Girl Scouting, and with lesbians in general. I was afraid at first and unsure how to work with her. This volunteer has the kind of leadership abilities that can mold and shape public opinion. I do not want our mutual discomfort to influence our professional relationship. But I know it does. I have worked hard to build a positive but very professional relationship with her. Our meetings focus on business, with little talk of life beyond Girl Scouting. When I am in her town, I still don't feel comfortable enough to spontaneously invite her for a quick cup of coffee. I will continue to try, though, to get to know her as a person, just as I want her to know me. Maybe that will make a difference.

The question of how much to tell volunteers has always been a challenge, particularly those volunteers in the community close to my home. The volunteers in my town see my family together regularly at all the usual centers of small-town life like the park and the grocery store. There are many Girl Scout families in my son's school, where my partner and I are active parent volunteers. In general, I don't tell unless they ask, and they almost never do, although there are several lesbian Girl Scout volunteers whom I've run into at various Pride events or who see the pink triangle on my car and draw me aside to say, "I like your triangle." I don't know if the phone calls spread through town like they did when troop leader Kathie had a fire in her back yard or town registrar Betty's daughter broke her arm. I smile as I picture the calls . . . . "Sorry to interrupt you during supper, but you'll never guess what I

Beth Toolan, 1972

heard about Beth . . . ." I believe that probably most people know, even if they are not yet comfortable uttering the word lesbian. I don't think that most people care much.

I believe that I can model inclusion and pluralism; I believe that it should be as easy for me to confront homophobia as it is racism, sexism, and classism. I believe that Girl Scouting has an incredible opportunity, both nationally and locally, to teach tolerance, to fight prejudice, and to be truly affirming to all girls. But I also know that for me, speaking out about lesbian issues still feels risky in some settings. I know, intellectually, that in Massachusetts, the law protects my job. But the reality is that people have lost and do lose jobs, either directly or indirectly because of sexual orientation.

Last fall, my partner of six years, Kathryn, and I held a Holy Union Ceremony. Although Kathryn comes with me to office parties, and our son, Julian, loves to visit me at work, I was nervous about telling people. Ever since my days as a Brownie, it has always been important to me to be liked. I knew I didn't have anything to worry about, but I still worried when I invited my Girl Scout coworkers.

On the day of the ceremony, our church was filled with family, friends, the

Girl Scout Executive Director, Assistant Executive Director, and several colleagues from my council. One of my favorite photographs is of them, my office friends, sitting together at one of the two completely heterosexual tables in the room—the other was the parents' table—making the three-fingered Girl Scout sign at my lesbian wedding. I like this photograph because it demonstrates to me that for now, at least, two of the most important elements of my life, family and work, are integrated, sustaining, and welcoming.

I have always received support from my coworkers at our Girl Scout Service Center. When a lesbian in Virginia lost custody of her son solely because of her sexual orientation, I could tell these coworkers that sometimes I am scared of losing my son. Over lunch, we talked about the *Ellen* "Coming Out" episodes—about how Ellen's struggles mirror those of many other gay people. They asked me if my parents are supportive, and I can happily say that they are—totally. When a local church withdrew meeting places for several troops because they believed that Girl Scouting promoted lesbianism, my office mates shared my frustration and anger.

I have talked to my colleagues about my ongoing process of coming out and that helps to make it real. I have told them about being a part of the Women's Center at college, about telling my parents the first and second times, about losing friends and making new ones, about wearing my Girl Scout T-shirt to a Gay Pride March, about finding my life partner. When we read about the disproportionately high rate of suicide among gay and lesbian youth and hate crimes in high schools, we talk about these problems, not in terms of percentages, but in terms of real people. We wonder if the young women who make up the teen suicide, substance abuse, and runaway statistics might have chosen different paths if even one adult had told them they were okay. I believe that talking about these issues, although certainly not the solution, is one of many steps along the way.

Being involved in Girl Scouting has been important in many phases of my life. As a child, Girl Scouting helped me challenge myself, to do my best, and to feel good about myself even if I could not always accomplish my goals. I learned that a few good friends are more valuable then many acquaintances. I learned to be part of a group and to express my opinions even if they are not popular.

The past four years as a professional Girl Scout have been ones of growth, both personally and professionally. I have learned acceptance of others as they have learned acceptance of me. I have lost some of the radical passion of my younger days and have gained a better understanding of my role in the world and the responsibilities that role carries. I have swapped stories about marital spats with my straight colleagues around the water cooler. Kathryn joined the group of staff and spouses who got seasick during a staff party on a boat. One Halloween, Julian and I baked peanut butter cookies and reverse trick-or-treated through my office, delivering the cookies.

My Girl Scout Council has demonstrated to me a solid commitment to being a sister to every Girl Scout. I am very lucky about that. But it also presents me with a challenge that I extend to everyone who reads this, Girl Scout or not. Be the one person who reaches out, the one person who listens, the one person who affirms. Be the person who helps someone learn that who you love is less important than that you love. Teach the girls in your troop—and in your life—to celebrate the uniqueness of everyone.

Beth Toolan and son Julian

POSTSCRIPT

* * *

If Girl Scouts of the U.S.A. wants to work against institutionalized homophobia, it might use as a model its decades-old commitment to eliminate institutionalized racism from the Girl Scout movement. It could recall its sustained efforts to make scouting available to minority girls. In the 1930s, for example, when Girl Scouting started in Arizona, one of the first troops was on a Hopi Indian Reservation. In the 1940s and 1950s, even though it was unlawful in some states for black girls and white girls to meet together, Girl Scout mixed troops broke the taboo. During that same era, before the integration of schools, Girl Scout camp was one of the only places where black girls and white girls could be together.

The organization also could note a recent achievement: nearly one third of Girl Scouts of the U.S.A. management positions are filled by people of color[1] (as compared to 14.3 percent national average for nonprofit organizations[2])

Finally, the organization could build on its current position of nondiscrimination against lesbian women by taking the next steps: acknowledging the gap between position and practice, apologizing for past injustices, and implementing a plan, perhaps similar to the one outlined in the letter which follows.

A Letter of Reconciliation I Wish Girl Scouts of the U.S.A. Would Write

Nancy Manahan

Dear Girl Scouts of America:
The National Council of Girl Scouts of the U.S.A. is writing to any Girl Scout, present or former, who has experienced homophobic prejudice in Girl Scouting. GSUSA wants to personally and publicly apologize if you have ever been treated with disrespect or made to suffer in any way because of your actual or perceived sexual orientation. We are sorry the organization has not always lived up to its ideals of fairness, honesty, and respect for every person. We are sorry if the organization you trusted, worked for, and believed in hurt you because in doing so, it betrayed its own values.

We have heard reports of lost professional and volunteer positions with the Girl Scouts during purges or because of rumors or accusations. We are making a commitment. Never again will the national organization openly, or tacitly, condone homophobia. Never again will we tolerate a witch-hunt. Never again will we stand by silently while losing some of our best and brightest members because of ignorance or hatred.

These are not idle promises. Girl Scouts of the U.S.A. has adopted, and the national membership has approved, a nondiscrimination plank that will be implemented in every local Girl Scout council.

1. GSUSA will not tolerate discrimination based on perceived or actual sexual orientation.

2. GSUSA will add sexual orientation to its non-discrimination policies and to its diversity training at all levels of the organization.

3. GSUSA will include accurate information about sexual orientation in its adult training materials and handbooks. The assumption that all people are heterosexual and the consequent erasure of gay parents, troop leaders, camp counselors, and Girl Scouts themselves will be eliminated from all GSUSA publications.

4. GSUSA will not tolerate discrimination toward volunteers or employees, nor will it refuse a volunteer or paid position to someone based on that person's assumed or known sexual orientation.

5. GSUSA will extend same-sex domestic partner benefits to any employee who qualifies.

6. All GSUSA employees will be expected to contribute to an atmosphere of safety and respect for all lesbian adults and youth in the organization.

7. GSUSA will publish this pledge and circulate it in every council in the United States, making it known that Girl Scouts of the U.S.A. is truly an inclusive organization, committed to justice and equality for all.

We take these steps in the knowledge that we will be accused by some of abandoning our ideals and of corrupting our mission. (Having weathered the outcry over our decision to permit a substitution for the word "God" in the Girl Scout promise in recognition of religious pluralism in our society, we know we can survive a similar backlash.) We believe that attempting to eliminate institutionalized homophobia renews our commitment to our ideals of fairness, honesty, respect for all people, and service to the broadest spectrum of American girls.

In addition to being more consistent with our values, taking these steps will help us serve girls by modeling acceptance of diversity. We are committed to helping girls learn to interact with other people with sensitivity to their feelings and respect for their rights. We cannot teach what we do not consistently practice. Girl Scouting, the largest voluntary organization of girls and women in the world, is for all girls. Taking these steps will also help us serve the estimated three to four million girls being raised in gay and lesbian households.

Secondly, we make this committment in the knowledge that some parents may withdraw their girls from Girl Scouting. This is our greatest fear: in doing what is right, we may be prevented from serving as many girls as possible. We remind such parents that we are the same principled organization we always have been with the same dedicated paid staff and volunteers we always have had. The only difference is that we are strengthening our pledge to end prejudice within the organization, to be more honest and more fair.

Finally, we take these steps in the recognition that our funding may suffer. Local Girl Scout councils depend upon the good will of community funding agencies such as United Way. They depend on churches, individuals, and cookie and calendar sales. The organization at every level may suffer from funding losses. It is, in part, this fiscal threat that has, for years, prevented us from taking a stronger stance in support of our lesbian members.

We are no longer willing to let fear take precedence over justice. We have built a prudent reserve in anticipation of this action. We estimate that the organization can sustain a moderate loss of funding for a decade. We predict that before the decade is over, discrimination on the basis of sexual orientation, like discrimination on the basis of race, will be not only illegal but unacceptable in this society.

In closing, we would like to invite any lesbian adults or youth who have avoided the Girl Scouts because of the organization's homophobia to give Girl Scouting another chance. We value your experience and your contributions. If anyone questions your right to be a Girl Scout, we will be there to support you. We ask for your help in entering the twentieth-first century with a policy–and practice–of zero-tolerance for discrimination.

It's a simple matter of justice.

Sincerely,
National Council
Girl Scouts of the U.S.A.

I hope that On My Honor: Lesbians Reflect on Their Scouting Experience *hastens the day when Girl Scouts of the U.S.A. will write such a letter.*

---

[1] *Human Resources Department, Girl Scouts of the U.S.A., March 1997.*

[2] *Pier C. Rogers and John Palmer Smith, "Nonprofit Management and Leadership: The Status of People of Color," a report of the Nonprofit Academic Centers Council, January 1994, pp.23-24.*

APPENDIX I

✳ ✳ ✳

The Girl Scout
Promise and Law

The Girl Scout Promise
   On my honor, I will try:
   To serve God and my country,
   To help people at all times,
   And to live by the Girl Scout Law.

   Members may substitute wording appropriate to their own spiritual belief for the word God if they choose to do so when reciting the Girl Scout Promise.

The Girl Scout Law
   The Girl Scout Law was revised in October, 1996, following a vote at the triennial National Council Session in Fort Worth, Texas.

I will do my best to be:
    honest and fair,
    friendly and helpful,
    considerate and caring,
    courageous and strong, and
    responsible for what I say and do,
and to
    respect myself and others,
    respect authority,
    use resources wisely,
    make the world a better place, and
    be a sister to every Girl Scout.[1]

A pre-1996 version of the Girl Scout Law:
        I will do my best
        to be honest
        to be fair
        to help where I am needed
        to be cheerful
        to be friendly and considerate
        to be a sister to every Girl Scout
        to respect authority
        to use resources wisely
        to protect and improve the world around me
      · to show respect for myself and others
        through my words and actions.[2]

The version of the promise and law which many contributors to this book learned may be found in the 1947 and the 1953 editions of *Girl Scout Handbook Intermediate Program* as well as in *Scouting for Girls* (1923):

On my honor, I will try:
    To do my duty to God and my country,

To help other people at all times,
To obey the Girl Scout Laws.

1. A Girl Scout's honor is to be trusted.
2. A Girl Scout is loyal.
3. A Girl Scout's duty is to be useful and to help others.
4. A Girl Scout is a friend to all and a sister to every other Girl Scout.
5. A Girl Scout is courteous
6. A Girl Scout is a friend to animals
7. A Girl Scout obeys orders.
8. A Girl Scout is cheerful.
9. A Girl Scout is thrifty.
10. A Girl Scout is clean in thought, word, and deed.[3]

[1] *San Francisco Bay Girl Scout Council*, "Join Us: Membership Information," *June 28, 1997,* <*http://www.sfbgirlscouts.org/joinus.htm*> *(June 30, 1977).*

[2] *Girl Scouts of the U.S.A.,* "Who We Are," <*http://www.gsusa.org/whoweare/whoweare.html*> *June 30, 1997.*

[3] *Girl Scout Handbook: Intermediate Program*, Girl Scouts of the U.S.A., 1953, 1955, p. 2.

APPENDIX II

✳ ✳ ✳

Girl Scout Councils that Include Sexual Orientation in Their Nondiscrimination Policies

Editor's note: Girl Scouts of the U.S.A. states that it will not discriminate on the basis of age, race, color, ethnic background, sex, creed, national origin, socioeconomic status, or disability. Many of the 320 Girl Scout councils in the United States model their nondiscrimination policies after the national policy. At least twenty-two other councils have expanded the list to include (among other categories) sexual orientation. My apologies to any council that includes sexual orientation but inadvertently has been omitted from the list below. Please notify Nancy Manahan c/o Madwoman Press so that the list can be corrected and updated in any subsequent editions of the book.

California
Oakland - San Francisco Bay
Sacramento - Tierra del Oro
San Jose - Santa Clara County

Connecticut
Bridgeport - Housatonic
New Haven - Connecticut Trails

Illinois
Chicago - Chicago

Massachusetts
Middleton - Spar and Spindle
Boston - Patriots' Trail

Michigan
Ann Arbor - Huron Valley

Minnesota
Duluth - Northern Pine
Minneapolis - Greater Minneapolis
St. Cloud - Land of Lakes
St. Paul - St. Croix River Valley

New Hampshire
Manchester - Swift Water

New Jersey
East Brunswick - Delaware-Raritan
Montclair - Greater Essex
and Hudson Counties

Ohio
Cleveland - Lake Erie

Pennsylvania
Philadelphia - Southeastern
Pennsylvania

Vermont
Essex Junction - Vermont

Wisconsin
Eau Claire - Indian Waters
Madison - Black Hawk

Washington
Seattle - Totem

Additional councils, while not using the term "sexual orientation" or "affectional preference" in their policies, include phrases like "and any other protected class," which, if the council is in a municipality or state that prohibits discrimination on the basis of sexual orientation, may cover lesbian employees and volunteers. Among the Girl Scout councils that fall into this category are the following:

Los Angeles, California - Angeles
Washington, D.C., - Our Nation's Capital
La Cross, Wisconsin - Riverland

States That Prohibit Discrimination on the Basis of Sexual Orientation

California

Connecticut

Hawaii

Maine

Massachusetts

Minnesota

New Hampshire

New Jersey

Rhode Island

Vermont

Wisconsin

GLOSSARY OF TERMS

✳ ✳ ✳

Girl Scout terms and definitions are reprinted with permission of the Tierra del Oro Girl Scout Council, Sacramento, California. Terms defined by the editor are marked with an asterisk.

Badge
Round embroidered recognition for Junior and Cadette Girl Scouts to indicate increased knowledge and skill in a particular subject.

Bisexual
A persistent pattern of same and opposite sex attraction or arousal.

Buddy System
A safety practice in which girls of equal ability are paired to help and to keep track of each other.

Counselor-in-Training
A Senior Girl Scout who is taking a course to learn outdoor group leadership skills as a camp counselor.

Court of Awards
A ceremony that can be held any time during the year at which badges, recognitions, and awards are presented.

Day camp
Camping by the day for a minimum of four consecutive days.

Dunking, Ditty, or Dip Bag*
A mesh bag made by sewing two dishrags together into which a scout puts her washed camp dishes and silverware and, holding the pull cord, dunks the bag into boiling water for the prescribed sterilization time, and hangs it on a line to dry.

Fly-up
The ceremony in which a Brownie Girl Scout "graduates" to Junior Girl Scouts.

Girl Guides
The original name for Girl Scouts, still used in many countries.

Girl Scout Birthday
March 12 is the Girl Scout birthday because it marks the first meeting of Girl Scouts in the U.S.A in Savannah, Georgia, in 1912.

Girl Scout Handshake
A formal way of greeting other Girl Scouts by shaking left hands while giving the Girl Scout Sign with the right.

Girl Scout Sign
The official Girl Scout greeting. The right hand is raised shoulder high with the three middle fingers extended and the thumb crossing over the palm to hold down the little finger.

Girl Scout's Own
A quiet inspirational ceremony that has a theme and is planned by Girl Scouts and their leaders.

GSUSA
Girl Scouts of the United States of America.

Heterosexuality*
A persistent pattern of opposite sex attraction or arousal and a weak or absent pattern of same sex attraction or arousal.

Homophobia*
Fear and hatred of homosexuals and homosexuality entailing negativism in feelings, attitudes, or behaviors against bisexual, gay, lesbian, or transgendered persons. It consists of a belief in the inviolability of sex roles; xenophobia, the fear of difference; erotophobia, anxiety about sexuality; and heterosexism, belief in the superiority of heterosexuals and heterosexuality.

Homosexuality*
A persistent pattern of same sex attraction or arousal and a weak or absent pattern of opposite sex attraction or arousal.

Investiture
A special ceremony in which a new member makes her Girl Scout Promise and receives her membership pin.

Kaper Chart
A chart that shows the delegation of jobs and rotation or responsibility day by day and/or meal by meal.

Leader-In-Training
A Senior Girl Scout who is taking a course to learn leadership skills as a troop leader.

Low, Juliette Gordon (nicknamed Daisy)
Founder of Girl Scouting in the United States, she formed the first troop that met in Savannah, Georgia on March 12, 1912.

Motto
Be Prepared.

Patrol
A widely used form of troop government where the troop divides into small groups.

Program Aide
Cadette and Senior Girl Scouts who have been trained to assist younger Girl Scout groups with songs, games, crafts, ceremonies or skills.

Resident Camp
A sustained camping experience for a minimum of six days, with overnight sleeping at a council owned, leased, rented or borrowed facility.

Service Team
A group of adult volunteers responsible for organizing and delivering service to Girl Scouts directed by service unit manager.

Sit Upon
A cushion often made by Girl Scouts to use when the ground is damp or to keep their clothes clean.

Slogan
"Do a good turn daily."

Trefoil
The international symbol of Girl Scouting. The three leaves of the trefoil represent the three parts of the promise.

Wider Opportunity
Any Girl Scout activity that takes girls outside their own troop or council.

World Association of Girl Guides and Girl Scouts (WAGGGS)
An international educational association for girls with a membership of eight and a half million in 136 countries organized into five regional groups: Africa, Europe, Asia-Pacific, Arab, and Western Hemisphere

World Trefoil Pin
A pin worn by all Girl Scouts and Girl Guides.

World Centers
Four program activity centers owned by WAGGGS. The centers are located in Mexico, England, India, and Switzerland.

* Definitons of these terms provided by the Editor.

RESOURCES

✳ ✳ ✳

IndgoGS@aol.com is a moderated discussion list for those interested in sharing ideas and experiences about lesbians in Girl Scouting. The list began in May 1997.

CONTRIBUTORS' BIOGRAPHIES

* * *

Jamie Anderson is a singer-songwriter who lives in Tucson, Arizona, with her longtime partner Dakota and their family (four cats and a dog). She makes her living as an out-lesbian musician. Currently, she has four recordings on her own label, Tsunami Records. Girl Scouting strengthened her love for women and for music—the two things that are most important in her life.

Henri Bensussen is an older Jewish lesbian with a granddaughter in Brownies. She works at Stanford University, but once, in the mid-1950s, she was a Counselor-in-Training at Camp Osito in the San Bernadino Mountains. Henri has contributed pieces in *Women of the Thirteenth Moon: Writings on Menopause* and in *Sexual Harassment: Women Speak Out* and is also a published poet.

Jeanne Córdova is the author of *Kicking The Habit; A Lesbian Nun Story* and *Sexism: It's a Nasty Affair!* She was the founder and publisher of *The Lesbian Tide* and founded and currently publishes *Community Yellow Pages*, the gay and lesbian telephone book of California. A journalist and essayist, she has been published in *Out, Ten Percent*, the *Advocate* and the *Los Angeles Village View*. She is currently a columnist for *Icon*, California's lesbian newspaper, and is working on a third book, *The Apostles*. Jeanne lives underneath the *D* of the Hollywood Sign with her South African partner, Lynn Harris Ballen.

Margaret Cruikshank, Ph.D., teaches English, Gay/Lesbian Studies, and Women's Studies at City College of San Francisco and teaches at the University of Maine in the summer. She has edited several groundbreaking anthologies—*The Lesbian Path* (1980), *Lesbian Studies* (1982), *New Lesbian Writing* (1984), and *Fierce with Reality, An Anthology of Literature on Aging* (1995)—and wrote *The Gay and Lesbian Liberation Movement* (1992). She loves the Arizona desert, the Boundary Waters Canoe Area of Minnesota, and the islands off the coast of Maine.

Rosemary Keefe Curb, Ph.D., still yearns for the simple pleasures of clover and crickets. She spent seven years in the Dominican Sisters and another five as hetero wife and mother. Life adventures have included editing *Lesbian Nuns: Breaking Silence* (with Nancy Manahan, 1985) and *Amazon All Stars: Thirteen Lesbian Plays* (1996). After twenty-five years in academia, teaching literature and women's studies, Rosemary now heads a university English Department in the Ozarks, where she lives with her partner and twin cats. She is a grandmother.

Janet de Vries, a geologist in a past life, is currently a counselor. She has appeared as "dyke on display" in numerous university classes, speaking about gay youth, discrimination against gays and lesbians, and the controversy about what causes homosexuality. Janet and her partner Leanne travel extensively. (Leanne's goal is to visit all of the national parks.) For relaxation, Janet pets their cat Sarah, reads lesbian mysteries, and putters around the house. To recharge her batteries, she networks.

Jane Eastwood lives in St. Paul, Minnesota, where she tends flower gardens that cover most of her yard. She works in marketing and public relations. A poet as well as a canoeist, kayaker, and dog musher, Jane cohosted the first lesbian Girl Scout round-up (in Minneapolis-St. Paul) in the early 1980s. This piece pays tribute to some special women she knew through scouting, although she was not aware of their lesbianism or her own until after she left the Girl Scouts. Their role modeling made it easier for her to decide to live in the company of women as a lesbian.

Nancy Franz is a life member of the Girl Scouts and is active with the Northern Pine Girl Scout Council in Duluth, Minnesota. She serves as an adult trainer and committee member for camping and recreation in northern Wisconsin. Nancy lives on forty-five acres overlooking Lake Superior near Washburn, Wisconsin and enjoys reading, traveling, and silent sports outdoors. At a recent summer camp reunion, many of her favorite Girl Scout counselors attended with their female partners.

Roberta Garr, an American of Baltic Jewish descent, lives in Vermont with Maike Haaland and works as a social worker for Social Services. She has been a Girl Scout since 1959. She enjoys hiking in the mountains, skiing and traveling.

Maike Haaland is a Norwegian, currently living in Vermont and working at Goddard College. She has been a Girl Scout since 1964. Some of her passions are traveling, weaving, reading, hiking, skiing and being in open spaces, especially in the mountains and at the ocean. Maike loves the Chalet, but cannot imagine respecting the taboo against being an open lesbian in Girl Scouting.

Jorjet Harper has been writing for the gay and lesbian press for more than fifteen years, and has published more than 400 articles—news, features, reviews, interviews, and humor columns—in forty periodicals. Her books, *Lesbomania: Humor, Commentary, and New Evidence That We Are Everywhere* (1994) and *Tales From the Dyke Side* (1996) are published by New Victoria. Her work also appears in *Lesbian Culture: An Anthology* and *Best Contemporary Women's Humor*. Jorjet was a Girl Scout from the ages of nine through fifteen—a Brownie, Intermediate, and Senior.

Jill Kennedy is currently working professionally as a camp director/outdoor specialist for a Girl Scout council. She has been involved with Girl Scouts, mostly through resident camping, since the fourth grade. Jill lifts weights competitively with the American Drug Free Powerlifting Federation and is a member of Little People of America and the Dwarf Athletic Association of America, organizations for short-statured individuals. She spends her time reading, writing letters, E-mailing, listening to Public Radio, playing sports, and weight training.

Terry King is a Black lesbian in her fifties. She is working on a masters degree in therapeutic recreation at California Sate University at Hayward and hopes to work with people suffering from Alzheimer's. Elderly people, children, and animals are drawn to her, and she has compassion and understanding for them. She yearns to travel while owning her home and fulfilling her responsibilities to her animals. Terry is a Gemini torn in many directions.

Amanda Kovattana was born of an English mother and Thai father. She was raised in Thailand in a traditional matriarchal extended family, but she was educated in English schools. Amanda immigrated to California with her parents in 1968 at the age of ten. A freelance writer with essays published in *Dyke Life*, *Entre Nous* and the *Palo Alto Weekly*, Amanda has finished an autobiographical novel which explores the influences of the women in her family and her bicultural/biracial heritage. She lives in the San Francisco Bay Area with her lover Catherine and makes a living as a personal organizer.

Rosemary Le Page served on the California Governor's Advisory Committee on Children and Youth as the Girl Scout representative and was awarded the Governor's medallion for Outstanding Youth Service in 1966. She directed Girl Scout camps and programs and was a troop leader for two Senior Girl Scout troops during her twenties. Currently, Rosemary is a nationally certified school psychologist and school administrator working for the public schools in Marin County, California and for her local Unitarian Universalist Leadership School. She is out in her community and speaks to high school psychology and social issue classes about being lesbian.

Terry Martin, Ph.D., an alumna of Camp Four Echoes (located in the Inland Empire Girl Scout Council on Couer d'Alene Lake in Idaho) is currently an English Professor at Central Washington University. Her work has appeared in more than thirty publications. Most recently her poetry was published in *The English Journal*, *Voices from the Middle*, *Inland*, and *Poetry Motel*.

Judith McDaniel believes she began training for her career as a writer and political activist in scouting. She attended International Girl Scout Camps in Germany, England, and Denmark. As an adult, she led a troop of fourth graders, and from 1980—1982 guided Girl Scout canoe trips on rivers and lakes in upstate New York. Judith has written *Sanctuary: A Journey*, an account of a 1985 river trip when she was captured by the Contras in Nicaragua; *A Lesbian Couples Guide* (1995); three novels, including *Yes I Said Yes I Will* (1996); and three books of poetry, including most recently, *Taking Risks*. She lives with her partner in Tucson, Arizona.

Martha McPheeters, Ph.D., is a white middle-class wilderness guide and research scientist. She is the Associate Program Director at Voyageur Outward Bound School in northern Minnesota during the summer. Martha received a Ph.D. in neurobiology in 1981 and can often be found in a laboratory experimenting with the taste systems of mudpuppies or hamsters. She embraces bisexuality and polyamory as positive lifestyle choices.

Kim Messner lives with her two cats in southern Maine. Formerly employed as a truck driving instructor (eighteen-wheelers), she has recently graduated from a Technical College and is currently employed in the computer field. She loves the ocean, nature, traveling and computers.

Marcia Munson spends her winters working in San Francisco and her summers traveling the world in search of wilderness areas to explore and ex-Girl Scouts with whom to camp. Her writing has recently appeared in the anthologies *Dyke Life*, *Lesbian Friendships*, and *Sexualities*.

Judith Niemi is director of Women in the Wilderness in St. Paul, Minnesota, a "camp for grown-ups" that brings women together to travel in the Minnesota northwoods and in jungles, Arctic tundra, and deserts. Her essays have appeared in several magazines and anthologies, and she is author of *Basic Essentials of Women in the Outdoors* and coeditor with Barbara Wieser of *Rivers Running Free: Canoeing Stories by Adventurous Women*, reissued in 1997 by Seal Press. She lives with too many computers, a house full of books, and a partner who shares a love for wild places.

Laura L. Post, M.D., is a left-handed Jewish lesbian writer of mixed-class heritage whose fiction, poetry, features, syndicated columns, and reviews have appeared in *Ms.*, *Deneuve/Curve*, *The Advocate*, *Washington Blade*, *The San Francisco Chronicle*, *The Chicago Tribune*, and more than 200 other newspapers, magazines, journals, and anthologies in the U.S., Canada, U.K., and Australia. Her essay on lesbian battering won first prize in the 1995 Arizona Authors' Contest, and her anthology of interviews with women musicians, *Backstage Pass*, was published in 1997. She is chairperson of the Department of Psychiatry at Commonwealth Health Center in Saipan.

Kristen Renn is a Ph.D. candidate at Boston College and Assistant Dean of Student Life at Brown University in Providence, Rhode Island. She is not currently affiliated with the Girl Scouts, but is involved with campus and community education and activism on issues of social justice, including lesbian/gay/bisexual/transgender concerns. She lives beside her mother in a Victorian twin house in southeastern Massachusetts.

Susan Rothbaum is a writer, singer, and teacher living in Minneapolis. She recently recorded *Shekhinah, Shaddai, Shalom,* an album of original and traditional Jewish songs that highlight feminine imagery.

At Girl Scout Camp, **Carol (Heenan) Seajay** learned how to organize, get things done, imagine something that didn't yet exist, and make it happen—skills that have served her well as a feminist and an activist. In high school, she worked in a Girl Scout inner-city day camp. As college students, she and her lover were advisers to a Senior Scout troop. Always a reader, she fell in love with the possibility of a lesbian literature at twenty-three and has spent the last twenty-four years working in feminist bookstores and publishing Feminist Bookstore News (PO Box 882554, San Francisco CA 94188). She lives with her lover of ten years.

Krysta Sutterfield holds associate and bachelor degrees and is aiming for a masters in health. She is a member of the First Unitarian Universalist Church of Columbus, Ohio. Krysta enjoys baking bread, quilting, reading, and living re-creations of the Middle Ages. She dreams of one day building her own energy-efficient, solar-powered house.

Donna Tsuyuko Tanigawa is a *yonsei* (fourth generation) of Japanese ancestry from the sugar plantation town of Waipahu, Hawaii. Her mother was a Girl Scout leader, and the scouts in her life were her *ohana* (family). She and her partner, Lee-Ann Matsumoto, hope to raise girls of their own, and they look forward to having Brownies in their lives. Donna has an M.A. in American Studies, teaches women's studies at Leeward Community College, and is in a masters program in English at the University of Hawaii at Manoa.

Beth Toolan has worked for the past four years for the Spar and Spindle Girl Scout Council in North Andover, Massachusetts. She is currently the Director of Membership and Marketing in the Lynn, branch office. She lives in Salem, Massachusetts, with her family.

Holli Van Nest is a white lesbian from a working-class background. Originally from Pennsylvania, she currently lives in Boston with her partner of ten years. Girl Scouting gave her a belief in making a contribution to the world, and she has spent much of her life volunteering for feminist causes. She enjoys gardening, swimming, camping, hiking, and canoeing, which bring to her day-to-day life a spiritual presence which has been there since her Girl Scout camping days.

Cara L. Vaughn was raised on the northern edge of the New Jersey pine barrens. In 1982, she and her lover moved to the east side of the San Francisco Bay. For income, Cara managed public relations and communications at the University Health Service at the University of California at Berkeley. For leisure, she dabbled in the creative arts and wrestled with uninvited plants in her yard. In July of 1997, she died at home after an eight-year battle with cancer. She is survived by her lover of eighteen years, artist/writer Jean Sirius.

According to **Rachel Wetherill**'s mother's 1933 *Girl Scout Handbook*, "You who have followed the trail will never forget it. You will have memories that no one can take away from you of good comradeship, of all kinds of weather, of gay little happenings along the way, of flashlight flickering on trees at night, of camp fire songs, and good food eaten among friends with the sauce of hunger and laughter" (p. 346). Rachel would like to thank her mother, who died in 1995, for showing her the trail. Rachel continues her work as a rural mail carrier in the small town described in her piece.

The Editor

Nancy Manahan, Ph.D., was active in Girl Scouting for twelve years, attending the 1962 Roundup as a camper and the 1965 Roundup as staff. She coedited (with Rosemary Curb) *Lesbian Nuns: Breaking Silence*. Her writing has also appeared in *Mother Jones*, *Women's Studies Quarterly*, *Lesbian Connection*, *Common Lives/Lesbian Lives*, and in the anthologies *American Notes and Queries*, *The Lesbian Path*, and *Lesbian Studies*. She teaches writing and literature at a community college in Minnesota, lives with her partner, novelist Becky Bohan, and spends summers hiking in state parks and canoeing in the Boundary Waters Canoe Area with family and friends.

INDEX

✴ ✴ ✴

Other Books from Madwoman Press

On the Road Again
The Further Adventures of Ramsey Sears
by Elizabeth Dean

Irreverent magazine columnist Ramsey Sears tours America, finding adventure and romance along the way. This is the critically acclaimed sequel to *As the Road Curves*.

223 pp. $9.95   ISBN 0-9630822-0-5

That's Ms. Bulldyke to you, Charlie!
by Jane Caminos

Hilarious collection of single-panel cartoons that capture lesbian life in full. From dyke teenagers and lipstick lesbians, to the highly-assimilated and the politically correct. This Lambda Book Award finalist is a must read.

"These funny cartoons depict moments in lesbian life with a fine edge."

–Women Library Workers
$8.95   ISBN 0-9630822-1-3

Lesbians in the Military Speak Out
by Winni S. Webber

More than thirty women, representing all branches of the services, tell us about their experiences as lesbians in the military. Minerva Quarterly Report called it a healing book . . . "it documents voices previously silenced by legal and social censure . . . its purpose is to help build bridges, not barriers, to understanding. Webber's book stands as highly recommended reading amidst the confusing and often painful dialogue that accompanies questions concerning the role of gay and lesbian people in a democratic society."

133 pp. $9.95   ISBN 0-9630822-3-X

Thin Fire
by Nanci Little

It was nominated for an American Library Association Gay and Lesbian Book Award and called "compelling" by Lambda Book Report. We think you'll agree when you read this novel. It's the story of Elen McNally coming of age. She signed on for a three-year hitch in the Army, thinking it would get her a one-way ticket out of Aroostook County, Maine. What she got instead was a round-trip journey of self-discovery that took her to the scrub desert of Fort Hood, Texas, and back to the serenity of an isolated cabin in the Maine woods.

227 pp. $9.95   ISBN 0-9630822-4-8

Sinister Paradise
by Becky Bohan

When Britt Evans, professor of classical studies, arrives at Santorini she expects nothing more than lots of quiet time for research at its archaeological excavation. She hasn't counted on being dragged into the investigation of a mysterious death, nor being attracted to Cassie Burkhardt, a computer programmer at the dig. As the murder investigation intensifies, so do Britt's feelings for Cassie and together they are drawn into a spiral of danger and intrigue. This fast-paced adventure is set amidst spectacular scenery in the Mediterranean. Bohan weaves a tight drama that the Minneapolis Star Tribune called a ". . . riveting tale of love and greed in a country of olives and deep blue water."

211 pp. $9.95   ISBN 0-9630822-2-1

Mrs. Porter's Letter
by Vicki P. McConnell

In this first book of the Nyla Wade mystery series, you'll meet Nyla, who is recently divorced and starting a new career as a reporter. She discovers a packet of letters buried deep within an old desk she's just bought. They turn out to be passionate love letters between W. Stone and Mrs. Porter. Are Stone and Mrs. Porter still alive and can Nyla return the letters to them? Driven by her curiosity, she embarks on a search which reveals more surprises and danger than she ever imagined.

210 pp. $9.95   ISBN 0-9630822-6-4

Double Daughter
by Vicki P. McConnell

Nyla Wade, reporter and detective, returns to Denver where her heart lies, only to discover clouds of menace hanging over the lives of gay friends, old and new. Although the threats appear to be the work of a well organized hate group, Nyla suspects the source could be closer to home. As she gets nearer the truth, she finds herself the next target!

196 pp. $9.95   ISBN 0-9630822-5-6

The Burnton Widows
by Vicki P. McConnell

Lesbian journalist Nyla Wade has moved to Burnton, Oregon, where she has a new job as a reporter at the local newspaper. When she arrives in the costal community she discovers a limestone castle, old murders and a town too anxious to obliterate the castle and its history: the generations of lesbians who have lived there. Nyla's unwanted probing re-opens old wounds, unleashes local gay activists and uncovers the truth about what happened the night of the murders.

246 pp. Naiad version $10.95   ISBN 0-9630822-7-2

Fool Me Once
by Katherine E. Kreuter

Meet Paige Taylor, mystery writer and private eye. She's intelligent, urbane, and can't resist a pun or the chance to travel. When she makes an appointment with Los Angeles dentist, Bill Barrett, she discovers that she has a problem tooth, but that he has much more serious troubles. His receptionist and ex-lover, Carol Oliver, has just died, and his wife, Sally, has disappeared with a half-million dollars worth of Krugerrands. With the help of her assistant, Dick Kessler, and her lover, Patricia Towne, a professor of French at UCLA, Paige sets out to find Sally and the money. In Paris, Pat Towne finds some clues to Sally's real identity. In Hawaii and Alaska, Dick discovers that Sally has an accomplice whose identity surprises them all. Paige, meanwhile, follows Sally's trail to China and Hong Kong. But someone is plotting the perfect murders, and as Paige gets closer to the truth her name is added to the list of targets. *Fool Me Once* is the first in a series of Paige Taylor mysteries.

211 pp. $9.95   ISBN 0-9630822-8-0

Fertile Betrayal
A Nedra Wells, D.V.M., Novel
by Becky Bohan

The transition from big-city to small-town life had been hard enough. Then veterinarian Nedra Wells found herself facing devastating crises at work and at home. The mysterious deaths in a local cattle herd baffled her, and long-time companion Annie was threatening to leave. As the crises deepened, she wondered if all her training and good efforts would be enough to salvage her reputation and her relationship.

227 pp. $10.95   ISBN 1-886231-00-1

The Grass Widow
by Nanci Little

Unmarried and pregnant in the unforgiving year 1876, nineteen-year-old Aidan Blackstone is banished in shame from the civilized life she's known in New England. She's sent to stay with cousins on a remote Kansas farm, but when she arrives in the tiny frontier community, the Bodett family—mother, father, and both sons—have all died in an outbreak of influenza. Daughter Jocelyn (Joss) Bodett is the only survivor. Joss is determined to hold on to her family's farm, running it alone if she must. Aidan, trained to be a rich man's wife, seems at first to be only one more obstacle. Joss's fierce independence, preference for men's clothing, and rough manners mark her as singularly unconventional, and a woman misplaced in her time. But fate isn't entirely cruel, and in Aidan's presence Joss finds first support, then friendship, and finally love.

246 pp. $12.95   ISBN 1-886231-01-X

You can buy Madwoman Press books at your local women's bookstore or order them directly from us. We welcome orders from individuals who have limited access to stores carrying our titles. Send direct orders to Madwoman Press, Inc., P.O. Box 690, Northboro, MA 01532-0690. Please include $2.50 for shipping and handling of the first book ordered and $.50 for each additional book. Massachusetts residents please add 5% sales tax. A free catalog is available upon request.